Dear Fellow Shareholders...

OVER 30 YEARS OF WIT, WISDOM, AND VALUE INVESTING INSIGHTS

MARTIN J. WHITMAN

Contents

Foreword

MARTIN J. WHITMAN

Dear Reader:

Dear Fellow Shareholders... contains copies of Shareholder letters in which I wrote about fundamental finance from 1984 through 2015. Principal conclusions, which are explained more fully in the letters, include the following:

In passive investing in common stocks, it is my belief that a good method of investing encompasses four elements:

1. The company should be eminently creditworthy
2. The common stock to be purchased should be priced at, at least, a 20% discount from readily ascertainable Net Asset Value (NAV)
3. There should be full, meaningful disclosures including reliable audited financial statements, and the common stocks ought to be traded in markets where regulators provide meaningful protections for minority, non-control stockholders
4. There should be reasonable prospects that NAV growth over the next three-to-seven years will not be less than 10% compounded annually after adding back dividend payout

Financial statements, whether issued under Generally Accepted Accounting Principles (GAAP) or the International Financial Reporting System (IFRS) provide the analyst with vital Objective Benchmarks, not Truth.

The trained financial analyst has enough background in financial accounting, securities law, tax law and corporate law so that the analyst can at least be a well-informed client.

If there is a priority of anything subsequent to the 2008 economic meltdown, it is creditworthiness, not the periodic income account which embodies periodic earnings and/or periodic cash flows from operations.

For most economic entities, whether corporate or governmental, debt in the aggregate is almost never repaid. Rather, maturing debt is refinanced and debt is increased insofar as the economic entity enjoys increasing credit-worthiness.

In Modern Security Analysis, there exist three types of price efficiencies: transaction efficiency, value efficiency and process (or lack of process) efficiency. Transaction markets tend to be highly efficient price-wise; the other markets not so. Transaction markets constitute only a teensy part of what happens on Wall Street.

Long-term buy-and-hold investors differ markedly from shorter term traders in terms of factors deemed important in an analysis. Shorter term traders tend to focus on a primacy of the income account, near-term changes in market prices, top-down analysis and equilibrium pricing (i.e., the market price reflects all-encompassing values). Long-term buy-and-hold investors tend to analyze in the same or highly similar ways as do control investors, distress investors, credit analysts and first and second stage venture capitalists.

Over the long-term economic entities that enjoy earnings, (i.e., creating wealth while consuming cash) need access to capital markets whether credit markets, equity markets or both.

No one not receiving promotional compensations outperforms markets consistently. Consistently is a dirty word meaning "all the time." Many outside passive minority investors (OPMIs) do outperform on average, most of the time and over the long-term.

Chapter 11, especially pre-packs and Section 363 transactions have become a most valuable tool for reorganizing troubled debtors.

Diversification is only a surrogate and usually a damn poor surrogate, for intimate knowledge of an economic entity, control of that entity and price consciousness (a denial of equilibrium pricing). However, if the investor lacks intimate knowledge about the issuing company and its securities, elements of control or price consciousness, it is important to diversify.

A margin of safety embodies not only quantitative considerations (e.g., discounts from NAV) but also qualitative considerations (e.g., strong financial position).

Companies and their securities should be analyzed as both going concerns and investment trusts.

Book values tend to be more meaningful in an analysis when the companies are well-financed and important assets are separable and salable without diminishing much from a going concern value.

Management ought to be appraised looking at, at least, three factors:

1. Management as operators
2. Management as investors
3. Management as financiers

Enjoy the read.

Martin J. Whitman

Introduction

For over 30 years, Marty Whitman has written comprehensive shareholder letters that provided readers with thorough lessons in his investment philosophy, security analysis and value investing. The collection of excerpts from letters in this book comprise the "best of" Marty's writings organized thematically to give readers an opportunity to dive into specific topics of interest.

The book's first section, "The Roots", includes Marty's proxy solicitation to the shareholders of the Equity Strategies Fund (EQSF) written in 1984. Marty and his colleagues at M.J. Whitman effected a takeover of EQSF, a closed-end registered investment company. We included the letter of solicitation for the proxy vote and a section from the proxy statement which outlined the investment philosophy that would be the foundation for Marty's future investments. In 1990, EQSF was closed to new investors and a successor fund, the Third Avenue Value Fund, was launched.

Marty was the portfolio manager for the Third Avenue Value Fund for the next 22 years and wrote some of the industry's most lauded shareholder letters. He continued to write the Chairman's Letter after his retirement as Portfolio Manager of the Fund in 2012. Since that time, Marty has managed his family's money in the Whitman High Conviction Fund, a private investment Fund that adheres to the strict value discipline outlined in this book.

We hope you enjoy reading these excerpts compiled from the past 30 years and find them as insightful and witty as we do.

PART 1

THE ROOTS

"We are bottom-up investors....Put simply, we analyze companies and individual securities, not markets and economies."

April 1989

CHAPTER 1

Equity Strategies Fund Proxy Vote

JANUARY 1984

M.J. Whitman & Co., Inc.
171 Madison Avenue, Suite 1600
New York, NY 10016

January 23, 1984

Dear Fellow Shareholders:

My name is Martin J. Whitman and I am President of M.J. Whitman & Co., Inc., a member firm of the National Association of Securities Dealers, Inc. which beneficially owns 44,200 shares of the Common Stock of Equity Strategies Fund, Inc. (the "Corporation"). I have also recommended the purchase of the Corporation's stock to clients of my firm. Messrs. Zohar Ben-Dov and Eugene M. Isenberg are beneficial owners of 69,650 and 66,050 shares of the Corporation's stock, respectively. We have formed a Committee and own in the aggregate more than 25% of the Corporation's common stock. Pursuant to the Corporation's By-Laws, Section 1.02, a Special Meeting may be called on written request of shareholders entitled to cast at least 25% of all the votes entitled to be cast at a meeting. We have exercised this right and have made a demand for a Special Meeting for the purposes of removing the present directors of the Corporation, and electing a new Board of Directors.

The Board of Directors has acknowledged our demand and has called a Special Meeting which will be held in Room 312, Sheraton Grand Hotel, 333 South Figueroa Street, Los Angeles, California on February 13, 1984 at 1:30 P.M.

If a majority of the shareholders in interest of the Corporation, votes FOR the removal of the present Board of Directors by attending the meeting or by proxy by marking the appropriate space provided on the enclosed Proxy Card and by signing, dating and promptly returning the Proxy Card in the enclosed envelope then the present directors will be removed from office.

If a majority of the shareholders in interest of the Corporation present at the meeting and entitled to vote either in person OR by proxy, votes FOR the elections of the new Board of six directors named in the annexed Proxy Statement, by attending the meeting or by proxy by marking the appropriate space on the enclosed Proxy Card and by signing, dating and promptly returning the enclosed Proxy Card in the enclosed envelope, then such new Board shall be elected provided only the present Board has been removed.

If you do not wish to replace the Board of Directors then you should vote against both proposals, or alternatively, not vote at all. In the event that either or both of the above proposals are not approved by the requisite vote, then the present Board will remain in office.

Your prompt return of the enclosed Proxy Card may spare the necessity and expense of further solicitation in order to insure a quorum at the Special Meeting. I urge you to attend the Special Meeting, at which time you may vote in person, even if you previously mailed a Proxy Card.

Martin J. Whitman, President
M.J. Whitman & Co. Inc.

January 23, 1984 Proxy Statement Selection

Probable Change in Fundamental Investment Policy of the Corporation

If the new Board of Directors is elected, it is the present intention of each of the nominees to seek, at the Annual Meeting scheduled to be held on April 11, 1984, shareholder approval for a change in the fundamental investment policy of the Corporation.

The Corporation was organized on August 14, 1981. The present investment policy of the Corporation is to attain as high a level of return as possible, focusing primarily on purchasing equity securities, writing covered listed call options, purchasing listed call options, purchasing listed put options, and purchasing money market instruments and other short-term debt securities. At present, the Corporation is managed by Security Pacific Investment Managers, Inc. ("Adviser"), which provides investment advice and investment supervisory services pursuant to a Management and Investment Advisory Agreement ("Investment Advisory Agreement"). The Investment Advisory Agreement is terminable on sixty days' written notice by any party thereto.

The nominees, if elected, presently intend to propose at the next Annual Meeting of the Corporation, the adoption of a new fundamental investment policy. The proposed new investment policy will be based essentially on a buy-and-hold strategy emphasizing long-term investment, in which the portfolio will consist largely of debt and equity securities which have special, non-general market characteristics as follows:

It is anticipated that, if the new investment policy is adopted, a substantial portion of the Corporation's portfolio may be invested in securities having relatively inactive markets. It is also likely that at any time that new purchases are being made, such purchases will be made in the securities of companies in the industries which are depressed. For example, if substantial new investments were to be made at present, such investments would be concentrated in the equity securities of companies in the energy, real estate and financial industries, as well as in the debt securities of certain issuers attempting to reorganize under the Federal Bankruptcy Code. It is the intention of the nominees, if elected, to seek investments in the equity securities of companies where debt service consumes a small part of such companies' cash flow. Investments may also be made in companies which could benefit from reorganization under the Bankruptcy Code, which would result in a reduction in debt service requirements. The Corporation will invest, on a long-term basis, in the securities of an issuer when it believes that either its debt securities will provide an above-average return, or when the market prices of its equity securities reflect, in management's estimation, a substantial discount from the net asset value of the issuer. Net asset value represents the fair market value of assets less the fair market value of liabilities. Net asset value is not necessarily the same as book value because, for the most part, book value is derived from historic cost, not estimates of market value. Of necessity, this investment approach means de-emphasizing consideration of near-term outlooks and current conditions in securities markets.

Based upon the most recently issued quarterly report for the Corporation dated September 30, 1983, the total percentage of common equities and options in the Corporation's portfolio was 90.7%. It is anticipated that in the event that the proposed investment policy change is effectuated, none of the Corporation's assets will be invested in options. At present, the change in proportion of investment in equity securities to debt securities cannot be estimated, as all investments resulting from the proposed change in investment policy will be based upon their individual characteristics in relation to the general and non-general considerations discussed above.

Research efforts in connection with the proposed new investment policy will emphasize analysis of documents, especially stockholder mailings and Securities and Exchange Commission filings by issuers. In the case of equity issues, four criteria in selecting investments would generally be stressed:

1. Strong financial position.
2. Responsible management and control groups, especially in terms of their apparent recognition of the rights of outside shareholders.
3. Availability of financial and related information.

4. Availability at a market price which management believes is below its estimate of net asset value.

In contrast with equity investment, in investing in debt securities, the proposed new investment policy, if adopted, would result in concentration in debt securities which management believes provide either above average current yields or yields to maturity, or the opportunity for the realization of capital gain because the debtor may be reorganized, restructured or liquidated. In this connection, management is likely to analyze issuers which either sought relief under the bankruptcy statutes or are candidates for such relief, in an effort to select debt securities which will benefit from changes arising out of the reorganization. Such changes could include reductions in debt service for the issues, which may result in the creditors' receipt of equity securities in exchange for part or all of their debt, and/or in the deferral or reduction in interest payments, and/or the extension of the maturity of the debt.

Accordingly, it is possible that if the proposed new investment policy is adopted, a considerable portion of the Corporation's portfolio would be invested in the securities of issuers which have sought relief under the Federal Bankruptcy Code, or companies which may seek such relief. Such investments carry special and substantial risks. In the case of any particular issue, it is very difficult to estimate prospects for the issuer emerging from bankruptcy, the period of time that may be involved and how much the particular issue will be worth either as a unimpaired claim under the Federal Bankruptcy Code, as a participant in a reorganization or as a participant in a liquidation.

It is also the intention of the new Board of Directors, if elected, to seek shareholder approval for changing the Corporation from a diversified management investment company to a non-diversified management investment company, pursuant to Section 13(a) of the Investment Company Act of 1940, in order to permit the Corporation to have more portfolio concentration, and less portfolio diversification than is now permitted.

The nominees, if elected, will formulate specific implementation procedures only upon shareholder approval of the new fundamental investment policy. The officers of the Corporation will not begin utilizing the new policy until the Board has reviewed and approved definitive procedures. Any specific plans developed will be intended to comply with applicable regulatory requirements. No assurance can be given that the proposed change in investment objectives, if implemented, will result in the appreciation of the Corporation's assets. If the new directors are elected and the shareholders of the Corporation subsequently disapprove of the proposed change in investment policy, the new directors will continue the present investment policy of the Corporation.

CHAPTER 2

Equity Strategies Fund Investment Philosophy

APRIL 1989

Our Investment Philosophy

The publication of the Equity Strategies Fund 1989 Annual Report affords good opportunity to discuss with all shareholders the underlying investment principals: what we see as the potential and the problems with our investment programs. The discussion below is divided into four topics:

1. Troubled Issues
2. Mezzanine Securities
3. Equity Securities
4. Business Development Investments

Troubled Issues

A troubled issuer is a company which has either defaulted on money payments due creditors, or where there appears to be a high degree of probability that such a default will occur. If the Fund is going to invest in the securities of troubled issues, it has been and will be as a senior creditor, preferably a secured creditor. Fund investments in these credits in recent years have included Anglo Energy Secured Income Notes (now Nabors Industries), Johns-Manville Debentures,

Mission Insurance Group Notes, LTV Steele Trade Claim, Public Service Company of New Hampshire Second Mortgages and Public Service Company of New Hampshire Third Mortgages.

This has been a fertile, relatively non-competitive investment field for the Fund where returns have probably averaged well over 20% per year compounded including situations (e.g. Mission Insurance Group) where the workout has proved to be difficult and time consuming. The relative non-competitiveness of the field arises, I think, out of the fact that our analysis focuses on different variables than almost everyone else's. All credit analysis and most security analysis, e.g. Graham & Dodd, are concerned solely with how to avoid investing in credit instruments where there might be a money default. Our emphasis, on the other hand is on what will occur in the event there is a money default. Frankly, most analysts have neither the background nor the access to qualified professionals to be able to be effective in dealing with defaulted securities.

In general, the senior debt of troubled companies is of two types: issues which will participate in reorganization and issues which will not participate in reorganization. Judgements as to whether a troubled credit will or will not participate in a reorganization involve analysis by people relatively experienced in workouts. Issues which will not participate in a reorganization are true credit instruments which will remain pretty much as is after a reorganization (whether or not that reorganization occurs voluntarily or in Chapter 11), and which, even during a Chapter 11 reorganization, may never even miss an interest payment. The Fund tries to acquire such non-participating credits at current yields of 18% – 20% or better, and with yields to "an improved credit rating" of not less than 40% annually. Such non-participating investments by the Fund have included the LTV Trade Claim, Public Service Company of New Hampshire Second Mortgages, Public Service Company of New Hampshire Third Mortgage Industrial Revenue Bonds, and probably NACO Financial Notes. Non-participating credits of troubled issues remain a promising area for Fund Investments.

Credit instruments that are going to participate in the reorganization of troubled issues pose a different set of problems. The basic rule (and law) in reorganization is that a senior creditor participating in a reorganization is entitled to receive "Full Value" before anyone junior to the senior creditor receives anything at all, unless a requisite vote is obtained in a Chapter 11 case and, as a result of that vote, the class of senior creditors agrees to accept less than full value. Full value need not be paid in the same or similar credit instruments, but might be paid in all sorts of considerations ranging – in whole or in part – from cash, to other assets, to new debt instruments, to common stock and warrants. The U.S. Bankruptcy Code contemplates that Plans of Reorganization be consensual, i.e. negotiated between creditors and parties-in-interest. By and large, those negotiations determine whether or not an individual creditor will get full value, and in what form such value, whether full or less than full, is to be paid. Fund investments in these participating credits have included Anglo Energy secured Income Notes, Johns-Manville Debentures and Trade Claims, Mission Insurance Group Unsecured Notes, Petro-Lewis Secured Debentures and Public Service Company of New Hampshire 13 ¾% Third Mortgage.

If investments in these participating credits are going to work out well for an investment company, the investment company has to be in a position to ride the coattails of an activist. The very nature of consensual plans requires hard, active negotiating – and legal posturing – if a class of creditors is to receive a satisfactory value in a satisfactory form. Being active is a very expensive proposition, especially looking at the rates lawyers, investment bankers, and accountants charge nowadays. In my view, active investing is inappropriate for companies such as Equity Strategies which is a Registered Investment Company under the investment Company Act of 1940, as amended. This does, however, remain an attractive investment field for the Fund. Equity Strategies will continue to make investments as a senior creditor where it hopes to participate in reorganization. However, it will generally do so only as a coattail-rider of third party activists whom we believe are highly competent, and only when there can be no question but that the Fund is a passive investor.

Mezzanine Securities

Mezzanine securities, under our definition, are instruments which based on our purchase price show promise of giving the Fund an annual pre-tax cash return, or zero-coupon return of in excess of 20%, and where there does not appear to be large risks of either a money default or of a contemplated transaction including liquidations, not closing. In the event of a money default, mezzanine securities have to accept a junior position. Under our definition, any junior security can be a mezzanine security as long as it has reasonably well defined contractual terms and/or reasonably well defined workout terms. Fund investments in mezzanine securities have defined workout terms. Fund investments in mezzanine securities have included Adobe Resources Preferred Stocks, Empire Gas Subordinated Debentures, First Pennsylvania Corp. Common Stocks, National Loan Bank Common Stock, Royal Palm Beach Colony, L.P., Texas American Energy Subordinated Debentures; Vyquest, Inc. Subordinated Debentures and Weatherford International, Inc. Preferred Stock. While Equity Strategies appears to have done satisfactorily investing in mezzanine securities, it is unlikely that such investments are ever going to become a large part of the Fund's portfolio even if many issues become available at ultra-attractive prices. It is just too unsettling swimming in the mezzanine swamp, as contrasted with either being a senior creditor, a holder of high grade equities, or an investor involved with business development. The basic problem with mezzanine investing is that each issuer tends to have specific weaknesses and if something does go wrong, it frequently is hard to protect the Fund's investment position.

Equity Securities

Equity securities are issues which have residual rights and are, in effect, ownership interests in going concerns. With only the most minor exceptions, all Fund investments in equity securities have the following characteristics:

1. The Company has an extremely strong financial position.
2. The Company appears to be reasonably well (or at least honestly) managed.
3. There is a plethora of documentary information about the Company which is available to us and is understood by us.
4. The equity security is available for purchase by us at a price which we believe represents a substantial discount from what the Company is worth as a private business.

Equity security investments have included the common stock of Adobe Resources, Capital Southwest Corp., Digital Communications Associates, Exxon, Ford, GATX Corporation, various genetic engineering companies, Kentucky Central Life Insurance Company, Liberty Homes, Penn Central and Perini Corp.

In our type of equity investing, there are two separate areas that one can look to: performance and value. In performance investing we not only follow the four criteria listed above but, in addition, look for a catalyst – a hostile take-over, friendly merger, restructuring – that will cause the common stocks (or its equivalent) to appreciate in the relatively near term. In value investing only an attractive price is sought; there does not have to be a catalyst.

By and large, Equity Strategies, insofar as it is an equity investor, is a value investor not a performance investor. I am not against performance investing but it tends to be a lot harder to do successfully than value investing. This is due, in great part, to the fact that most equity investors are looking for catalysts. If you want to be a successful performance investor, most of the time you have to be prepared to pay up, i.e. pay higher prices than that at which comparable values may be available. This tends to be hard for us to do.

Value Investing has its problems. The biggest single one seems to be that the companies invested in frequently are run by conservative, deeply entrenched managements and control groups who care a lot less than Equity Strategies shareholders do about when good stock market price performance will occur. Even given this, I believe that a portfolio of well selected value equities ought to earn reasonably satisfactory returns and ought to entail reasonably small investment risks.

The more I am around value equity investing, the more convinced I become that bargain purchases are created at least as much by past prosperity for companies (which does not get reflected in the market price for a company's common stock) as they are by bear market. Regardless of the level of markets, good analysts ought to be able to uncover pretty good value most of the time.

One final word about equity investing by Equity Strategies. We are bottom-up investors not top down and the Fund also is a "good enough" investor, not a profit maximizer. Put simply, we analyze companies and individual securities, not markets and economies. If we think the internals for a company and its securities are good enough to meet our hurdle rates – a pre-tax return of 30% or better without meaningful investment risk; we ignore market risk completely. For example, we do not hesitate to buy Kentucky Central Life Common at 12, even though somebody's technical approach to the market indicates that the common stock might sell down to 7 or 8. We worry about being wrong about the Kentucky Central Life business and about what the real value of the Kentucky Central subsidiaries might be; we do not worry about how the Kentucky Central Life Common Stock will perform. We assume – usually correctly – that if we are right about the Kentucky Central Life business, the market will catch up sooner or later. Market timing is a luxury we cannot afford. Business analysis is tough enough without overlaying it with market analysis; something we feel usually is not less than 99.44% mumbo-jumbo.

Business Development Investments

Business development investing entails funding a company either directly or indirectly through exchanging debt for common stock with the result that the company becomes strongly capitalized, and Equity Strategies becomes a holder of a significant percentage of that company's equity. To date, Equity Strategies has invested in two business development situations: Nabors Industries and KCP Holding. If Vyquest reorganizes, it too will become a business development investment.

The risk reward ratio for Equity Strategies can be quite good in business development investing, but most of the investments seem to involve a high "beta", that is big risk potential, big reward potential.

CHAPTER 3

Equity Strategies Fund Launches Third Avenue Funds

OCTOBER 1990

Dear Fellow Shareholders:

At October 31, 1990, the unaudited net asset value attributable to the 2,435,394 shares of Common Stock outstand was $25.44 per share, compared with unaudited net asset values of $30.82 per share at July 31, 1990 and $20.37 per share at October 31, 1989. At November 30, 1990, unaudited net asset value was $25.48 per share.

The fluctuations in net asset value are attributable, by and large, to swings in the market prices of Nabors Industries Common Stock, which thus far in calendar 1990 has ranged from a high of 7 ¼ to a low of 3 ¼; at November 30, Nabors Common closed at 5 ¼. While the Nabors common stock is likely to continue to fluctuate at least over the near term, the Nabors business seems to be making steady, admirable progress. The Company remains extremely well financed; I would not be surprised were the tax sheltered earnings from operations to exceed $0.60 per share in the fiscal year to end of September 30, 1991. Based on the Funds carrying value (a ½ point discount from market), Nabors Common accounted for 86% of total Fund assets at October 31. Equity Strategies owns 5.15 share of Nabors Common Stock for each one share of Equity Strategies Common Stock outstanding.

There were a few significant changes in the portfolio during the October quarter. The Fund established new positions in the Home Insurance Company Preferred Stock; Digital Communication Associates Common Stocks; and First Constitutional Financial Corp. Common Stocks. The Home Insurance Preferred equity affords a current return of about 23% based on the Fund's cost; we expect this issue, which is senior to all holdings company debt, including bank loans, to continue to be a performing instrument. Digital Communications Associates is an extremely well-financed computer peripheral manufacturer whose common stock is selling near historic lows at a material discount from net asset value. First Constitution is a New Haven Connecticut saving bank holding company. First Constitution has $1.8 billion portfolio consisting mostly of Connecticut real estate mortgages about $1 billion on which are secured by single family residences. The Company remains in capital compliance for all regulatory purposes despite severe write-offs; however, non-performing loans continue to increase; our purchase price of 1 ¼ compares with a stated net asset value at September 30, 1990 of $13.16 per share. Although real estate conditions continue to decline in Connecticut, First Constitution seems much better capitalized that almost all if its competitors. I think First Constitution is very likely to be a survivor.

At October 31, the Fund had liabilities for deferred taxes on unrealized appreciation of about $12.7 million, or approximately $5.25 per Equity Strategies share. This tax liability will never actually become payable unless profits are realized upon the sale of securities, especially Nabors Common Stock. Given this "phantom liability", your Board concluded in 1986 that is would be prejudicial to existing shareholders if Equity Strategies instituted a continuous offering of Equity Strategies Common shares to that the number of Common shares outstanding would increase. In that case, new shareholders buying common stocks at net asset value would receive a bargain versus existing shareholders since the price new shareholders would pay, would reflect a 100% deduction for these deferred tax liabilities which might never, in fact, become payable. To overcome this prejudice against existing stockholder of Equity Strategies Fund, and still permit new investments into a mutual fund, a new Fund, Third Avenue Fund, has commenced operations. Third Avenue has the same management and Board of

Directors of Equity Strategies. Third Avenue Fund, Inc. has a continuous offering of its common shares with a minimum subscription amount of $1,000.

CHAPTER 4

Inaugural Third Avenue Funds Letter to Shareholders

OCTOBER 1990

Dear Fellow Shareholders:

Welcome! This is the first Annual Report of the Third Avenue Fund, Inc., (TAF). TAF was established to follow the same general investment strategies as Equity Strategies Fund, Inc. under the aegis of the same Board of Directors and the same management. The crucial difference between the two funds is that TAF makes a continuous offering of new shares. Equity Strategies, on the other hand, is closed to new investors. As the accompanying audited financial statements show, TAF had made no securities investments, as of October 31, 1990, the close of TAF's first fiscal year. At October 31, 1990, the net asset value was $10.00 per share.

TAF commenced its investment operations on November 1. We anticipate that TAF will be close to fully invested by calendar year-end. At December 19, 1990, net asset value was $10.18 per share. The Fund's unaudited portfolio consisted of the following securities as of that date:

Face Amount/Shares	Issuer
$400,000	Louisiana State Agricultural Authority 8.25% Bonds due 10/1/96
$1,000,000	Adams County (Colorado) IDR Bonds 9.00% due 11/1/96

$2,000,000	AmBase Corp. Senior Subordinated 14 7/8% Notes due 7/15/98
15,000 shares	Home Insurance Company $2.95 Series A Preferred Stock
7,000 shares	Elders IXL (Canada) Retractable Preferred Stock
20,000 shares	Presidential Life Corp. Common Stock
20,000 shares	Broad, Inc. Common Stock
177,000 shares	National Asset Bank Common Stock
50,000 shares	National Loan Bank Common Stock
70,000 shares	First Constitutional Financial Corp. Common Stock

Management believes that most of the securities owned by TAF are selling at prices that appear to reflect panic on the part of the sellers. Indeed, we don't think prices have been this attractive since 1974 for the types of securities of most interest to TAF. Low prices ought to reflect both reduced risk and large appreciation potentials for TAF. Of course, while we believe these holdings are appropriate for TAF, given its investment program, the following discussion should not be read as a general recommendation to other investors. A brief review of the rationale for each of TAF's holdings follows:

The Louisiana State and Adams County Industrial Revenue Bonds are backed by Guaranteed Investment Contracts, or GICs, issued by Executive Life Insurance Company of California ("Executive Life"). TAF acquired both securities at an approximate 50% yield to maturity and a 37% current yield. Executive Life's parent, First Executive Corporation, appears to be hopelessly insolvent. Executive Life, though, appears reasonably solvent, able to meet its obligations, in part, because its junk bond portfolio seems to be materially less junky than average. An issue has been raised that these GICs would be subordinate to other policy holder claims in the event that Executive Life ever is placed in conservatorship, (i.e., an insurance equivalent of Chapter 11). It is unlikely that a subordination claim can ever be perfected because, in our view, there appears to be little legal basis for any such claim. In any event, we expect Executive Life to stay out of conservatorship and that these bonds will continue to pay interest and principal without a money default. On the other hand, if Executive Life is ever taken into conservatorship, we expect that the ultimate rehabilitation of Executive Life would result in a workout for these issues at prices that would give TAF a quite satisfactory return on its investment.

AmBase Corporation ("AmBase") is the parent of Home Insurance Company ("Home"), owning 41% of Home Preferred Stock outstanding and 100% of Home Common Stock outstanding. AmBase has announced an agreement to sell its entire Home position to a group headed by a subsidiary of TryggHansa, a large Swedish insurance company. The Indenture governing the Bonds owned by TAF requires that if AmBase is no longer a "substantial owner" of Home, AmBase is required to tender for these bonds at a price of 100% of par, and that condition cannot be waived without each bondholder's consent. We believe that, in the event AmBase does not honor this condition, it will be either because the acquirer of Home can succeed in assuming these Notes despite the plain language of the Indenture, in which case the Notes will become a performing loan yielding about 47%; or AmBase seeks relief under Chapter 11. We feel in that case, this issue still ought to work out better than TAF's cost basis of less than 23% of par. This issue is only subordinated to $400 million of bank debt and $102 million of 113/4% Debentures, a relatively small amount compared to the value of the Home position. Most of the other claims against AmBase are for employee compensation, which in Chapter 11 may be subordinate to TAF's position under theories of equitable subordination. It has been hard for bankruptcy courts to allow claims for equitable subordination in the past. In the AmBase case, however, we believe there is a strong claim for equitable subordination (and voidable preferences) given the AmBase management and their compensation packages.

Home Insurance is operating well, and does not appear to be infected with the AmBase disease. Home Insurance Preferred Stock is senior to AmBase Bank Debt, and may, in fact, be comparable to securities rated Baa or maybe A. At TAF's cost, the Preferred held by TAF offers a 25.1% current return. If a buyer of the Home desires to refinance this high dividend preferred, say in two years, the buyer would have to call the issue at $20. If that were to occur, the yield to maturity for TAF would be about 53%.

Elders Preferred is ratably secured with the bank debt of the parent company, Elders IXL Ltd. (Australia) ("Elders"). At TAF's cost, the yield to maturity at the 1992 redemption date is about 30%. Elders is a wellfinanced, profitable brewer with interests in beer operations in Australia, the United Kingdom and Canada. Presidential Life ("Presidential") is a New York domiciled life insurance company. TAF acquired its position at less than two times earnings and at above a 57% discount from net asset value.

Presidential Life has a junk bond problem. We believe that problem has been vastly overblown in the marketplace. Indeed, we think Presidential is a conservatively capitalized company. However, if we are wrong, the ultimate downside for TAF's position in Presidential Life Common is much greater than would be the case for the other insurance investments discussed above, Executive Life, AmBase, and Home Insurance.

The TAF position in the equity of Broad, Inc. ("Broad"), a financial services company, was acquired at less than five times earnings and at 57% discount from net asset value. We haven't figured out what is wrong with Broad, Inc. Common Stock, other than a general malaise toward financial institution equities in the financial community. After two face-to-face visits with Broad management, we remain highly impressed with them.

National Asset Bank and National Loan Bank are debt free companies which are continuing to liquidate portfolios of troubled Texas bank loans. TAF acquired its positions at prices which appear to be discounts of at least 50% from conservatively estimated present values for those bank loans. We remain particularly impressed with the management at National Asset Bank. That management is attempting to convert the company from a liquidating bank to a nonbank going concern. If they succeed, they may be in a position to build premium values, well in excess of liquidating values, into the company.

At September 30, 1990, First Constitutional Financial Corp. ("First Constitution"), a unitary savings bank, had a net asset value of $13.16 per share, was in capital compliance for all regulatory purposes, and was suffering cash losses from operations of perhaps $1 million per year. TAF's cost basis for its First Constitution position is $0.94 per share. We believe that First Constitution may be one of the few survivors among banks doing business in southeastern Connecticut. Practically all the other banks appear to be basket cases. If First Constitution proves to be a survivor, it might well take over a substantial amount of profitable business from competing banks, starting in 1991. It appears as if the appreciation possibilities for First Constitutional Common Stock may be huge, although there may be some risks.

We suppose that many people who read this letter will conclude that the TAF portfolio is speculative. Certainly all the conventional thinkers believe TAF is speculative. We disagree. Unconventional, sure. But given the prices at which the various securities were acquired, and given the extensive, in-depth research that went into the decision making process for each investment, speculative versus conservative ought not to be measured only by what is cosmetically acceptable, and what rating services say. Rating services and conventional thinkers pay no attention at all to price. From the TAF perspective, we believe that there ought to be, at the least, a price component in measuring whether an investment is either speculative or conservative. There also ought to be a quality of research component. TAF will try to stay conservative by these measures even though the portfolio is unlikely to ever be cosmetically correct.

PART 2

INVESTMENT PHILOSOPHY

"In common stock investing, the sole, or almost sole, focus is on buying into well-financed companies at steep discounts from readily ascertainable NAV where there are reasonable prospects for double digit NAV growth over the next five-years or so."

July 2009

CHAPTER 5

Third Avenue Value Investment Philosophy

OCTOBER 1992

The Third Avenue Value Investment Philosophy

It ought to be constructive for shareholders if I explain the Fund's investment approach in some detail, describing both what Third Avenue Value Fund (TAVF) does and does not do. While I refer to myself in the narrative below as the Fund's manager, it is important to remember that I function as manager under the supervision and direction of TAVF's skilled and dedicated Board of Directors. Our investment philosophy encompasses two disciplines; one used in acquiring and holding credit instruments, and one used in acquiring and holding common stocks. Since Foster Brewing (Canada) and Reading & Bates matured, TAVF has been basically a common stock fund. At October 31, 1992, the portfolio broke down as follows:

Asset	% of Total Assets
Cash and Equivalents	26.7%
Credit Instruments	10.3%
Common Stocks and Equivalents	63.0%
	100.0%

By the end of calendar 1992, the percentage of Fund assets in cash and equivalents is likely to be reduced materially because of several buying programs currently under way, both for credit instruments and common stocks. Credit instruments acquired by TAVF are strictly performing loans which I believe will continue to be performing, though one can never know for certain. The Fund tries to restrict such purchases to securities which afford a current yield, or a yield to maturity, at least 500 basis points above what comparable credits are selling for in the general market. Moreover, such instruments have to have strong covenant protections so that in the event of a money default TAVF will realize a profit, or at least not suffer any loss, on its investment in the consequent workout. The two credits held by the Fund — US Trails 12% Senior Notes due 1998 and Olympia & York Maiden Lane Finance Corp. 10 3/8% First Mortgage due 1995 — both benefit from having a first lien on underlying assets. To us, credit analysis is not so much a process of measuring the probabilities of whether money defaults will or will not occur, but rather measuring how the creditor will fare in a reorganization or liquidation if a money default does occur.

In acquiring common stocks, TAVF focuses on four characteristics:

1. The issuer has to have a strong financial position measured not only by balance sheet data but also measured by off balance sheet liabilities and contingencies, whether or not disclosed in footnotes to financial statements.
2. The issuer should be run by reasonable control groups and managements, as gauged by managerial competence as operators and investors, as well as by an apparent absence of intent to profit at the expense of stockholders.
3. The business has to be one I understand, which generally means that the numbers reported (which are usually in accordance with Generally Accepted Accounting Principles) have to be reliable as objective benchmarks to aid in my understanding the business, its values and its dynamics.
4. The price the Fund pays for a common stock ought to be no more than one-half of what I believe the issuer is worth as a private company.

TAVF is a buy-and-hold investor. The businesses in which the Fund invests, whether as a creditor or equity participant, are characterized by staying power. Fluctuations in market prices for securities tend to be ignored. General market, as distinct from fundamental, factors are always ignored. One reason is that the "market" tends to emphasize different things than TAVF does. For example, most analysts in research departments appear to be interested in current earnings and short-term earnings forecasts (this is especially true for computer stocks such as Apple Computer and Digital Equipment). TAVF is interested in long-term basic earning power. Another reason is that the Fund's investments tend to grow out of intensive research. If I do not believe that I know much more than the "market" about a particular investment, the Fund ought not to be in that investment.

Our policy for selling positions held by TAVF has a number of components. First and foremost, the Fund sells promptly when I find a mistake has been made either because the future is unpredictable or the analysis that preceded the investment was faulty. However, the validity of an analysis ought to be gauged by events within the business, not by market price fluctuations. The Fund will also sell if I believe a security reaches prices that result in a gross overvaluation. Modest overvaluation is not a reason to sell, especially if the Fund continues to grow so that it always has new moneys to invest. I find that the TAVF type of analysis is much better suited to identifying attractive securities, then it is to identifying overvalued securities. I suppose this is so because there is a concentration on worst case scenarios in a TAVF type analysis rather than measuring realistic upside potentials. My guess would be that most of the Fund's "sells" over time will come from situations working out, i.e., credit instruments maturing or portfolio companies becoming involved in asset conversion events such as mergers, acquisitions, restructurings and liquidations. For example, since the end of the October quarter, National Loan Bank announced an intent to wind up its liquidation by early 1993. Using management's current estimates of likely realizations, the compound annual return to TAVF from this investment, based on its cost, should be not less than 20%.

Another principal reason why "sell" decision making is so tough is that corporate values are anything but static. Reasonably managed businesses which are reasonably well-financed, almost by definition, increase in value over long periods of time as the businesses progress. Insofar as this is so, bargains are created more by past corporate prosperity than by bear markets. The Fund's position in Capital Southwest common stock, for example, has appreciated by about 27% since the Fund acquired its position. Yet Capital Southwest common stock is selling at the same, or a greater, discount from net asset value than existed when TAVF acquired its position. A well-defined sell strategy makes sense, theoretically, for money managers who: a) are trying to maximize profits; and b) are trying to outperform the market. I don't try to maximize profits, but rather try to do "good enough"; and I definitely do not try to outperform the market.

The managements of many of the companies in which TAVF invests are ultraconservative — that's where those huge cash positions come from in the first place. In many instances, I believe these managements are overly conservative. Also, many, if not most, of the managements and control groups of the Fund's portfolio companies could not care less about the price of the common stocks of the companies they run. By virtue of their balance sheets, these are not companies seeking access to capital markets, nor are their principal owners seeking to sell out.

In some cases, insiders may have a strong incentive to keep the price of the common stock low. Principal owners of Forest City Enterprises, for example, may be faced with inheritance taxes. If so, it would be advantageous for them to have Forest City common stock valued, for estate tax purposes, at market on the American Stock Exchange at $17 per share; rather than at the values management and their real estate appraisers believe exist, a minimum of $80 per share, at January 31, 1992. In other cases, e.g., Dart Group and Penn Central, controlling owners have had transactions with the companies which, while they might meet tests of fairness, were not, by definition, arm's length. Overall, though, I do not think that the managements running the TAVF portfolio companies compare unfavorably with the managements of public companies in general. In any event, I certainly prefer overly conservative managements to overly promotional managements. Because of various state laws and court decisions over the past 10 or 15 years, managements in general now have, in my view, considerably less incentive to foster the interests of outside, passive minority stockholders, than had been the case previously.

Large cash positions are more than a source of safety for companies, they are also a source of investment income. TAVF's portfolio companies are cash-rich. However, earnings on that cash are now at a low point. Frankly, cash, as an earning asset, is now less attractive than it has been at any time in the last 40 years.

The Fund acquires all sorts of securities that meet its criteria. Some are actively traded issues of large companies — such as Apple Computer, Digital Equipment, Kemper Corp., Penn Central. Others are "penny stocks" — including First Constitution Financial Corp. and National Loan Bank. And others are hardly marketable at all within twenty-four hours — for example, Capital Southwest, Liberty Homes, Consolidated Tomoka Land, NAB Asset Corp., Public Storage Properties, and Dart Group, even though I believe each of the positions could be liquidated at around current market in seven days. These relatively unmarketable issues are what I call "Roach Motel" securities. It is easy to check in (buy), but you can't check out (sell) on a day-to-day basis. It is very important in acquiring "Roach Motel" positions that the fundamental analysis be sound if draconian downsides are to be avoided.

TAVF does not pay much attention to diversification, other than to comport with regulatory and income tax requirements so that the Fund can qualify as a registered investment company under Subchapter M of the Internal Revenue Code and not be a taxable entity. Put simply, diversification is only a surrogate, and frequently a poor surrogate, for knowledge and control. Lacking control, unlike for example promoters of leveraged buyouts, common sense dictates that the Fund diversify to some extent. On the other hand, since our investments are based on specific knowledge, there is far less need to diversify than is the case for most mutual funds, especially those that are top-down investors using factors such as industry or country identification, indexes or market timing systems as a basis for investment decisions.

Also, in the Fund's type of investing, identifying particular industries is something we underweight compared with the typical portfolio manager. Given TAVF's investment criteria, it is more accurate to view the situation as the industry selecting the Fund, rather than TAVF choosing the industries in which to invest. One way of looking at the Fund's industry selections is to observe that at October 31, 1992, TAVF was concentrated in the common stocks of financial institutions, real estate enterprises and computer companies. Such industry concentrations did not occur because of conscious forethought. Rather, this is where the Fund was able to acquire at attractive prices the securities of companies which appear to have substantial staying power and substantial long-term earning power.

TAVF's analyses concentrate strictly on "what is" in terms of understanding a company and its securities. In contrast, most other analysts give considerable weight to attempting to fathom "what the market thinks," best described by John Maynard Keynes as gauging "the average opinion of the average opinion." There is an economic reality to these "average opinion" searches from a company point of view, since, if a company needs periodic access to capital markets, whether credit markets or equity markets, then what the market thinks has a lot to do with whether, or not, a company and its security holders will prosper. In the case of the Fund, though, a need for access to capital markets for the companies whose common stocks are in the portfolio is virtually nonexistent. The companies in which TAVF has common stock investments are largely self-financing, net cash generators. This leaves me free to concentrate on "what is."

TAVF pays no attention to macro factors such as stock market levels, general interest rates, and business cycles: the various top-down factors on which most analysts concentrate. I, like almost all others, am not very good at predicting macro factors. Furthermore, such factors historically have not been of overriding importance to dedicated investors — and business people concentrating on a bottomup approach. It's difficult to spend a lot of time learning the "nitty gritty" facts about an issuer and its securities; on the other hand, it's easy to have opinions about things like the outlook for the overall economy.

I am frequently asked to contrast the TAVF investment style with that of Graham & Dodd. There are similarities, but the differences are far more important. In terms of credit analysis, TAVF is covenant driven; Graham & Dodd is not covenant driven, but rather emphasizes quantitative analysis on an overall basis and seeks to avoid investing if there is any probability at all of a money default. In equity investing, Graham & Dodd concentrates on postulating a series of good caveats to follow if you really do not know much about the company in which you are investing. TAVF, on the other hand, concentrates on knowing much. One practical area where this shows up is the assessment of the importance of common stock cash dividends. Graham & Dodd view cash dividends as highly important. TAVF ordinarily ignores cash dividends as an investment consideration, and when it does consider them, the existence of a cash dividend is much more likely to be viewed as a negative, rather than a positive factor.

Academic finance, too, is relatively unimportant to TAVF. Put simply, modern finance theory is valuable in dealing with situations such as derivative securities, and merger arbitrage where there are a limited number of variables to be examined. The underlying assumptions of academic finance tend to be unrealistic or misleading when applied to the complex situations in which TAVF invests.

Timing of purchases is not a consideration in the TAVF scheme of things. If a security is cheap enough, it is acquired. Arguments might be made logically to elevate timing of purchases to an important consideration in making an investment decision about an individual security. Such arguments, though, have much less validity in the management of an entire portfolio. If the analysis of underlying values is correct, one or more of the issues in the Fund's portfolio ought to be working-out periodically, say every six months or so; this ought to take care of any timing consideration.

TAVF views risk and reward quite differently than is conventional. The common view is that there is an elementary tradeoff: you have to take risks to obtain rewards. In the TAVF view, there is no such trade-off but, rather, the cheaper you buy, the greater the reward and the cheaper you buy, the less the risk. In conventional thinking there are two components of the measure of degrees of speculation: quality of the issuer and terms of the issue. TAVF emphasizes a third consideration: price of the issue. Conventional wisdom assumes that securities prices at any moment of time are in equilibrium, i.e., the price is right. TAVF's underlying assumption is that the price is wrong.

It probably is a mistake to talk about general risk. Rather the focus should be on specific risks — market risk, investment risk, interest rate risk, currency risk, etc. The Fund tends to take huge market risks in that no attention is paid to predicting near-term market prices. Indeed, I know from long experience when acquiring securities that no matter how low I think a price can go, it can, and usually does, go a lot lower. In contrast, TAVF goes to great lengths to try to avoid investment, risk, i.e., even using worst case scenarios the underlying values attributable to the securities in which TAVF invests ought to be greater than the Fund's cost basis after allowing for a considerable dissipation of future values as events unfold.

In trying to avoid investment risks as a component of obtaining an increased upside potential, TAVF is like most active investors and business people. Most of the great fortunes probably have been built by activists who avoided risk. Activists avoid risks by getting paid off the top. In contrast, TAVF tries to avoid risks by buying cheap. Such risk avoiders include fund managers in managing their own businesses, who collect cash fees off the top; LBO promoters, who, by arranging attractive senior financing, get cheap, or free, common stock (plus cash fees); and by real estate entrepreneurs, who arrange nonrecourse mortgage financing. In contrast, TAVF tries to avoid risks by buying cheap.

I am also asked if TAVF acquires growth stocks or foreign issues. Sure we do, if the price is right. As a sort of topdown rule of thumb, TAVF looks at acquiring growth issues of unseasoned companies provided the price at which the common stock is available approximates the price that a first tier venture capitalist would pay. That price is almost always a small fraction of the Initial Public Offering price. No growth issues per se are in the TAVF portfolio at present. Foreign issues have to meet our basic criteria. As a practical matter, this means the particular issue has to be registered with the U.S. Securities and Exchange Commission. TAVF has no foreign issues in its portfolio at present, unless one deems Digital Equipment, well over half of whose revenues are derived from offshore sources, to be a foreign issuer.

TAVF differs from many other very fine and capable value investors in that if I think a value is good enough without reference to other factors, the Fund will buy. In contrast, others want not only value, but also a catalyst, i.e., evidence that something is going to happen within a determined period of time. For example, the Fund holds a position in St. Joe Paper, a storehouse of value which holds, among other things, 3% of all the land acreage in the State of Florida. Others would rather not own St. Joe Paper until there is some tangible evidence that values will be realized for the benefit of St. Joe shareholders in the foreseeable future. The objective of the Fund is to earn a satisfactory return for its investors, say 20% compounded annually. Whether or not we outperform other funds or the general market is not of great moment. It might be noted that the insiders hold substantial investments in TAVF Common Stock. My family and I own 149,129 shares, or 6.4% of the shares outstanding at October 31, 1992. The Board of Directors and Officers of the Fund, together with my family, hold 176,774 shares or 7.6% of the outstanding issue.

CHAPTER 6

Third Avenue is Different

OCTOBER 1993

Third Avenue is Different From Top-Down Mutual Funds

The vast majority of investment companies, as well as the dollar value of funds, are managed by disciples of modern capital theory, i.e., believers in an "efficient market." Modern capital theory, in turn, is based upon the views that investors always know less than the "market"; that the principal factors to study are the behavior of securities prices and the behavior of security markets (i.e., a technical and chartist approach); and that appropriate diversification and asset allocation are the means to guard against risk (i.e., the market price of a security is always the right price and, therefore, it is impossible to guard against risk by buying cheap). These views may have validity in risk arbitrage type situations where one can forecast a reasonably determinate workout in a reasonably determinate period of time and when you keep score only by looking at closing prices every night.

The Third Avenue Value Fund (TAVF, "The Fund") engages in little, or no, risk arbitrage; the Fund gives little weight to daily market prices and market price fluctuations. The Fund, purely and simply, rejects modern capital theory as totally invalid for buy-and-hold value investors. It is difficult to imagine TAVF making any investment if I did not believe, based on the factors that are relevant for the Fund (and these relevant factors do not include short run trading considerations), that Fund management knows much more than the "market" about the particular investment. To TAVF, the only two factors to study are the fundamentals of the business and the securities issued by the business. Specific risk for the Fund is measured by the quality of the issuer, the terms of the issue, the price of the issue, and, probably above all, the staying power of the issuer in the event that unforeseeable adversities occur. The historic behavior of securities prices and securities markets are pretty much an irrelevancy. Diversification and asset allocation, in the TAVF scheme of things, are merely surrogates for knowledge and control. One of the striking differences between the Fund and "plain vanilla" asset managers is that TAVF does not focus on the same criteria as those types of asset managers in making buy, or not buy, decisions. Insofar as I can tell, the typical fund manager emphasizes an issuer's industry identification, reported earnings or cash flows from operations (especially those forecast for the quarter or year ahead), and Wall Street sponsorship, if any. The idea behind that approach is to try to forecast the relative immediate price performance of the security being examined, comparing how a particular security might perform relative to similarly situated issues or markets. The Fund, on the other hand, emphasizes the quality and quantity (i.e., net asset value) of the resources in the business, and then tries to estimate how those resources might be converted into earning power over a relatively indeterminate future.

Earning power will not necessarily be evidenced by earnings as reported for accounting purposes, but might also be measured by increases in unrealized, and therefore unreported, appreciation (e.g., St. Joe Paper), by increased cash flows (e.g., Forest City Enterprises), or by a company becoming an attractive sales, merger or acquisition candidate (e.g., Constellation Bancorp). The Fund does not try to forecast near-term security price performance; rather, it tries to gauge the ability of a business to build long-term values while minimizing long-term investment risks, at least for security holders. Comparative analysis is deemphasized; it will probably be good enough if the Fund, over a long period, can earn total returns of 20%, or better, compounded annually, without worrying about how that return compares with general market indices or other funds. TAVF's concentration on the quality and quantity of resources in a business, rather than immediately forecasted earnings and cash flows for that business has a number of unique advantages from an analyst's point of view. First, there is an absence of competition for identifying attractive securities. Second, one probably can make as good, or even better, forecasts of future earnings or cash flows, by using net asset value, rather than the past earnings record, as a starting point. Although some — modern capital theorists, for example — maintain that book value is unimportant, they forget that you need to have a book value figure in order to calculate the return on equity (ROE) figure, which they do regard as important. In fact, both a business' past operating record and its current resources are essential tools of valuation, and one is not a substitute for the other. (If it were, I would prefer resources.) Incidentally, however, large amounts of resources in a business, such as airlines or meatpacking, may be more indicative of onerous overhead than of large future earning power; hopefully, this potentially negative aspect of large resources is not applicable to any of the equity issues in the Fund's portfolio. A partial explanation for TAVF's emphasis on balance sheet resources, rather than income account earnings flows and cash flows is that, unlike most funds, TAVF research has a very large corporate finance component and, unlike others, is not grounded in research performed for outside, passive, minority investors. In corporate finance one looks at resources and examines the ways in which superior returns might be achieved from those resources by obtaining new finance or refinance and/or by changing the way in which those resources are employed or managed. In contrast, outside passive minority investors, and modern capital theorists, assume implicitly that most resources will continue to be employed by the same managements in the same ways in which they historically were. Although this is occasionally a realistic assumption as it has been, say, for most electric utilities, it is just not the norm for most American public companies in any three-to-five-year period.

Because the Fund invests the way it does, its performance seems to have been, and I think likely will continue to be, independent of what happens in the general market. For the first three years of its existence, TAVF's total annual return for its initial investors averaged approximately 30% compounded. I think it may be very difficult for the Fund to sustain 30% annual returns independent of the general market. A principal reason for the level of the Fund's success over its first three years of life was that TAVF's portfolio had no big losers, meaning no poor underlying business performances which then were reflected in securities prices. Avoiding big losers over long periods of time is almost certainly impossible for passive investors, at least for TAVF. Its managers are just not that good at predicting the future. This does not mean that I am anything but optimistic about the results the Fund is likely to obtain, given our investment discipline and regardless of the general level of securities prices. It does mean that I think it will be exceedingly difficult for TAVF to do as well in the next three years as in the last three, even though the Fund is operating with a manifestly lower expense ratio now, compared with that which existed when TAVF was much smaller.

The IPO Phenomenon and The Fund

Two watershed phenomena in the last 15 to 20 years, in my view, have altered materially the incentives for key players in the financial community. The first change involves the amounts of compensation available for securities sales forces following the elimination, in May 1975, of fixed commissions on securities traded on a secondary basis. The second change relates to a change in the manner in which investment banks employ their own funds.

One result of these changed incentives is the likelihood that Initial Public Offering (IPO) booms, and their related speculative excesses, may recur more frequently than in the past. The Fund's investment in Sen-Tech Common, through a private placement, is designed, in part, to enable TAVF to profit from the next IPO boom, if not from the next boom's speculative excesses. Put simply, we acquired our position in Sen-Tech at a price reasonably related to private business value. An IPO value for the Sen-Tech position, on the other hand, should be well in excess of its private business value. In any event, the prospects of SenTech's ever going public are enhanced, and the IPO pricing in that event will be better, because of the excellent quality of Sen-Tech's Wall Street sponsorship and ownership.

The elimination of fixed commissions on "May Day" 1975 has resulted in greatly increased emphasis being placed on financial products which compensate securities sales persons quite handsomely, i.e., products with very large gross spreads including, but not limited to, tax shelter limited partnerships, load mutual funds, and new issues of municipal bonds, junk bonds and common stocks. The sales representative at Prudential, Merrill Lynch or Bear Stearns, for example, really doesn't have to compete with Charles Schwab for discounted commissions in the secondary market. Rather, he or she can collect as much as 2/3 of a 5% to 10% gross spread from selling IPOs — instead of arguing with a customer over whether the commission on the purchase or sale of existing publicly traded issues should be two cents or four cents per share. Further, IPOs tend to be an easy sale.

Although the rule of thumb is that a company won't go public, and probably can't go public, if a common stock issue can be priced only at or below private business value, once a typical, private company does go public, it ordinarily does so at a price which represents not only a substantial premium over private business value but, more importantly, also represents a meaningful discount, usually based on comparative analysis spread sheets, from anticipated market prices for the new issue. There is a conscious attempt to create an ebullient after-market for IPOs, which make them easy sells.

The changed investing practices of leading investment banks reinforces the tendency toward the creation of IPOs Before the late 1970s-early 1980s, most investment banks worked only for fees, while employing their own capital only in their own investment banking/ brokerdealer activities. Now, in contrast, virtually all investment banks are merchant bankers — owning equities in companies they hope to sell, merge or take public. As a result, investment banks have become enthusiastic sponsors of IPOs because, in general, they own interests in the private companies which are going-public candidates.

Admittedly, IPO markets are especially capricious. There are times when it may be tough to sell any new issue, such as in 1989-1990. And there are times when the public falls over itself to buy "garbage" at outrageous prices, for example, 1993. Yet, if TAVF can acquire equity interests in well managed, wellcapitalized, private businesses early on, at prices which are no greater than, and probably less than, private business values, and where there is reasonable Wall Street sponsorship, then it is likely that, sooner or later (perhaps within the next two to five years), opportunities will exist to create an IPO for one or more of the Fund's portfolio companies at attractive prices. To a great extent, this type of analysis drives the entire venture capital industry. I certainly believe it is a valid analysis for Sen-Tech, and Sen- -Tech type investments. In these cases, the returns to the Fund ought to be pretty good.

It should be noted that TAVF, like any mutual fund, is not permitted to have more than 15% of its net assets, measured as of the time the last investment is made, committed to securities that are not readily marketable. Such nonmarketable securities include not only Sen-Tech type investments, but also bank debt investments such as Eljer Bank Debt.

Finding Bargains From the Bottom Up

In October, I addressed the Miami Bond Club in a talk entitled, "Finding Bargains from the Bottom Up." The premise of my remarks was that despite the roaring general bull market from 1974 through 1993, numerous bargains continually were being created for investors such as TAVF through a) highly specific industry-wide depressions, b) favorable corporate operations which tend to be ignored by top-down investors, and c) the creation of financially strong companies through providing those businesses with access to junior capital in the form of junk bonds or IPOs at pricing levels that might have been extremely attractive both for the issuing company and for equity security holders who did not have to pay the high IPO prices. I think it will be worthwhile to share with you that October paper (reprinted below), particularly because the points were made by reference to various securities in the TAVF portfolio.

It is apparent to me that regardless of the general level of securities prices, past events are creating continually attractive investment opportunities for fundamentalist investors who follow a bottom-up, rather than a top-down, approach to securities analysis. A bottom--up approach emphasizes the study of individual issuers and specific securities. A top-down approach, in contrast, emphasizes the study of securities prices, general market histories, investor psychology, the level of interest rates, business cycles, overall industry trends, and other technical factors. Most Outside, Passive, Minority Investors (OPMIs) are top-down; virtually all activists such as those engaged in mergers and acquisitions, hostile takeovers, and leveraged buyouts are bottom-up. Academic finance is exclusively top-down. Indeed, academia is best described as consisting of stock market technicians with Ph.Ds.

Let me demonstrate the point about value creation being independent of general market levels by reviewing various investments that currently make up, or have in the recent past been, a significant part of the Third Avenue Value Fund portfolio.

As a bottom-up value investor, Third Avenue Value Fund follows two general investment criteria. Insofar as the Fund acquires performing loans, those instruments have two characteristics:

1. A yield to maturity of at least 500 basis points more than performing credits of comparable quality.
2. Protective covenants so that in the event of a money default, the Fund has reasonably good prospects of recovering at least its cost.

Insofar as the Fund acquires common stocks, or comparable equities, the issuing company, and the security, combine four characteristics:

1. The company enjoys an exceptionally strong financial position as measured by an absence of liabilities, whether on balance sheet, in footnotes, or off balance sheet; and as measured by the company's ownership, or control, of high quality assets.
2. The company appears to be reasonably well managed.
3. The company is readily understandable, which in practice means that the issuer complies with the filing requirements of the Securities and Exchange Commission, and issues financial statements which are meaningful and reliable.
4. The price at which the common stock is available is no greater than 50% of what I believe the equity would be worth were the issuer a private, rather than public, business.

Implicit in the Third Avenue Value Fund approach is the belief (proven again and again over time) that many, if not most, financial forecasts will prove to be wrong because the forecasts were too optimistic. Thus, the Fund tries to buy "what is" cheap, rather than relying on forward looking information. Further, insofar as it acquires credits, the Fund wants covenant protection in the event that forecasts are wrong and a money default occurs. Insofar as the Fund acquires equities, it wants the businesses to have staying power.

Conventional market indices measure the extent of the enormous bull market in general securities that has occurred since 1974. The Dow Jones Industrial Average, which opened at around 880 in 1974, is now at approximately 3600. During the same interim, the Standard & Poor's 500 Stock Average increased similarly during the same interim from about 99 to approximately 460. Yet, during the past 19-20 years, large proportions of Corporate America (and Real Estate America) were being savaged, going through experiences as devastating, or even more devastating, than had occurred during the Great Depression of 1930s for many industries. These draconian events affected, among others, most of the country's manufacturing base, including automobile manufacturers and suppliers; integrated steel mills; aluminum smelters; base metal companies; airlines; real estate (twice); savings and loans (twice); energy; agriculture; computer hardware; defense suppliers; home builders; and department stores.

Despite the buoyant general market, each of these debacles resulted in the securities of victimized companies becoming available at ultralow prices, even though many of the companies and securities, whether distressed credits or equities, met Third Avenue Value Fund criteria. For example, the Fund reached the analytic conclusion that despite the plethora of bad loans (mostly real estate) made by most depository institutions, many of such banking companies were not only inherently profitable but also very good takeover candidates provided that they could become "adequately capitalized" for regulatory purposes. The way to make these inherently profitable institutions "adequately capitalized" was to directly infuse equity into the banks; put otherwise, it made much more sense to buy newly issued bank common stocks from depository institutions, rather than already outstanding common stock from bank stockholders. This the Fund was willing to do provided that the Fund received freely tradable securities; and also acquired its position at a price that was no greater than 75% of proforma book value, and preferably at a discount from market. Thus, Third Avenue Value Fund acquired equity positions in Constellation Bancorp, People's Heritage Financial Group, Crossland Federal Savings Bank, Glendale Federal Bank, and UnionFed Financial Corp. The game plan is for these banks to be run conservatively for five years, or so, during which period they ought to earn at least 10% per annum on equity. If at the end of that period, an institution is acquired in a stock swap at, say, two times book (the average deal now takes place at more like 2

½ to 3 times book), the compound average annual return to the Fund will exceed 35%. Most of the bank managements of the companies in which the Fund has invested seem to concur with this agenda; there seems little question that the wave of bank mergers and acquisitions will continue. Hard times in the lending and real estate industries created these investment opportunities in the midst of a bull market for most other securities. The Fund also had opportunities in the two years to acquire real estate equities in companies unquestioned staying power at ultralow prices compared with reasonable, long-term appraisal values.

At any given time, the best performing equities in a market will be those that are reporting improving earnings per share quarter to quarter, those that have the most popular industry identification, and those that are most heavily promoted by insiders and members of the financial community. These three market factors are ignored by the Fund. Rather, Third Avenue Value Fund focuses on quality of the financial position and quantity of resources in the business relative to the security's price. Quality of financial position plus quantity of resources, incidentally, translates into long-term earning power, whether that earning power evidences itself as unrealized and, therefore, unaccountable for appreciation of undeveloped land (St. Joe Paper); growing cash flows (Forest City Enterprises); enhanced attractiveness as a takeover candidate (Constellation Bancorp or DCA); or rapid increases over long periods in earnings per share as reported for GAAP purposes (SunAmerica).

It is the past prosperity enjoyed by these businesses that created the earning power values the Fund is interested in, rather than bear markets. For a large portion of the Fund's equity portfolio, tremendous business values were created by past corporate prosperity. In a few cases, e.g., Apple Computer and Digital Equipment, much of the corporate wealth created seems to have been dissipated by current difficulties; but the businesses remain quite strong, and they seem to have quite large resources relative to the prices of their equities. Equities in the Fund's portfolio which appear to have created large corporate wealth through good operations in the past include Penn Central, SunAmerica, USLICO, Danielson, Consolidated Tomoka, Forest

City Enterprises, Capital Southwest, Liberty Homes, Dart Group, St. Joe Paper, Apple Computer, Digital Equipment and Fund American Enterprises.

Another extremely important source of corporate wealth creation is access to outside capital on an ultraattractive price basis (i.e., at price levels far higher for the purchaser than would be available in normal commercial transactions involving private businessmen and private lenders). Such attractive access to outside capital has been available as never before for many companies in the past two years who have tapped the "junk bond" and IPO markets. The IPO market sells to relatively unsophisticated OPMIs, individual or institutional, who are basically traders and will immediately sell any security which no longer has market momentum because of a disappointing quarterly earnings report (Syntellect), or because an industry falls out of favor (e.g., medical equipment). Yet, raising money through IPOs gives many of these companies considerable financial strength. The prices at which the common stocks of IPOs which disappointed momentum investors are available frequently are no greater than that which a first stage venture capitalist would pay, even though the company is well financed and already public. The Fund, for example, recently ran a spreadsheet on all Compustat listed companies which were selling at not more than a 60% premium over book value, and whose cash holdings alone equaled not less than 80% of total book liabilities. 172 issuers made the list, the vast majority of which were cratered IPOs. Third Avenue Value Fund took positions in 13 of these companies: Central Sprinkler, Handex Environmental, Integrated Systems, Interphase, Meadowbrook Rehabilitation, Micronics Computers, PharmChem Laboratories, Photronics, Syntellect, Telco Systems, UTILX, VLSI Technology and Zygo Corp.

Passive investing on a bottom-up basis, it seems to me, is a lot easier than being a trader, or trying to do what academics focus on for OPMIs — beat the market continuously.

The bottom-up investor can average down with impunity. The bottom--up investor with cash reserves can invest with aplomb when markets are in vicious down drafts or there are, for example, large amounts of tax loss selling. The bottom-up investor buys when he believes prices are good enough, not when he thinks the market has hit bottom.

While the bottom-up investor, like the Fund and predecessor investment vehicles, will be wrong about almost a certain percentage of investments over the long term, most of the investments ought to work out "good enough" regardless of what happens in the general market.

Timing is not a problem when managing a bottom-up portfolio. While no individual security bought on a bottom-up basis can be expected to work out in a given period of time, if specific securities in an overall portfolio are not working out from time to time, say every six or nine months, that means that the fundamental analysis was probably bad to begin with.

Bottom-up value investing seems to be quite different than top-down performance investing. For one thing, each tends to focus on different variables (e.g., corporate staying power vs. quarterly earnings as reported for GAAP purposes). Probably the worst dilemma facing the top-down analyst, and quantitative analysts, in general, is the worry about "what does the market know that I don't?" or "what is the message the market is sending?" For the Bottom-up these are not great problems. Frequently, the analyst can be confident that he, or she, knows more about a particular situation than the "market" does. In any event, in bottom-up investing the strong tendency is to focus on different information, and different time horizons, than is usual for those involved with the general market.

While the bottom-up investor has to spend considerable time on research, I think the workload is manifestly lighter than it is for top--down analysts who have to worry about day-to-day price movements and who have to spend a lot of time studying and opining about "will-o'-the wisp" matters such as the historic behavior of markets (i.e., BETA), the direction of interest rates, and other things they can't possibly know much about.

There are problems with being a passive bottom-up investor:

- Few analysts have the requisite training
- It can be a risky business if conducted with borrowed money
- It is out of the mainstream; you are viewed as a speculator because most of your investments may not be cosmetically correct. There is

little appreciation of the underlying fact that the best way to not speculate is to buy cheap; the best way to maximize profits is also to buy cheap. Believers in the efficient market state that you cannot buy cheap; believers in the efficient market are mostly "looney tunes," as I demonstrate in other papers. But they seem to be the cosmetically correct majority view.

Bottom-up investing entails focusing on the same valuation variables as activists. Frequently, activists will preempt those values for themselves by causing changes in credit agreements, or by the forced acquisitions of common stocks in leveraged buyout and going-private transactions. In such force-out transactions, the activist has many advantages, not the least of which is complete control of timing. Suppose the private business value of Company X, attributable to its common stock, is $10; X Common initially trades at $5; bear market, or poor quarterly earnings, causes X Common to sell at $2; activist proposes cash merger at $3; passivist is screwed.

Nothing is perfect. But I submit that bottom-up investing is a very attractive activity. Appropriately done, it ought to obtain good results for investors independent of what happens to general securities markets. Those of you stuck with top-down disciplines certainly ought to consider investing a portion of a portfolio's funds in a bottom-up portfolio if for no other reason than it ought to be market neutral.

CHAPTER 7

Consistent Performance and Averaging Down

APRIL 1995

Consistent Performance and Averaging Down

As part of my day-to-day chores, I've now read a fair amount of the mountains of literature, both books and articles, published by people involved in Academic Finance. Almost all of those materials are, in my opinion, badly flawed insofar as they purport to describe and analyze buy-and-hold, or control, investing. One source of badly flawed analysis revolves around the establishment of a comparative analysis "strawman," to wit, the thesis that all investors should be judged solely by the extent to which their results outperform, or equal, the performance of a related market or index consistently. "Consistently" means short run, whether daily, weekly, monthly or quarterly. Whatever the merits of such a standard for traders without much, if any, fundamental knowledge of what they are investing in, this consistency standard is totally inapplicable to The Third Avenue Value Fund (TAVF), and other buy-and-hold investors who rely on fundamentals. Academic Finance is a technical-chartist approach to investing which focuses only on the study of prices and markets as they relate to Outside, Passive, Minority Investors (OPMIs).

There is no way that TAVF will outperform any market consistently, nor does the Fund try to do so. Rather, TAVF tries to acquire equities in companies that have good long-term growth prospects, are well-financed, are reasonably well-managed, and whose equities are available at prices that are cheap relative to a long-term, or indeterminate-term, valuation of the enterprise as a private business or takeover candidate. Put otherwise, TAVF tries to avoid investment risk. Avoiding investment risk involves a very meaningful trade-off, in that the Fund seems to take huge market risks, at least as measured against trying to attain superior levels of near-term market performance. Indeed, as to almost all of TAVF's investments since the Fund started investing four and a half years ago, either the issuer's recent earnings performance was poor, or the near-term outlook was clouded at the time TAVF invested in the equities –hardly prescriptions for outperforming the market consistently. The TAVF record is replete with examples of this. The Fund's principal real estate investments were made in 1991 and 1992 when the near-term outlook could hardly have been more dismal. The same was true for the Fund's acquisition of bank equities in 1991 and 1992; the common stocks of financial insurers and title insurers in 1993 and 1994; regional broker-dealer equities in 1994; Inverse Floaters in 1994 and 1995; and Destec Common in 1995.

Given that the companies in which TAVF invests have tremendous staying power, and that I try to be quite knowledgeable about each issue, it is relatively easy to average down when specific issues are poor market performers. My underlying investment thesis for TAVF is 180 degrees opposite to that of Academic Finance, which assumes that there is universal price efficiency in OPMI markets for control of companies. My view, in contrast, is that if I did not know more than the OPMI market about the companies in which the Fund has invested, or at least about those characteristics of the portfolio company and its securities that are of greatest interest to the Fund, then TAVF ought not to have been in those securities in the first place. Furthermore, these characteristics that most interest the Fund, e.g., strong financial position, tend to be quite different from the characteristics on which OPMIs trying to outperform the market consistently focus, e.g., recent reported or currently forecasted quarterly earnings. The TAVF approach just does not lend itself to consistent outperformance of the market. However, the TAVF approach should allow an investor to average down with far greater comfort than exists for most other investment "styles" in instances where there has been poor OPMI market performance for an issue unaccompanied by evidence of deterioration in the long-term fundamentals of the business.

TAVF's goal is to try to earn 20% compounded on a long-term basis, whether or not the Fund outperforms specific markets or indices. There is nothing magical about 20%. Most non-investment company issuers have target returns on equity (ROE), without particular reference to the ROEs being earned by other businesses which may, or may not, be comparable. A pre-tax 20% ROE goal for TAVF seems reasonable as is the case for many other businesses in many other industries. For its 4 1/2 years of existence, TAVF's average annual rate of return has been 21.39%.

Management Entrenchment

My principal reason for writing about this topic is to share with you my thoughts about how corporate takeovers are likely to affect the TAVF portfolio, or at least the equity portion of the portfolio, in the years just ahead.

In the TAVF scheme of things, the ultimate bail-out for equity investments comes from either improvement in going concern operations over the long-term, or from what I call Asset Conversion activities; i.e., the realization of substantial premiums over OPMI market prices in merger and acquisition transactions, hostile takeovers, leveraged buyouts, restructurings or capitalizations, sales of assets and liquidations. In the period ahead, it seems likely to me that there will be an explosion in Asset Conversion activities if present general economic and financial conditions persist.

As I have noted in previous quarterly reports, the environment for Asset Conversion activities became buoyant after 1993, as secured financings from commercial banks became plentiful and access to capital markets, especially for junk bonds and junk preferreds, improved. Now an additional factor has been added — the weak dollar.

If there is any efficiency to markets, it seems all but inevitable that companies and other strategic buyers located in countries with strong currencies will be buying up significant pieces of corporate America. Even at premiums of 75% to 150% over OPMI market prices, companies which are well-financed, reasonably well-managed, and have strong franchises, such as, for example, MBIA, Forest City Enterprises, First American Financial and Alex. Brown, must appear to be unusual bargains for buyers who would acquire such businesses for prices measured by these buyers in Japanese Yen, German Marks, or Swiss Francs. The parts of corporate America that will be bought up ought to be those companies which have the same characteristics that made them attractive investments for TAVF.

In Asset Conversion analysis the key factor to consider is not so much whether a particular security is attractively priced in the OPMI market but, rather, whether a particular deal is doable. Whether a particular deal is doable depends primarily on whether or not management wants the transactions; and if not, management's ability to resist. For reasons discussed below, many, if not most, attractively priced securities probably will not turn out to be doable deals.

TAVF is quite specifically in the pre-deal business, acquiring securities which are attractively priced, but where no evidence may exist indicating that the attractive security might be converted into a doable deal. Insofar as a portion of the Fund's portfolio of attractive equity securities becomes converted into doable deals, TAVF's overall long-term performance is likely to be better than it otherwise would have been. To identify whether any appreciable portion of the Fund's portfolio might be subject to Asset Conversion activities in the years just ahead, it is instructive to gain insights not only into the current takeover climate in the U.S., but also the relationships that seem to exist between corporate managements and OPMI shareholders, as well as the pricing parameters that seem to apply to Asset Conversion activities.

In trying to understand the Asset Conversion climate, it is essential to be attuned to three fundamental economic and sociological factors. First, all relationships between incumbent managements and OPMI shareholders combine both communities of interest and conflicts of interest. Whether communities of interest will tend to be predominant, or the conflicts of interest will tend to predominate, will vary with the particular situation.

Second, in almost any Asset Conversion situation the justified pricing covers a very broad range. At the minimum, OPMI investors, as willing sellers, are happy to receive premiums over recent OPMI market prices. At the maximum, a strategic control acquirer, as a willing buyer, can be satisfied with those prices and terms which represent a modest discount from what the willing buyer believes the acquisition is worth to him, her, or it. The variables dominant in determining OPMI market prices such as reported earnings (especially near-term forecasted earnings), industry identification, dividends, sponsorship, stock promotion activity, market liquidity for the particular security, chartist-technical approaches, views about general levels of credit and equity markets, short-term macro economic outlooks, and comparative analysis are either different or weighted differently than the variables dominant for the control buyer — namely, ability to finance the transaction, strategic fit, and long-term outlook.

Third, any financial practice that is not subject to the imposition of meaningful disciplines is going to be characterized by excesses and abuses. These disciplines are imposed by the operation of competitive markets, by law and regulation, and by other means, such as the operation of the Internal Revenue Code or the hard work of informed, involved, independent members of Boards of Directors. By and large, there are very few, if any, meaningful disciplines imposed on the top managements of public corporations in terms of limits on management compensation, whether such compensation arises out of strict going concern activities, Asset Conversion activities, or terminations of employment. Top management compensation is an area that has been characterized by gross abuses. Here, there are inherent conflicts of interest between top managements and OPMI shareholders. The almost universal existence of management entrenchment devices, such as those discussed below, contribute to the continuation of these gross abuses by top management.

Since the passage by the Federal Government of the Williams Act in 1968, regulating the purchase for cash of 5% or more of a class of a public company's voting securities, there has been a strong trend, especially by the States and State courts, with Delaware chief among them, toward removing from OPMI stockholders the power to decide about Asset Conversion activities and giving it, instead, to Boards of Directors. In most cases, it appears as if the principal constituencies of these Boards have been incumbent managements. The outside directors serving on these Boards seem mostly to have been inattentive and compliant, rubber stamping management proposals.

If management entrenchment devices, i.e., "shark repellents" did not exist, then acquirers could gain control of companies by: a) buying for cash 50% or more of the outstanding common stock in the open market, in private transactions, and/or via a tender offer; b) by acquiring control through the use of a voluntary exchange of securities to acquire 50% or more of the outstanding voting stock; or c) by soliciting proxies where a majority vote would deliver control. There never has existed a level playing field in contests for control of companies, especially where voluntary exchanges and proxy solicitations have been involved; incumbent managements always have had a big edge. However, the acceptance of "shark repellents" during the last 25 years increasingly has tipped the playing field toward incumbent managements irrespective of which playing field — whether, cash purchases, voluntary exchanges or proxy solicitations – although certain proxy solicitation rules promulgated in 1992 have made vote solicitations a trifle easier for outsiders.

From the TAVF point of view, this abdication of shareholder rights to Boards of Directors has had mixed results even in cases where the communities of interest between managements and OPMI shareholders are predominant, such as would tend to be the case in a negotiated merger with an independent third party. On the one hand, in the case of Asset Conversion deals, Boards of Directors, insofar as they engage in arm's length dealings, (i.e., the control buyers are not insiders), are likely to obtain better prices and terms than would the OPMI investor groups which could not negotiate and would settle for only a premium over OPMI market prices. On the other hand, there are likely to be fewer transactions than would occur were the decision making process to be left solely in the hands of shareowners, because managements and Boards of Directors are likely to cause difficulties for non-management control buyers, whether friendly or hostile.

The vast majority of transactions are friendly, negotiated deals which result in OPMI shareholders realizing a substantial premium over market. However, the existence of "shark repellents" which enable managements and Boards to discourage any unfriendly "change of control" activities tends to have an importance that far transcends the hostile takeover arena. Purely and simply, the absence of the pressure from hostile transactions causes many managements to prefer the status quo in any case, thereby eliminating desires to become involved in all types of Asset Conversion events, whether friendly or unfriendly.

From TAVF's perspective as a buy-and-hold investor involved mostly with investments in going concerns that are going to remain going concerns, the mechanism of market price in the OPMI market does nothing to distinguish between good managements, which a buy-and-hold investor would want to remain in office, and bad guys who ought to be kicked out. As a matter of fact, what the Fund defines as "good management" tends to be different from what the OPMI community might define as good management. TAVF tends to dislike managements which are highly promotional and short run conscious; managements which, for example, massage earnings to obtain near-term market performance, or managements which forego attractive long-term investment opportunities, because they might have an immediate negative OPMI market impact. From a corporate point of view, promotional managements deliver very important benefits to companies which need current, or relatively continual access to capital markets, especially through the sale of new issues of equity. However, as a result of the TAVF's criteria that its portfolio issuers have strong financial positions, most of the companies in which the Fund invests are essentially self-financing businesses without compelling pressures to access capital markets.

Against such a background there is much to be said for requiring outsiders to negotiate with Boards, rather than deal directly with stockholders, since in many instances dealing with Boards of Directors results in shareholders, such as TAVF, receiving materially more consideration than they would if outsiders could appeal directly to shareholders by offering them a premium over market.

All management entrenchment devices are promulgated under the rubric of stockholder (or creditor) protection — whether in the form of supermajority provisions, fair price provisions, freeze-out provisions, cash-out provisions, control share acquisition provisions, poison pills, staggered boards, disgorgement statutes, parachutes, blank check preferreds, or change of control provisions in loan documents.

However, despite the lip service paid to stockholder protection, conflicts of interest are almost always present. All too frequently the underlying intent in establishing management entrenchment devices is not to get better pricing for OPMI shareholders, but to insulate management in office. Here, the inherent conflicts of interest predominate.

"Shark repellents" tend to be waived when the acquirer is a friendly. A lot of friendlies are insiders in going private management buyout transactions. The negotiations, here, seem frequently to revolve only around giving the OPMI a premium over market, especially in the case of smaller, less well publicized transactions. Additionally, the insider buyer always controls the timing of transactions. Going private buyout proposals tend to be made by insiders when the OPMI market price for a particular issue is relatively depressed compared with a contemporaneous business value. Here, conflicts of interest predominate, especially for the long-term, buy-and-hold investor, because the willing buyer (the insider) who seeks a low price is also a fiduciary charged with improving returns for OPMIs.

For example, say the common stock of a publicly owned company has a private business value of $10; a TAVF-type investor acquires a position for $5; and a bear market causes the common stock to sell at $2, even though there has been no deterioration in business fundamentals. The insider fiduciary picks that bear market moment to go private at $4. To the outside world, all the stockholders, including the TAVF-type investors, receive a 100% premium over the OPMI market. What is their gripe? Plenty, I think, from a TAVF point of view, even though Academic Finance and arbitrageurs understandably would disagree. This type of pricing phenomena, where insiders absolutely control timing and can choose to force outsiders to sell, is a reality that is going to be present in a portion of any buy-and-hold, long-term investment portfolio, including the TAVF portfolio. It is a built-in long-term disadvantage that TAVF is just going to have to live with.

The *Revlon* line of cases in Delaware is important because of its general tendencies to encourage better pricing for specific deals but also fewer deals in the aggregate. *Revlon* defines the duty of a Board to become auctioneers, and get the best price and terms for OPMI shareholders when a company is going to be sold and there will be a change of control. *Revlon*, therefore, puts companies into play and requires competitive bidding, even though reasonable bust-up fees for an initial bidder are allowed. The result is a relatively level playing field in the auction. Revlon is a godsend in terms of improving prices, even though the *Revlon* line of cases are far from universal. A notable exception to *Revlon* was *Time Warner* where Delaware courts, through tortured and unworldly reasoning, found that the Time, Inc.-Warner Communications merger did not involve a change of control because majority voting remained in the hands of OPMIs. The Delaware Courts failed, in *Time Warner*, to realize that in voting situations involving OPMIs, control does not belong to OPMI voters, but rather to whomever has meaningful elements of control over corporate proxy machinery and corporate funds used to solicit proxies.

The downside of *Revlon* is that target companies are discouraged from doing any deals because negotiating a transaction, e.g., Paramount-Viacom, will just put the target company, Paramount, on the auction block. Given the nature of the TAVF portfolio, which I think is chock full of takeover candidates, the Fund's overall interest might better be served if there were more takeover transactions at lower premiums over OPMI market prices, rather than improved pricing for fewer individual transactions because an auction takes place on a relatively level playing field. This is of decreasing validity, however, insofar as the TAVF portfolio companies become growing going concerns which are increasing in fundamental value over time. This mitigates the need for any Asset Conversion transactions at all. However, where portfolio companies earn unsatisfactory economic returns on the inherent asset values, or where those companies would derive synergistic benefits from corporate combinations rather than remain a stand-alone going concern, there is a need for Asset Conversion activities, especially if the Fund is to earn its 20% bogey. I am sure that there are, and will be, quite a number of issues in TAVF's equity portfolio with large inherent asset values whose future earnings might be less as stand-alone going concerns than if those companies were combined in whole, or part, with other enterprises. Current examples of such portfolio companies could include St. Joe Paper, Apple Computer, Cray Research, Capital Guaranty, Datascope and Forest City Enterprises.

Delaware is the key corporate state, not only because more than half of the Fortune 500 is incorporated in Delaware but also because other State courts tend to follow the Delaware lead.

It is hard to engage in Asset Conversion activities unless one has a good concept of what a fair price is. A fair price is defined as that price, and such other terms, which would be arrived at in a transaction between a willing buyer and a willing seller, both with knowledge of the relevant facts, dealing at arm's length, and neither under any compulsion to act. The underlying factor that makes an OPMI a willing seller is a premium over OPMI market price. The underlying factor that makes a control buyer a willing buyer involves paying no more than a moderate discount from the present value of the benefits that the deal might bring strategically to the buyer, especially if the transaction can be financed on attractive terms. Thus, a fair price can, and usually does, encompass quite a broad range. In level playing field auction situations, the price arrived at tends to be close to the value of the willing buyer. In non-contested transactions, especially where the buyer is an insider, say a going private transaction, the price arrived at tends to be the premium over the OPMI market price that the willing seller will go along with. If OPMIs in Delaware perfect rights of appraisal, or in litigation there is a substantive appraisal of "entire fairness," the courts tend to focus on the willing seller environment, giving considerable weight to what an OPMI could have sold his stock for in the OPMI market.

Finally, given our views that fairness covers a broad range of pricing, the last thing to depend on, as a rule, are "fairness opinions" rendered by investment bankers. Traditionally, investment bankers have been perceived as the tools of the managements who hire them. Also, as a matter of habit, investment bankers tend to focus on OPMI market prices in all instances other than those where the investment bankers are hired by Boards whose managements want to resist change of control proposals. I rarely have found investment bankers to have a strong community of interest with the OPMI stockholders (versus managements) the bankers purport to represent.

Having said all of the above, I come down, net, in favor of moderate management protection provisions for the companies in the TAVF portfolio. Virtually all of the companies whose common stocks are represented in the portfolio have very strong financial positions. Many appear to enjoy valuable franchises. Most seem managed by reasonably competent people with relatively strong interests in the feasibility of the companies they manage. Further, I believe most give genuine weight to taking actions that will benefit the long-term welfare of the OPMI stockholder (and, though I cannot know for sure, I believe that few of the managements are thinking of using their control of timing to engage in Asset Conversion activities like going private at just the wrong time for TAVF). The existence of "shark repellents" ought to result in better terms most of the time than would exist if the purchaser/acquirer dealt directly with the shareholders rather than negotiating through the Board. The obvious trade-off seems to be that the existence of "shark repellents" will mean there will be fewer deals for TAVF overall than otherwise would be the case. Taking, say, a five-year perspective, rather than a one-year perspective, I have a hunch that there ought to be enough Asset Conversion deals done so that TAVF will fare well. If the Fund does not, it probably will be attributable much more to flaws in the Fund's fundamental analyses, rather than to the existence of a hostile Asset Conversion environment within the portfolio companies.

Incidentally, my views about the benefits of "shark repellents" in the case of the Fund's equity portfolio do not apply to all managements. It certainly is inapplicable to the many insiders who will seek to use their control of timing to force companies to go private at just the time when the underlying pricing is highly favorable to them and less favorable to OPMIs. Also, I am against using "shark repellents" to insulate in office most managements of financially troubled companies which can't or won't meet their obligations to creditors and are restructured either out of court or in Chapter 11. As a group, these managements generally are not entitled to any entrenchment from the point of view of their securities holders. However, the fact is that the vast majority of them enjoy considerable entrenchment.

CHAPTER 8

Value Investing at Third Avenue

OCTOBER 2001

Wealth Creation Companies

The pricing criteria used by the Third Avenue Value Fund ("The Fund") in acquiring the common stocks of wealth-creation companies bottomed on the fact that these issues seemed to be available at prices that represented discounts of at least 20% to 40% from readily estimable net asset values, and where Fund management believes there are reasonably good prospects for regular increases in net asset value over the long term. Common stocks which met this standard were Phoenix Companies, Alexander & Baldwin, BKF, Brascan, Catellus, Forest City, Legg Mason, MONY and Toyota Industries.

There seems to be a general misunderstanding about wealth creation companies in the financial community and in academic circles. First, there is scant recognition of the fact that outside of Wall Street, where one deals with privately owned businesses, the vast majority of economic endeavor involves striving to create wealth in the most tax effective manner. Where control persons have choices, they would rather create wealth by some means other than having ordinary income from operations simply because striving for cash flows or earnings from operations tends to be highly inefficient tax-wise. Second, in their new book, *Value Investing — From Graham to Buffett and Beyond* written by Bruce C.N. Greenwald, Judd Kahn, Paul D. Sonkin and Michael van Biema (Greenwald and van Biema are faculty members at Columbia Business School), the authors seem to have trouble identifying, and valuing, net assets. They state, "in the contemporary investment world net-nets are, only with the rarest exceptions, a distant memory." In fact, though, each of the nine wealth-creation common stocks Third Avenue acquired during the quarter is a net-net by any economic, non-accounting convention, definition of net-nets.

Greenwald, et al., define net-nets only by looking at accounting convention, not economic reality. They define net-nets as a common stock available at a price that represents a discount from a company's current assets after deducting all book liabilities, both short-term and long-term. The problem with this measurement is that for going concerns, much of their current assets are not current assets at all, but rather fixed assets of the most dubious value. For example, Sears Roebuck, like any other retailer, could not stay in business if it did not maintain inventories continually, which in Sears' case have a carrying value of over $5 billion. In the aggregate, these inventories are a fixed asset for the going concern, not a current asset. Individual inventory items do turn to cash within 12 months and thus are, for accounting purposes, called current assets. In fact, though, Sears' aggregate $5 billion investment in inventory is a permanent investment, particularly vulnerable to seasonal markdowns, theft, obsolescence and mislocations. Contrast this with Forest City's developed real estate projects. While Forest City's developed real estate is called a fixed asset, a substantial portion of these assets is really quite current, a source of almost immediate cash through sale or refinancing, without interfering with Forest City as a going concern. Forest City Common is a true net-net. The same is true for other wealth creation common stocks acquired during the quarter at substantial discounts from readily ascertainable net asset values — including the probable real estate values in Alexander & Baldwin and Catellus; the probable securities values in Brascan (including real estate), Phoenix Companies, MONY and Toyota Industries; and the probable values of Assets Under Management (AUM) for BKF and Legg Mason.

Value Investing at Third Avenue

The back of the Greenwald book describes the investment approaches of a number of highly competent value investors: Warren Buffett; Mario Gabelli; Glen Greenberg; Robert H. Heilbrum; Seth Klarman; Michael Price; Walter and Edwin Schloss and Paul D. Sonkin. It's a worthwhile read. Third Avenue, in its practices, seems to have much in common with these investors. The front of the Greenwald book, though, describes underlying theories about value investing. These theories seem to have nothing to do with the basic assumptions under which Third Avenue operates. Contrasting the Third Avenue approach with the Greenwald approach ought to be helpful in getting investors to understand the Third Avenue modus operandi.

A major difference between the Greenwald approach and the Third Avenue approach revolves around valuing a company and valuing a security. Greenwald, et al., state, "There is general agreement that the value of a company is the sum of the cash flows it will produce for investors over the life of the company, discounted back to the present."

The Greenwald approach is far too general to be useful for Third Avenue. For TAVF, there exist four factors which contribute to corporate value and three factors which determine the theoretical value of a security.

The four elements of corporate value:

1. Free cash flow from operations available for the security holder. Very few companies ever actually achieve such free cash flows on a reasonably regular basis. While for any individual project to make sense it has to return a cash-positive net profit over its life, this is not true for most companies (as distinct from stand-alone projects), especially expanding companies. Most businesses consume cash. TAVF likes to invest in the common stocks of those few companies in a position to create cash flows on a regular basis. The principal area where this takes place in the Fund's portfolio is in money management companies: BKF, John Nuveen, Liberty Financial and Legg Mason.
2. Earnings: Most prosperous going concerns create earnings, not free cash flows. Earnings exist where a company creates intrinsic wealth from operations while consuming cash. Since most going concerns consume cash, their earnings streams may be of limited value unless such flows are also combined with access to capital markets, either credit markets or equity markets or both. TAVF, in acquiring the common stocks of earnings companies, limits its acquisitions to businesses with exceptionally strong financial

positions. This means, most of time, that the companies have far less need to have access to capital markets during any given period than run-of-the-mill, less-well-capitalized, going concerns. More importantly, though, the companies whose issues the Fund acquires have rather complete control over the timing as to when they want to access debt markets or equity markets. Capital markets are notoriously capricious in terms of both pricing and availability. TAVF tries to avoid investing in the common stocks of less well-capitalized companies, in part because such issuers frequently are forced to raise outside capital at the most disadvantageous times. Well-capitalized-earnings companies whose common stocks were acquired by TAVF during the quarter include Energizer, Trammell Crow, American Power, Applied Materials, AVX, Credence, Electro Scientific, KEMET, MBIA, Nabors, and Vishay. Most Wall Streeters and most academics, including Greenwald, et al., subscribe to a primacy of the income account point of view and believe that the dominant, and sometimes even the sole, sources of corporate value are flows from operations — both cash flows and earnings flows. At TAVF, we have a balanced approach. Indeed, we think more corporate wealth is created in the U.S. by the two factors discussed below than by flows, even though frequently there tends to be a close, symbiotic relationship between flows, whether cash or earnings, on the one hand, and asset values and access to capital markets, on the other.

3. Resource conversion activities. These activities encompass repositioning assets to higher uses, other ownership or control, or all three; the financing of asset acquisitions, the refinancing of liabilities or both; and the creation of tax advantages. Resource conversion activities take the form of mergers and acquisitions, contests for control, leveraged buyouts, restructuring troubled companies, spin-offs, liquidations, massive securities repurchases, and acquiring securities in bulk through cash tender offers or exchange offers. Within the Third Avenue portfolio, it appears as if some 3% to 5% of the common stocks held are subject to takeover bids of some sort by control investors every quarter. Common stock issues acquired during the quarter which may very well be involved in getting taken over in the years ahead include Energizer, Phoenix, Alexander & Baldwin, BKF, Catellus and MONY, albeit Fund management has never been really good

at identifying which companies will be "in play" at any given time in the future.

4. Access to capital markets at super-attractive prices. There seems little question that far more corporate wealth has been created in this country by taking advantage of attractive access to outside capital than by any other single source. The Greenwald book, and indeed virtually all economic literature, ignores this factor as a source of wealth, or a source of franchise. Unfortunately, as a passive value investor, the Fund does not often get to benefit from super-crazy prices that exist in equity markets from time to time. To benefit from these super-crazy prices as a price-conscious value investor, TAVF would have to become a venture capital investor seeking IPO bailouts; something that seems to be outside Fund management's sphere of competence. Fortunately, though, many of the companies in whose common stocks Third Avenue has invested have super-attractive access to credit markets where they are able to obtain low-interest, long-term, non-recourse financing for major portions of the projects which they build, or in which they invest. Companies whose common stocks the Fund invested in during the quarter, with such attractive access to capital markets, include Alexander & Baldwin, Brascan, Catellus and Forest City.

The language used by all academics, including Greenwald, et al, that securities values are a function of the present worth of "cash flows" is unfortunate. From the point of view of any security holder, that holder is seeking a "cash bailout," not a "cash flow." One really cannot understand securities' values unless one is also aware of the three sources of cash bailouts.

A security (with the minor exception of hybrids such as convertibles) has to represent either a promise by the issuer to pay a holder cash, sooner or later; or ownership. A legally enforceable promise to pay is a credit instrument. Ownership is mostly represented by common stock.

There are three sources from which a security holder can get a cash bailout. The first mostly involves holding performing loans. The second and third mostly involve owners as well as holders of distressed credits. They are:

1. Payments by the company in the form of interest or dividends, repayment of principal (or share repurchases), or payment of a premium. Insofar as TAVF seeks income exclusively, it restricts its investments to corporate AAA's, or U.S. Treasuries and other U.S. government guaranteed debt issues.
2. Sale to a market. There are myriad markets, not just the New York Stock Exchange or NASDAQ. There are take-over markets, Merger and Acquisition (M&A) markets, Leveraged Buyout (LBO) markets and reorganization of distressed companies markets. Historically, most of TAVF's exits from investments have been to these other markets, especially LBO, takeover and M&A markets.
3. Control. TAVF is an outside passive minority investor that does not seek control of companies, even though we try to be highly influential in the reorganization process when dealing with the credit instruments of troubled companies. It is likely that a majority of funds involved in value investing are in the hands of control investors such as Warren Buffett at Berkshire Hathaway, the various LBO firms and many venture capitalists. Unlike TAVF, many control investors do not need a market out because they obtain cash bailouts, at least in part, from home office charges, tax treaties, salaries, fees and perks.

I am continually amazed by how little appreciation there is by government authorities in both the U.S. and Japan that non-control ownership of securities which do not pay cash dividends is of little or no value to an owner unless that owner obtains opportunities to sell to a market. Indeed, I have been convinced for many years now that Japan will be unable to solve the problem of bad loans held by banks unless a substantial portion of these loans are converted to ownership, and the banks are given opportunities for cash bailouts by sales of these ownership positions to a market.

Greenwald, et al., have a monolithic approach to analysis using three tools to analyze all companies: replacement cost of assets, earnings power, and franchise value. TAVF, on the other hand, analyzes different businesses differently, ranging from analyzing strict going concerns by giving heavy weight to earnings power, as for example AVX or Nabors; to analyzing businesses which are really investment companies masquerading as something else. Here, heavy weight is assigned to readily measurable asset values as well as an appraisal of managements' abilities to increase these net asset values over the long term. Catellus, Forest City, Hutchison Whampoa, Investor AB, and Toyota Industries are examples of such situations.

Greenwald, et al., like almost all academics, consciously or unconsciously, look at companies as substantively consolidated with shareholders. This tends to be a non-productive approach almost all the time. At the Fund, companies are analyzed as stand-alones or parent-subsidiary. The common stock for TAVF is a different constituency from the company, or its management — separate and apart.

Most academics pay much attention to an artificial calculation: the Weighted Average Cost of Capital (WACC). WACC measures the cost of outside capital to a company as a blend of after-tax interest rates and capitalization values for common stocks based on references to current common stock prices in public markets. Interest is, of course, a cash cost, while capitalization rates for publicly-traded common stocks have nothing to do with most companies, since they do the bulk of their equity financing by retaining earnings rather than by selling new issues of common stock to the public. More importantly, though, WACC is not very meaningful for companies who have rather complete control of the timing as to when, or if, to access capital markets. Such companies will access outside sources of capital at the time WACC type pricing is most attractive to them. These are the companies in whose common stocks TAVF invests. A contemporaneous calculation of WACC for these companies tends to be not meaningful.

Greenwald, et al., discuss risk in general but do admit that relative price volatility in the securities market may not be an adequate measure of risk. For TAVF, the word risk cannot be used without putting an adjective in front of it. There is no general risk. There is market risk, investment risk, currency risk, terrorism risk, inflation risk, failure to match maturities risk, commodity risk, etc. The Fund tries to avoid investment risk, i.e., that the companies in whose securities we have invested will suffer permanent impairments. The Fund ignores market risk, i.e., that the trading prices of the securities held will fluctuate.

Greenwald, et al., assume, quite properly, that an overpriced common stock will attract new competition. Greenwald, et al., however, ignore something that may be much more important. An overpriced common stock, in the hands of a reasonably competent management, is frequently a most important corporate asset. Much of the small cap/high tech investments of the Fund are in companies which were able to build up huge cash positions by taking advantage of the crazy prices that existed in IPO markets in the late 1990's.

CHAPTER 9

The Concept of Net-Nets

JANUARY 2006

Over 80% of the Fund's common stock portfolio are in the issues of extremely well-capitalized companies that were acquired at prices, which at the time of acquisition, represented meaningful discounts from readily ascertainable net asset values. These net asset values became readily ascertainable insofar as the specific assets consisted of cash and equivalents; investments in marketable securities and performing loans; income-producing real estate; land suitable for development; and intangibles such as mutual fund assets under management. Rarely (except for cash and equivalents) were these readily ascertainable asset values classified as current assets under Generally Accepted Accounting Principles (GAAP). The Fund's definition of Net-Nets is taken from Graham and Dodd's *Security Analysis*, but with a few twists. Graham and Dodd relied on a GAAP classified balance sheet to define current assets in order to ascertain if a common stock was a Net-Net. Third Avenue Value Fund (TAVF) uses its own judgment rather than GAAP classification to define current assets in order to decide what is a liquid, i.e., current, asset.

Graham and Dodd describe Net-Nets in the 1962 edition of *Security Analysis* on pages 561 and 562:

> **Net-Current-Asset Value:** *We feel on more solid ground in discussing these cases in which the market price or the computed value based on earnings and dividends is less than the net current assets applicable to the common stock. [The reader will recall that in this computation we deduct all obligation sand preferred stock from the working capital to*

> *determine the balance for the common.]From long experience with this type of situation we can say that it is always interesting, and that the purchase of a diversified group of companies on this 'bargain basis' is almost certain to result profitably within a reasonable period of time. One reason for calling such purchases bargain issues is that usually net-current-asset values maybe considered a conservative measure of liquidation value. Thus as a practical matter such companies could be disposed of for not less than their working capital, if that capital is conservatively stated. It is a general rule that at least enough can be realized for the plant account and miscellaneous assets to offset any shrinkage sustained in the process of turning current assets into cash. [This rule would nearly always apply to a negotiated sale of the business to some reasonably interested buyer.] The working capital value behind a common stock can be readily computed. Consequently, by using this figure (i.e., net-net asset value) as the equivalent of 'minimum liquidating value' we can discuss with some degree of confidence the actual relationship between the market price of a stock and the realizable value of the business."*

While Graham and Dodd seem to have invented the idea of Net-Nets, TAVF uses that idea with a number of modifications. First, the Fund is not interested in Net-Nets unless the company is extremely well-financed. A large quantity of current assets, especially if they consist of inventories, costs in excess of billings, or receivables from less than creditworthy customers, probably cannot help the common stock of a company which cannot meet its obligations to its creditors. Second, many current assets classified as current assets under GAAP are really fixed assets of the worst sort. Take department store merchandise inventories. If the department store is to be liquidated, merchandise inventories are indeed a current asset, convertible to cash within 12 months at prices that conceivably could be close to book value, although much less than book value may be realized if the merchandise is disposed of in a GOB (Going Out of Business) sale. On the other hand, if the department store is a going concern, merchandise inventories are a fixed asset of the worst sort. The merchandise inventories have to be replaced, are hard to value, and are subject to markdowns, obsolescence, shrinkage, seasonality and mislocation. The Toyota Industries portfolio of marketable securities seem to be much more of a current asset than department store merchandise inventories even though, for GAAP purposes, Toyota Industries' marketable securities are not considered a current asset. Third, the Graham and Dodd formulation does not account for off balance sheet liabilities which may, or may not, be disclosed in footnotes, nor do Graham and Dodd take into account excessive expenses or losses; at TAVF such expenses or losses are capitalized and added to liabilities. Fourth, Graham and Dodd only seem to recognize partially that certain fixed assets, e.g., property, plant and equipment, can sometimes create cash. For example, under Section 1231 of the U.S. Internal Revenue Code, the sale at a loss of such assets used in a trade or business, usually gives rise to an ordinary loss for income tax purposes. In that case, a corporation may be able to apply the loss first to reduce current year taxes and any excess loss might be used to get "quickie" cash refunds from the IRS with regard to taxes paid in the prior two years.

The identification of Net-Nets has not proved that difficult for the Fund, even though most of the new investments now are outside the United States. The toughest problem faced by TAVF, by far, is to identify managements and control groups of these Net-Nets who are both able and conscious of the interests of outside, passive, minority investors such as Third Avenue. So far, the Fund's results in this area seem to have been pretty good, though, of course, mistakes have been made. When all is said and done, however, TAVF management owes an enormous debt of gratitude to Graham and Dodd for introducing the concept of Net-Nets. It remains the most important single part of the Fund's common stock portfolio.

CHAPTER 10

The Third Avenue Formula for Investing

JULY 2009

1. The company in which Third Avenue Value Fund (TAVF) would invest has to be extremely well-financed.
2. The common stock has to be available at a meaningful discount from readily ascertainable net asset value (NAV), usually over 25%.
3. We consider the Company to have favorable prospects for growth of better than 10% compounded per annum over the next five-to-seven years, without diluting the currently outstanding common stock.

All other systems – whether Graham & Dodd fundamental analysis, or Modern Capital Theory, or Technical-Chartist Approaches – are involved with predicting near-term price movements for securities. TAVF is so involved only in the relatively rare instances when it is involved in risk arbitrage, i.e., investing in securities where there will be relatively determinant work-outs in relatively determinate periods of time.

As a practical matter, Third Avenue rarely takes any course of action, or has any opinions as to what near-term price movements might be for individual securities or markets in general. Rather, in common stock investing, the sole, or almost sole, focus is on buying into well-financed companies at steep discounts from readily ascertainable NAV where there are reasonable prospects for double digit NAV growth over the next five years or so.

If the analysis is close to correct, long-term market performance ought to be pretty good either because of resource conversion activity (changes of control, mergers and acquisitions, recapitalizations, spin-offs, share repurchases); or because NAV for the going concern continues to grow. If NAV does grow, capital gains are assured as long as the discount from NAV does not widen materially.

There is no question but that over any short run, general market factors will more than anything else influence what individual securities prices will be day to day. The sole reason why TAVF Management does not pay any attention to general market factors, is that we are no good at making such prognostications. We don't think anybody else – perhaps with the exception of a few geniuses who are unknown to us – is any good at it either. It seems as if the actions of the general market are truly a random walk.

In the analysis of many companies, short-term considerations can be very important. This tends to be true for companies that are not well financed, especially those that need relatively continuous access to capital markets. These are the types of companies in whose common stocks TAVF does not invest.

Resource conversion, in our opinion, is much more likely to occur in North America than in Hong Kong or Japan. In North America, there exists a good body of law about resource conversion activities, but above all, there exists an army of highly skilled, highly paid, investment bankers who are out there creating, encouraging and abetting various resource conversion deals. In contrast, it seems likely that the gains TAVF might realize from most of its East Asian investments would be attributable primarily to growth in NAV rather than resource conversion. It is Fund Management's opinion that growth prospects in East Asia, especially mainland China, are considerably better than they are in North America at the present time.

It is absolutely ludicrous to suppose that TAVF faces an efficient market in its common stock investing, where an efficient market is defined as one in which rational pricing exists. Market prices in OPMI markets seem to be set by market participants focused on short-run outlooks and trying to pick market bottoms; technical chartist considerations; predictions about stock market movements over the near term; general stock market predictions at the expense of company analysis; emphasis on earnings per share, cash flow and dividends to the exclusion of balance sheet considerations, especially creditworthiness.

Such market participants include day traders, chartist-technicians; asset allocators; market participants financed with borrowed money; participants untrained in fundamental analysis; participants who don't read disclosure documents; believers in Modern Capital Theory (The Efficient Market Hypothesis & Efficient Portfolio Theory); behaviorists and psychologists.

Why would anyone conclude that these market participants, with their investment criteria, would ever set prices, directly or indirectly, that would reflect efficient prices for Third Avenue? Assuming Fund Management doesn't screw up, we believe TAVF has the potential of performing as it has in the past; outperforming indexes and benchmarks on average, most of the time, and over the long term. There is no way TAVF will ever outperform indexes and benchmarks consistently, i.e., all the time. The Fund will always be subject to the same poor performance that afflicted it in 2008. Fund Management, though, operates on the assumption that 2008s will recur only in 15-to-25-year intervals. If, by and large, the Fund can generally avoid possible permanent impairments like MBIA –where Fund Management discovered that it was dealing not only with toxic liabilities (the extent of insurance losses could be far higher than MBIA's reserves on its books), but also, in Fund Management's opinion, was dealing with toxic management –performance ought to be okay.

Third Avenue and 363 Sales

A 363 sale is the sale of assets by a company in bankruptcy in accordance with Section 363 of the Federal Bankruptcy Code. The process starts with a "stalking horse" bidder that enters into a purchase agreement for the assets. This provides a "floor bid" and serves as a basis for conducting an auction. As recognition of the expense and risk associated with entering into this agreement, the stalking horse bidder is entitled to a break-up fee and expense reimbursement if it is not the successful bidder. In conjunction with court approval of the stalking horse bid, dates are set for a bid deadline, auction and court hearing to approve the winning bid. If other bidders submit "qualified bids" by the bid deadline, they are permitted to participate in the auction, which typically is conducted by the law firm representing the debtor. Following the auction, both the winning bid and an alternate bid are approved in a bankruptcy court hearing. During the quarter, we were actively involved in two 363 sales processes:

Nortel. As we discussed in the last two letters, the Fund purchased $100 million (face) of Nortel Senior unsecured debt at an average price of 17% of claim following its bankruptcy filings in January 2009. We attended the auction of a portion of Nortel's Carrier Networks business (its Code Division Multiple Access and Long Term Evolution assets) on July 24, 2009, at the office of Cleary Gottlieb Steen and Hamilton LLP (Nortel's bankruptcy counsel). Nokia Siemens was the stalking horse bidder, a position that it earned by entering into a purchase agreement on June 19th to buy the assets for $650 million. The debtors (Nortel) determined that this agreement represented the best opportunity to maximize value for the assets and serve as a basis for conducting an auction. On June 29th and June 30th, respectively, the Canadian and U.S. bankruptcy courts approved Bidding Procedures, including a break-up fee of $19.5 million and expense reimbursement of $3 million if Nokia Siemens was not the successful bidder, and a July 21st deadline for competing bids. Additionally, a minimum overbid of $5 million was established.

Two additional parties, MPAM Wireless, Inc. (an affiliate of MatlinPatterson, a Nortel bond holder) and Ericsson submitted qualified bids prior to the deadline. These bids were required to exceed the stalking horse bid by the sum of the break-up fee, expense reimbursement and minimum overbid. The auction on July 24th consisted of seven rounds of bidding with no bids received in the last round. Ericsson's sixth round bid of $1.13 billion was the Successful Bid, and Nokia Siemens' $1.03 billion fifth round was the Alternate Bid. This was a terrific result for the Fund as Nortel bondholders, as Ericsson's bid represented a 70% improvement compared to the stalking horse bid, even adjusted for the payment of the break-up fee and expenses.

Fleetwood. During the quarter, we entered into a stalking horse bid to acquire manufactured housing assets from Fleetwood Enterprises along with our strategic partner, Cavco Industries. Such assets would be acquired by FH Holding, Inc., a jointly-owned corporation. Fleetwood Enterprises, which filed for Chapter 11 protection on March 10, 2009, is the second largest producer of manufactured homes behind Berkshire Hathaway-owned Clayton Homes. Industry shipments have declined from a peak of 373,000 in 1998, when the industry benefitted from an easy credit environment much like what drove the site-built housing bubble of 2005-2006, to a current run-rate of around 50,000. Our stalking horse bid of $18 million (plus or minus net working capital) included seven operating manufacturing facilities and one non-operating facility, all of which someone from Third Avenue visited during the quarter. We believe that these facilities, which are operating at close to break-even levels during the current industry depression, are among the best in the industry, with extremely high quality and loyal work forces. Most importantly, we believe that our strategic partner, Cavco, is the best-managed company in the industry, led by Chairman and CEO Joe Stegmayer, who was formerly Clayton's Chief Financial Officer.

The bidding procedures for our stalking horse bid entitled us to a $450,000 break-up fee, a $400,000 expense reimbursement and a minimum overbid of $100,000. Therefore, any other bid had to exceed ours by at least $950,000 (5.3%). Importantly, the bidding procedures also enabled us to credit bid our break-up fee. A subsidiary of Clayton Homes submitted a bid of $18,950,000 by the August 8th deadline, prompting an auction on August 10th at the offices of the debtors' counsel in Irvine, CA.

We won the auction with a bid of $21.8 million (including a $450,000 credit bid) for the operating assets plus $4.8 million for an idle facility in Woodland, CA. Based on the $800,000 of value ascribed to our bid from purchasing this facility, which Clayton was unwilling to purchase, our net bid of $22,600,000 was determined to be superior to Clayton's final cash bid of $22,500,000 (plus $400,000 for our expense reimbursement). Despite the $3,350,000 (19%) increase in the value of the operating assets from our stalking horse bid, we were very pleased with this result. Our purchase price represented a discount to the real estate value of the properties and ascribed no value to Fleetwood's brand name or strong independent retail distribution network.

Advantages of 363 sales

363 sales can be preferable to corporate acquisitions for both buyers and sellers. Buyers benefit from asset purchases that are "free and clear" of all liabilities other than those that are expressly assumed (such as warranties). This simplifies the diligence process and enables buyers to avoid difficult-to-quantify liabilities such as retirement benefits and pre-petition litigation. Additionally, valuations in 363 auctions are typically attractive, based primarily on asset value supported by tangible assets, such as real estate, receivables and inventory, as opposed to going concern value.

Sellers benefit from a fair auction process in which price will usually be the sole factor in determining the winning bidder. This typically is not the case in corporate deals when management often drives the process to their benefit. For example, Instinet's management and a private equity investor purchased the company's agency brokerage business for $207 million, a discount of $100 million from what Third Avenue offered, and sold the business one year later to Nomura for $1.2 billion. Companies such as GM and Chrysler that are burning significant cash from operations before debt service (not the case with Fleetwood or Nortel) may not experience a fair auction process, particularly if existing creditors are unwilling to fund additional losses. In these situations, the field of bidders is limited (only the US Government in the case of GM and Chrysler) and liquidation can be the only alternative to a fire sale. Fund Management seeks to avoid being creditors of these companies.

Ideas for Government Reform

The United States is a mixed economy. Both the private sector and the government have to be involved in economic activity. The government has a great role to play in providing incentives to non-government entities so that these other entities can become more productive.

Politics aside, two topics have emerged in the last year in Third Avenue's investment process where it has become obvious that the government can do much to improve national productivity.

1. **Amend Section 382 of the Internal Revenue Code.** The change of ownership requirement should be eliminated so that new providers of equity capital will not jeopardize a company's ability to utilize its tax attributes. Section 382 limits the use of net operating loss carry-forwards for companies that undergo a change of ownership. At a time when the government should be encouraging private investment into troubled companies, this limitation has the opposite effect. We recommend that companies that receive cash infusions or conversions of debt to equity be exempt from Section 382 limitations insofar as the equity infusions involve changes in ownership. This would enhance immensely the ability of troubled companies to attract capital from the most dynamic elements existing in the private sector.

2. **Infrastructure spending should be credit-enhanced by the private sector with the U.S. Government acting as the ultimate financial guarantor.** Monoline insurers, such as MBIA and Ambac, could provide underwriting and administrative services and assume first loss coverage protection. The U.S. Government should be the ultimate financial guarantor after the private sector absorbs the first losses; also, the government should charge fees that enable it to generate an attractive underwriting profit. The cost to issuers would be more than offset by the significant savings from lower financing costs. Credit enhancement has become an essential component of infrastructure financing because the purchaser of bonds knows that a competent party, the insurer, has investigated thoroughly, and because of the credit insurance the bonds become marketable. The United States government now has to be the ultimate guarantor because it is the only AAA credit left standing.

CHAPTER 11

Net-Nets on Steroids

JULY 2010

I remain enthusiastic about the Third Avenue Value Fund's (TAVF) current portfolio, the vast bulk of which seems best described as Graham & Dodd "Net-Nets" on steroids. However, it may be hard for investors to understand the TAVF investment approach unless the investor has some sense of the uses and limitations of financial accounting, especially as it pertains to value investing. Thus, in this quarterly letter I discuss "The Uses and Limitations of Financial Accounting for the Value Investor".

The first rule to remember is that financial accounting can't tell "The Truth." Financial accounting systems such as Generally Accepted Accounting Principles (GAAP) have to be based on a relatively rigid set of assumptions that cannot in all (or even most) contexts reflect economic reality. What economic reality is must be determined by the user of GAAP (the analyst) not the preparer of GAAP financial statements (the CPA). Yet GAAP or other accounting systems such as International Financial Reporting Systems (IFRS) or Statutory Accounting Systems for U.S. insurance companies, are essential, irreplaceable, tools for the value analyst. GAAP and GAAP-like financial statements are virtually the only quantitative objective benchmarks available to the analyst in the vast majority of situations. The value analyst uses these objective benchmarks to ascertain his or her determinations of what economic reality is.

The second rule to remember is that financial statements, unadjusted by the user, almost always will be misleading in one context or another.

Accrual accounting, the basis for most of GAAP, tends to mislead because of the failure to reflect good estimations of the cash flow experience, whether positive or negative. (Financial textbooks such as Brealey and Myers' *Principles of Corporate Finance* overestimate the importance of internally generated cash flows.)

Cash accounting tends to mislead because it doesn't reflect any estimation of the wealth creation, or wealth destruction, experience.

The third thing to remember in value investing is that there is no Primacy of the Income Account despite its general acceptance on Wall Street, even by Graham & Dodd in their various editions of *Security Analysis; Principles and Technique*. Rather, every accounting entry can be important in a value analysis. There is recognition of the accounting cycle fact that every accounting number is derived from, modified by, and a function of, other accounting numbers. This grows out of the recognition by the value analyst that corporate value is created in a multiplicity of ways, sometime related to each other, sometimes not. At TAVF, for purposes of analysis, we recognize four different ways in which corporate values are created:

1. **Cash flows from operations available to securities holders.** This, while not uncommon, seems rarer than most commentators seem to believe.
2. **Earnings, with earnings defined as creating wealth while consuming cash.** This seems to be what the vast majority of businesses and the vast majority of governments do the vast majority of the time. For the vast majority of entities, it is hard for earnings to deliver good results to shareholders over the long term, unless the entity has access to capital markets or has created saleable assets. As a practical matter, for earnings to create corporate value, the entity has to remain, or become, creditworthy.
3. **Resource conversion results in the creation of corporate wealth through asset redeployments, liability restructurings, and changes of control.** These are accomplished through mergers and acquisitions, liquidations, investments in new areas,

cash purchases of control blocks of securities, voluntary exchanges, spin-offs, debt restructurings, repurchases of outstanding common stocks (either leaving the issuer a public entity or going private).

4. **Having access to capital markets on a super-attractive basis.** Probably more corporate value has been created this way than any other, especially when such super-attractive access is combined with an ability for the entity to benefit from an absence, or relative absence, of income tax burdens. Such super-attractive access to capital markets includes both equity markets and credit markets. A primary example of an equity market where corporations had super-attractive access (free money if you wish) was the pre-2000 dot com bubble. Credit markets which are super-attractive include the availability of non-recourse mortgage loans for a long term at low, fixed-interest rates issued to finance the ownership of income-producing real estate.

A good example of the difficulty in prescribing GAAP rules that reflect economic reality revolves around accounting for financial instruments, whether those instruments should be carried at amortized cost less impairments, or at lower of cost or fair value (with fair value usually equaling market price). The Financial Accounting Standards Board (FASB) is considering the matter currently. FASB's current position seems wise – disclose both amortized cost and fair value. One disclosure would be in the financial statements themselves and the other would be in the footnotes to the financial statements. The real-world scenarios for accounting for financial instruments are so complex, I'd leave it up to corporate managements to decide whether fair value ought to be in the financial statements or footnotes; ditto for amortized cost, of course. Whichever management chooses becomes a good tool to help value analysts appraise management, e.g., how promotional are they?

Take a look at the complexity involved in accounting for financial instruments. In appraising a portfolio of non-control, marketable common stocks, there is no question that the appropriate standard is fair value. In appraising a portfolio of high quality performing loans which the holder intends to hold to maturity, the preferred standard should be amortized cost. But even this is complicated. Assume, in the case of an equity portfolio, that the holder has designs on getting control of some of the issuers whose common stock is in the portfolio. Fair value here can be misleading since from the point of view of the holder, the lower the fair value (i.e., market price) the more favorable to the holder. Assume that the portfolio of performing loans is financed almost wholly by interest bearing liabilities, the collateral for which is the performing loan portfolio. Here the liabilities would be worth their principal amount, unless that holder had other resources which he could use to acquire the liabilities at a discount, if available. In this case, fair value seems a much better measure for the performing loans than amortized cost, simply because it is possible that an event of default on the performing loans will be measured by fair value rather than amortized cost.

It ought to be noted that concerning events of default, there exist two, not one, general tests of insolvency. First there is the balance sheet test – does the fair value of the assets exceed the claim value of the liabilities? In the above leveraged balance sheet, the fair value of the performing loan portfolio could have flunked the balance sheet test. Second, there is the income test – will the borrowing entity be able to service its liability obligations as they become due? Normally, in gauging insolvency, the income test is far more important than the balance sheet test. Maybe the performing loan portfolio would pass the income test with flying colors while flunking the balance sheet test. If so, I'd postulate that amortized cost were the more important measure; if not, I'd opt for fair value, However, it should be noted that whether or not an event of default exists would be determined by the covenants in loan agreements and bond indentures.

Note that fair value measures can have perverse effects for an analyst. Take portfolios of performing loans that are financed by liabilities that are not interest bearing. This is the situation that exists for insurance companies and pension plans. Most insurance companies and most pension plans are continually reinvesting money received from maturing obligations into new obligations and also investing new moneys into new obligations, the vast bulk of which will be performing loans held to maturity. Assume interest rates rise sharply. Fair values will decrease dramatically but future net investment income will be much greater than would have been the case if interest rates had not risen. Which should be weighed more heavily – the current reductions in fair value or the prospective increases in investment income? That is something for the analyst, not the accountant, to decide.

I learned a great lesson about inflation accounting in the late 1970s and early 1980s. At that time, the accounting authorities together with the Securities and Exchange Commission (SEC) put in place as a financial statement supplement, "Inflation Accounting," i.e., Current Value Accounting. Inflation accounting was designed to ameliorate the effects of overstated earnings caused by companies in a highly inflationary environment taking inadequate depreciation charges for expenditures they would have to make to replace aging property and equipment. At the time, I thought this brought some truth to accounting, never realizing other effects of rampant inflation. Because costs increased so rapidly, there were huge benefits to many companies with large amounts of "sunk costs." New competitors couldn't afford to enter the industry and existing companies found it hard to expand. Net, net, probably competitive relief because of rampant inflation was more important than materially inadequate depreciation charges. There was no way GAAP could handle both.

It is much more important for the U.S. economy to have its accounting systems geared toward informing creditors in a meaningful fashion than it is to have accounting systems directed toward meeting the perceived needs of Outside Passive Minority Investors (OPMIs). First, there is a lot more credit outstanding in the economy than there is net worth. Second, creditors use accounting to help determine the creditworthiness of a company by estimating whether that company will be able to generate cash internally, both long- and short-term, to pay its bills, and by estimating whether that company is likely to have relatively continual access to capital markets, especially credit markets. In contrast, OPMIs tend to place overemphasis on one accounting number – reported earnings – in order to predict what stock market prices in the immediate future might be. Bluntly, accounting systems do not seem as if they can really be very helpful as a tool for predicting near-term equity prices in OPMI markets. As far as I can tell, near-term market prices for common stocks in non-arbitrage situations will continue to be a "random walk".

Cash payments are very different from stock options from a creditor's point of view. Cash payments by a company can affect the creditworthiness of a business. Cash payments, therefore, are a company and a creditor problem. With minor exceptions, the issuance of stock options has no effect whatsoever on the creditworthiness of a company. Instead, stock options result presently, or prospectively, in the dilution of existing stockholders' ownership interests. Stock options are not a company and creditor problem. They are a stockholder problem.

Those who think of options as an expense have it wrong, at least from the Company and Creditor points of view. Warren Buffett is quoted as saying, "If options are not a form of compensation, what are they? If compensation isn't an expense, what is it? And if expenses shouldn't go into the calculations of earnings, where in the world should they go?" Frankly, the Buffett statement is an overgeneralization, even though most finance academics seem to be wholly in concurrence. Stock options are not compensation from the points of view of the company itself, or its creditors. Stock options certainly are "compensation" when looked at strictly from the point of view of stockholders. The issuance of options results in present, or potential, dilution of common stockholders' interests.

Assuming stock options are to be treated as a company expense, what should that expense be? Presently, the disclosure required under GAAP assumes that the cost of options to the company equals the theoretical value of the options to the recipients. However, it is utterly ludicrous to suppose that the value of a benefit to a recipient has any necessary relationship to the cost to a company to bestow that benefit. It is as if a sales clerk who has a 40% off employee discount buys a $100 sweater from her department store for $60 and the store then states that it incurred a cost of $100 because that is what the sweater is worth to the clerk, even though the company's actual cost for the sweater might be, say, $35. The real cost of an executive option to the company (rather than to its stockholders) equals the present value of the probability that option program will reduce the company's future access to capital markets, especially equity markets. I would not know how to measure such a cost. In fact, there should be an offset to this cost, namely the present value of the probability that the options program increases the retention of talent and/or motivates that talent's productivity.

The cases where stock options become a company problem as well as a stockholder problem seem few and far between. Options are a company problem long-term, insofar as they either cause the company to pay out cash (or property), or, if their issuance reduces access to capital markets. In general, those cases where stock options become a company problem seem to encompass the following:

1. The company is committed, or required, to pay out an ultra-high percentage of future earnings as cash dividends to common stockholders. Such companies include Real Estate Investment Trusts (REITs).
2. The potential issuance of common stock through the exercise of stock options reduces the company's future access to capital markets to raise new funds.
3. The company is committed to having the amount of common stock outstanding relatively fixed, and therefore, acquires for cash, or property, enough outstanding common stock to cover the new issuance of common stock through the exercise of stock options.

Over 80% of the TAVF portfolio is invested in the common stocks of companies I like to think of as Graham and Dodd Net-Nets on steroids. The reason for steroids is that we believe the prospects seem bright that over the next five-to-seven years, the net asset values (NAVs) of the TAVF portfolio companies will increase by not less than 10% to 20% per annum compounded. TAVF Net-Nets count as current assets high quality assets, surely convertible to cash in a year or so. Graham and Dodd, in contrast, define current assets only as assets conventional balance sheets.

Other things being equal, the Graham and Dodd Net-Nets held by TAVF are susceptible to resource conversion activities, especially changes of control, and going privates, i.e., insider buyouts. This is so because the common stocks are so cheap relative to business values and each company enjoys a super-strong financial position. I have no question that TAVF's Hong Kong-based Net-Nets would be highly attractive to various Chinese mainland entities. However, there will never be a change of control in any of our Hong Kong Net-Nets unless it results from a friendly, negotiated transaction. Insiders in each company own enough common stock to thwart easily any hostile takeover attempts.

If there ever were to be a change of control in any of the Hong Kong Common Stocks owned by TAVF, the prices paid for these securities ought to reflect huge premiums over current prices.

While going-private transactions almost always are priced at substantial premiums over then existing market prices, this is far from always attractive for buy-and-hold investors, such as TAVF. This is because the buyer in the going-private transaction has complete control of the timing of the transaction. The buyer has incentive to propose a transaction when market prices for the common stock are depressed.

I have no idea as to whether or not changes of control or transfers of elements of control, or going privates ever will occur for any the Net-Nets held in the TAVF portfolio. Rather, a basic reason for owning these common stocks is that we believe the prospects appear to be so very good that NAVs will grow over the next five-to-seven years at rates of not less than 10% to 20% per annum compounded.

The Fund's common stock portfolio is invested in the issues of extremely well-capitalized companies that were acquired at prices that, at the time of acquisition, represented meaningful discounts to readily ascertainable NAVs. The NAVs became readily ascertainable insofar as the specific assets consisted of certain marketable securities: income-producing real estate; land suitable for development; and intangibles, such as mutual fund assets under management. Rarely (except for cash and equivalents) were these readily ascertainable asset values classified as current assets under GAAP. The Fund's definition of Net-Nets is taken from Graham and Dodd's *Security Analysis*, but with a few twists. Graham and Dodd relied on a GAAP classified balance sheet to define current assets in order to ascertain if a common stock was a Net-Net. TAVF uses its own judgment, rather than GAAP classification, to define current assets in order to decide what is a liquid, i.e., current asset.

Graham and Dodd describe Net-Nets in the 1962 edition of *Security Analysis* on pages 561 and 562:

> **Net-Current-Asset Value** *We feel on more solid ground in discussing these cases in which the market price or the computed value based on earnings and dividends is less than the net current assets applicable to*

the common stock. [The reader will recall that in this computation we deduct all obligations and preferred stock from the working capital to determine the balance for the common.] From long experience with this type of situation we can say that it is always interesting, and that the purchase of a diversified group of companies on this 'bargain basis' is almost certain to result profitably within a reasonable period of time. One reason for calling such purchases bargain issues is that usually net-current-asset values may be considered a conservative measure of liquidation value. Thus as a practical matter such companies could be disposed of for not less than their working capital, if that capital is conservatively stated. It is a general rule that at least enough can be realized for the plant account and miscellaneous assets to offset any shrinkage sustained in the process of turning current assets into cash. [This rule would nearly always apply to a negotiated sale of the business to some reasonably interested buyer.] The working capital value behind a common stock can be readily computed. Consequently, by using this figure (i.e., Net-Net asset value) as the equivalent of 'minimum liquidating value' we can discuss with some degree of confidence the actual relationship between the market price of a stock and the realizable value of the business.

While Graham and Dodd seem to have invented the idea of Net-Nets, TAVF uses that idea with a number of modifications. First, the Fund is not interested in Net-Nets unless the company is extremely well-financed. A large quantity of current assets, especially if they consist of inventories, costs in excess of billings, or receivables from less than creditworthy customers, probably cannot help the common stock of a company which cannot meet its obligations to its creditors. Second, many current assets classified as current assets under GAAP are really fixed assets of the worst sort. Take department store merchandise inventories. If the department store is to be liquidated, merchandise inventories are indeed a current asset, convertible to cash within 12 months at prices that conceivably could be close to book value, although much less than book value may be realized if the merchandise is disposed of in a Going Out of Business sale. On the other hand, if the department store is a going concern, merchandise inventories are a fixed asset of the worst sort. The merchandise inventories have to be replaced, are hard to value, and are subject to markdowns, obsolescence, shrinkage, seasonality and mislocation. The Toyota Industries portfolio of marketable securities and the Brookfield Asset Management portfolio of Class A Office Buildings seem to be much more of a current asset than department store merchandise inventories even though, for GAAP purposes, Toyota Industries' marketable securities, and Brookfield Asset Management's Class A office buildings, are not considered a current asset. Third, the Graham and Dodd formulation does not account for off-balance sheet liabilities, which may or may not be disclosed in footnotes; nor, do Graham and Dodd take into account excessive expenses or losses. At TAVF, such expenses or losses are capitalized and added to liabilities. Fourth, Graham and Dodd only seem to recognize partially that certain fixed assets, e.g., property, plant, and equipment, can sometimes create cash. For example, under Section 1231 of the U.S. Internal Revenue Code, the sale at a loss of such assets used in a trade or business, usually gives rise to an ordinary loss for income tax purposes. In that case, a corporation may be able to apply the loss first to reduce the current year taxes and any excess loss might be used to get "quickie" cash refunds from the IRS with regard to taxes paid in the prior two years (sometimes five years).

The identification of Net-Nets has not proved that difficult for the Fund, even though most of TAVF's investments now are outside the United States.

For most market participants, the most important accounting number is earnings per share reported for a quarter. There are times in corporate analysis where quarterly earnings deserve great weight. Those times exist for not-well-capitalized companies that need relatively continuous access to capital markets. Also, quarterly earnings can have a major impact on heavily margined portfolios. Neither of these conditions pertains to TAVF, which invests only in the common stocks of very well-capitalized companies; also, TAVF does not borrow funds. Quarterly earnings are highly important to TAVF, insofar as they provide evidence that a business has suffered, or is suffering, a permanent impairment. None of the current common stocks in the TAVF portfolio seem to be close to suffering a permanent impairment. Current tough economic times –especially– in North America and Europe, notwithstanding, Fund Management keeps a wary eye on probabilities of permanent impairment.

In examining probable directions financial accounting ought to take, I have a few suggestions:

1. The company is a stand-alone and its financial statements should reflect this fact. It is not the stockholders; it is not the management. If this were recognized there never would have been a "stock option" controversy in the first place.
2. Financial accounting should be directed, first and foremost, toward meeting the needs of creditors. There certainly should exist a modifying convention of conservatism. It is impossible to design a meaningful accounting system to meet the perceived needs of day traders and stock market technicians, whether market participants or financial academics.
3. Insofar as possible, financial accounts ought to be based on principles, rather than rules. Now, because of a focus on rules, GAAP has become as complicated as the Internal Revenue Code. What a waste!
4. Financial statements ought to be prepared on the assumption that users are intelligent, diligent, and reasonably well trained in understanding the uses and limitations of financial accounting.

There are investment areas where financial accounting is important, indeed, vital. For example, financial statements seem always to be a key in credit analysis. However, there are equity areas where financial statements become relatively unimportant. These areas include equity participations in new inventions and new discoveries; and, also, certain areas where issuers are sitting on huge amounts of unrealized appreciation, which unrealized appreciation is almost impossible to measure by any tool available to a non-control investor. Those seem to be areas where value investors ought to fear to tread. Unlike most general market participants, value investors are bottom-up participants, people who aren't interested in all securities. Many of such securities are just unsuitable and/or unanalyzable using value investing techniques.

CHAPTER 12

Fundamental Finance

OCTOBER 2012

The Third Avenue Management (TAM) mode of operation is to emphasize Fundamental Finance (FF), rather than trading strategies. FF encompasses Value Investing, Control Investing, Distressed Investing, Credit Analysis and First and Second Stage Venture Capital Investing. TAM is, of course, primarily a Value Investor that is a passive non-control investor.

FF approaches matters quite differently than do short-run traders. In FF in 2012, the emphasis is on creditworthiness, rather than earnings or cash flows. In FF, managements are appraised not only as operators, but also as investors and financiers. As Value Investors, the bulk of TAM efforts are directed toward investing in equities of financially strong companies which, over the long-term, have good prospects to grow readily ascertainable Net Asset Values (NAV). And also in FF, it becomes important to understand the motivations and practices of activists.

As such, FF tends to be quite different than activities revolving around trading, or academic finance as embedded in Modern Capital Theory (MCT). Also, as an FF disciple, I reject a number of commonly held beliefs including the concept of "too big to fail"; the definition of corporate failure; the belief that creditworthy entities, corporate or governmental, ever repay indebtedness in the aggregate; or the belief that a capital infusion into a private enterprise by a governmental agency is, *ipso facto* a "bailout" rather than an "investment".

It seems to me that almost all other approaches to investing and academic finance ranging from *Principles of Corporate Finance* by Brealey and Myers to *Security Analysis Principles and Technique* by Graham, Dodd and Cottle (G&D) to tracts on trading techniques focus on forecasting and explaining short-run market prices, especially on prices at which securities are traded in markets populated by Outside Passive Minority Investors (OPMIs). In sharp contrast, FF focuses strictly on explaining and understanding commercial enterprises and the securities they issue. To me, short-run market prices in OPMI markets are "random walks" except for the special cases of "sudden death securities", such as options, warrants, certain convertibles and risk arbitrage situations where there will be relatively determinant workouts in relatively determinant periods of time. As a consequence of the 2008 economic meltdown an FF approach to investing became more relevant, and MCT and G&D approaches seem to have become less relevant.

A contrast in approaches between academic finance and FF is contained in the introduction to Brealey and Myers *Principles of Corporate Finance* (McGraw Hill 1991) a leading finance text, where the authors state "there are no ironclad prerequisites for reading this book except Algebra and the English language. An elementary knowledge of accounting, statistics, and macroeconomics is helpful, however." To understand FF, however, the market participant ought to strive to become knowledgeable in several fields – knowledgeable enough to be an informed client. FF areas where knowledge is a prerequisite include the following:

- Securities Law and Regulations
- Financial Accounting
- Corporate Law with some emphasis on Delaware Law
- Income Tax

Other disciplines that might come into play depending on the particular situation being analyzed are Bankruptcy Law, Insurance Law and Regulation, Banking Law and Regulation, Environmental Law, etc.

To others, the default position embodies the MCT view that markets are efficient, to wit, the price is right. In FF, in contrast, most prices are quite wrong most of the time.

In FF, control issues and changes in control are a major consideration. Control issues are pretty much ignored by MCT and G&D. Control common stocks and passively owned common stocks are the same in form but control common stocks are, in fact, a vastly different commodity than non-control common stock, certainly priced very differently in their respective markets. Control issues are also highly important in restructuring troubled issuers. It appears as if subsequent to the 2008-2009 economic meltdown, an increased percentage of changes of control have occurred through recapitalization, asset sales and capital infusions involving troubled publicly-owned companies, rather than has occurred through acquiring common stocks or using the proxy machinery to effect changes of control of healthy companies.

The conventional thinking seems to be that one has to take huge risks to obtain huge rewards. I demur. Rather, the royal road to riches is not to take investment risks, but, rather, to lay off the investment risks on someone else. Great fortunes have been built by those who successfully laid off investment risk on others. These success stories include the following people:

- Corporate Executives
- Hedge Fund Operators
- Plaintiffs' Attorneys
- Bankruptcy Attorneys and Investment Bankers
- Securities Brokers
- Venture Capitalists

The best – but far from the only – way for OPMIs to lay off investment risk is to acquire securities that are high quality and have good prospects for growing NAV over the long-term.

The elements that go into investing in such common stocks encompass the following:

1. The issuer has to enjoy a super-strong financial position.
2. The common stock has to be available at, at least, a 20% discount from readily ascertainable NAV.
3. The company has to provide comprehensive disclosures, including complete audits, and also be listed or traded in markets in jurisdictions that provide strong investor protections. (The U.S., Canada and Hong Kong being examples).
4. After thorough analysis the prospects appear good that, over the next three-to-seven years, the company will be able to increase NAV by not less than 10% compounded annually after adding back dividends.

These are certain shortcomings to this approach. A strong financial position, especially in the 2012 low interest rate environment, means the OPMI is dealing with managements willing to sacrifice Return on Equity (ROE) and Return on Assets (ROA) in exchange for the insurance against adversity provided by a strong financial position; and the opportunism for companies that arise out of a strong financial position. Also, the OPMI market seems efficient enough so that a large discount from NAV almost always indicates an absence of catalysts that could result in immediate market appreciation.

There are many, many value investors who are quite competent competitors. As far as I can tell, however, none seem to put as much emphasis on strong financial positions as we at TAM do.

Another factor that others seem to ignore is the importance for companies to have access to capital markets, both credit markets and equity markets. Capital markets are notoriously capricious, sometimes not available at all (see the 2008 credit meltdown) and sometimes willing to give companies what might be characterized as "almost free money" (see the 1999 IPO boom).

The goal of most corporations and most (but not all) OPMIs ought to be wealth creation and it is important to note that there are four general ways to create wealth, not just the two seemingly cited by MCT and G&D. MCT and G&D believe in a primacy of the income account, i.e., creating wealth by flows – whether cash flows or earnings flows (earnings is defined as creating wealth while consuming cash). The four general ways of creating wealth –either corporate or individual – are as follows:

1. Cash flow from operations
2. Earnings from operations
3. Resource conversion, i.e., massive asset redeployments, mergers and acquisitions, liability restructurings, changes of control, spin-offs, and liquidations.
4. Having attractive access to capital markets.

It seems as if conventional securities analysis puts overemphasis on four factors which makes their approach much less useful in helping to understand FF in particular and business in general. The four areas of overemphasis are as follows:

1. Primacy of the income account (to the exclusion of balance sheet and financial position considerations).
2. Short-termism
3. Emphasis on top-down analysis and a consequent denigration of bottom-up analysis.
4. Equilibrium Pricing – i.e., the price at any moment of time represents an efficient market, and that price will change as the market digests new information.

G&D seem guilty on the first three accounts. MCT seems guilty on all four.

For us, much common wisdom is just plain wrong: Too Big to Fail is meaningless. The standard has to be "Too Important Not to Be Reorganized Efficiently and Expeditiously". The reorganization and/or capital infusions after 2008 into GM, Chrysler, CIT, Citigroup and AIG are good examples of efficient and expeditious reorganizations of very important companies.

Corporate failure is defined as a restructuring or liquidation where junior security holders are wiped out or almost wiped out. Chapter 11 does not define failure. Staying in business does not define success. After 2008, AIG and Citicorp both failed using our definitions of failure, though neither ever filed for Chapter 11 Relief.

In the aggregate, debt is almost never repaid by entities which remain creditworthy. Rather, it is refinanced and expanded insofar as the entity – whether corporate or governmental – expands its borrowing capacity, i.e., becomes more creditworthy. The difference between a bailout and an investment is that a bailout constitutes a capital infusion without any hope of a return, no matter how return is measured. If there are prospects of a return, as well as a return of principal, the capital infusion is an investment. The Troubled Asset Relief Program (TARP) instigated in 2008 to rescue U.S. banks was an investment by the government, not a bailout.

Three elements go into the determination of credit-worthiness for functional purposes.

> a) Amount of Debt
> b) Terms of Debt
> c) How Productive are the Use of Proceeds from Incurring the Debt.

Of the above, perhaps c) is the most important.

Also there are three tests of solvency, and most entities do not have to pass all three to be deemed solvent.

1. Does the fair value of the assets exceed the claims against those assets (a balance sheet test)?
2. Does the entity have the wherewithal to meet its obligations as they come due (an income account test)?
3. Does the entity have access to the capital markets to meet cash shortfalls (a liquidity test)?

In *Security Analysis*, on page 47, G&D opine on the difference between investment and speculation. "An investment operation is one which upon thorough analysis, promises safety of principal and a satisfactory return. Operations not meeting these requirements are speculative." At TAM, we agree wholeheartedly with G&D. The TAM approach described in this letter is designed to be an investment operation, not a speculation.

There are three general measures of investment risk:

1. Quality of the Issuer
2. Terms of the Issue
3. Price of the Issue. Diversification is only a surrogate, and usually a damn poor surrogate for knowledge, control and price consciousness.

The most talented value investors seem to graduate into distress investing and control investing. Such graduates include Warren Buffett, Sam Zell, Carl Icahn, Bill Ackman and David Einhorn.

The appraisals of managements ought to examine them not only as operators, but also as investors and financiers.

In FF there is no substantive consolidation but plenty of structural subordination. In particular the company is a stand-alone – it is not the management, it is not the stockholders. Every constituency in an economic entity in its relationships with other constituencies combines communities of interest and conflicts of interests.

Essentially stock options are a stockholder problem, not a company problem.

It is axiomatic that if an economic entity cannot be made creditworthy, sooner or later the entity has to be reorganized or liquidated. It seems as if no one is really doing anything on the sovereign front to make Portugal, Ireland, Italy, Greece and Spain creditworthy. For starters, at the minimum there is a need for efficiency rather that austerity.

For most portfolios of performing loans, time corrects the error of having bought at too high a price. In examining NAV, it is important to examine the dynamics of NAV, rather than just the statics of NAV. For almost all corporations, NAV will grow year by year almost continuously. Quality of NAV tends to be much more important than the quantity of NAV. Certain assets contained in book value reflect overhead unlikely to ever be recovered through earnings or cash flow. Those are the types of NAV common stocks TAM tries to avoid as an OPMI. There are valuable lessons to be learned from G&D's analysis of Net-Nets.

Payments to shareholders, either in the form of dividends or stock buybacks, has to be a residual use of cash most of the time, compared with using cash to expand corporate assets or reduce corporate liabilities. However, from a corporate point of view, it sometimes makes sense to pay large and increasing dividends, because that can give the corporations better access to capital markets than would otherwise be the case. Also, managements might consider large dividends simply because it is desired by so much of the company's OPMI constituency.

For the most part, the TAM approach is basically a buy-and-hold approach. Sales take place when the security becomes grossly overpriced, the analyst has made a mistake, corporate conditions change, or for portfolio considerations. For TAM, a principal goal is to buy growth, but, don't pay for it.

A security has value to a holder only insofar as it promises a cash bailout, control or both. A fair price is that which would be arrived at between willing buyers and willing sellers each with knowledge of the relevant facts and neither under any compulsion to act. Most going-private and leveraged buyout transactions are characterized by coerced seller–willing buyer. However, OPMIs become willing sellers when offered premiums over market prices.

CHAPTER 13

Third Avenue and the Efficient Market Hypothesis

OCTOBER 2010

November 1, 2010, marked the 20th anniversary of the launch of Third Avenue Management's (TAM) first mutual fund, Third Avenue Value Fund (TAVF, "Third Avenue" or the "Fund"). Much has been accomplished in the past 20 years by TAM, in providing sound investment advice and good results for the shareholders of our four funds, registered under the Investment Company Act of 1940, as amended, and managed by Third Avenue: TAVF, Third Avenue Small-Cap Value Fund, Third Avenue International Value Fund and Third Avenue Real Estate Value Fund. I am particularly proud and pleased by what has been achieved by my partners at Third Avenue and by all the employees of the firm. They really are a remarkable bunch.

Twenty Years of Value Investing

When the Fund first reported to shareholders on October 31, 1990, it had a portfolio of ten securities including municipal bonds, corporate bonds, corporate preferred stock and common stock. "We suppose that many people who read this letter will conclude that the portfolio is speculative," we wrote. "Certainly all the conventional thinkers believe the Fund is speculative. We disagree. Unconventional, sure. But given the prices at which the various securities were acquired, and given the extensive, in-depth research that went into the decision-making process for each investment, speculative versus conservative ought not to be measured only by what is cosmetically acceptable and what ratings services say. Rating services and conventional thinkers pay no attention at all to price. From the Third Avenue perspective, we believe that there ought to be, at the least, a price component in measuring whether an investment is speculative or conservative. There also ought to be a quality of research component. Third Avenue will try to stay conservative by these measures even though the portfolio is unlikely to ever be cosmetically correct."

For two decades, a hallmark of Third Avenue's style has been the search for safety in places where most investors would never look. In a mutual fund industry that has spawned narrower and narrower niches in response to the teaching of Modern Capital Theory (MCT) and the Efficient Market Hypothesis (EMH), Third Avenue has charted a unique path. Guided by an adherence to price consciousness and a deep understanding of underlying business fundamentals and asset values, Third Avenue managers have wide discretion to invest where and when they deem it appropriate. The results have been gratifying – returns that beat the market most of the time and over the long run. The experience has been unique. TAVF and its investors are rarely, if ever, invested alongside the galloping herds.

It was 1993 when the Value Fund first invested in Apple Computer. This was back when Apple's products served a decidedly niche audience and the company seemed destined to, at best, maintain its position as a relatively small manufacturer of personal computers, if not to be outright crushed by Microsoft and computer manufacturers making machines that ran its operating systems. When we initiated our position, we did not know how truly iconic and enduring a fixture Apple would become. What we did know, from our fundamental bottom-up analysis, was enough to understand what the company was worth at the time and how the market, in its momentary ignorance, had left its securities undervalued. Apple enjoyed a super strong financial position. TAVF invested in technology companies large and small throughout the 1990s. In almost every instance, cash alone exceeded total book liabilities. Our investments in smaller semiconductor capital equipment stocks led to the eventual formation of the Third Avenue Small-Cap Value Fund. We avoided the speculative dot com stocks of the day, (including new issues that we called "schlock" in 1999), but we didn't eschew investing in technology. Instead we invested in well-capitalized semiconductor companies, those that built the infrastructure of the Internet that endured, even as so many Internet pure plays fizzled into the ether. Outsiders were quick to judge us for not joining the dot com frenzy, with some wondering whether or not we were out of touch with a new era. We invested by the dictates of our philosophy and were ultimately vindicated. At the Value Fund we are now looking at some larger, undervalued American technology companies.

In the wake 2001's shock to the U.S. economy, Third Avenue returned to its roots in distress investing. We invested in the high-yield debt of several troubled companies, seeking returns of 25% or more. We owned unsecured debt in Kmart, which sought bankruptcy protection in 2002. TAVF purchased common stock to help fund Kmart's reorganization. Our Real Estate team determined that we were able to purchase Kmart common for less than the value of the company's real estate. We exited our position when we believed the stock had become egregiously overvalued.

In 2004 and 2005, TAVF began making a number of overseas investments in common stocks, including companies such as South Korean steel producer POSCO and also in Hong Kong real estate and investment companies. These remain in the portfolio today. At the time, we said that "other things being equal, we would prefer to invest in this country (the U.S.)," but our price consciousness dictated that we look abroad. Once again, price led us in the right direction. It now seems that any long-term investor should want to have a portion of their assets in companies headquartered in and doing business in the Far East, including Hong Kong. TAVF became an excellent way to gain that exposure through a portfolio of the strongest companies that are run by management teams whose interests are aligned with those of Outside Passive Minority Shareholders (OPMIs), even when those shareholders are situated abroad. Third Avenue was able to make such investments with confidence because we have a long tradition of global value investing.

In an industry where independent thinking, fundamental analysis and conviction-based investing have been abandoned by so many other managers, in order to force their investment strategies to match a benchmark or fit someone else's mandate or style box, I am proud to say that we have remained true to our investment philosophy for our entire 20 years. Every step of the way we have "eaten our own cooking," investing our personal money in our funds, alongside and on the same terms as you, our fellow shareholders. I guess that makes us biased. But we are biased on your side.

Efficient Market Hypothesis Revisited

While I have written about the subject many times over the past twenty years, it seems productive to write to you about the disparities that exist between the analyses that goes into the bulk of Third Avenue Management's (TAM) equity investments on the one hand, and the beliefs and analyses that pertain to the efficient market hypothesis (EMH) on the other hand. EMH is believed in by almost all academics – whether finance professors or economists and probably by most mutual fund managers – almost all of whom sign off on what is called MCT. Put simply, in the efficient market hypotheses, market prices for individual securities in markets populated by OMPIs almost always reflect some sort of universally accepted value.

In the last quarterly letter, for the period ended July 31, 2010, I discussed TAVF's investments in securities which I called Graham & Dodd net-nets on steroids. These securities account for about 60% of TAVF's net assets. The Graham & Dodd net-nets on steroids virtually all have the following characteristics:

- The companies enjoy super strong financial positions.
- The common stocks were purchased at prices that represented at least a 25% discount from readily ascertainable Net Asset Values (NAV), with the average discount probably closer to 35% to 40%.
- The disclosures available to OPMIs were, and are, comprehensive, complete and understandable.
- Past records of the companies were, and are, very good with most growing NAV (after adding back dividends) at compound rates during the previous five years of better than 10% – in fact closer to 15%.
- The prospects for growth in NAV in the next three-to-seven years at rates better than 10% compounded seem very good.
- Current earnings and cash flows are strong.

There is one other very important characteristic to all these Graham & Dodd common stocks whose names include: Brookfield Asset Management, Capital Southwest, Cheung Kong Holdings, Hang Lung Group, Henderson Land Development, Investor A/B and Wheelock & Co. That other characteristic is that in each instance, there are little or no prospects for changes of control. If there were prospects for changes of control, not only would the discounts from NAV disappear, but control buyers probably would pay control premiums (maybe substantial premiums) over NAV, in part, because given the super strong financial positions of the companies, most acquisitions could be financed on extremely attractive terms. Thus, it seems obvious that here OPMI market prices do not come close to reflecting underlying corporate values.

It is fair to argue that efficient market pricing reflects all relevant factors, not just underlying corporate value, and lack of prospects for changes in control are a very relevant factor in analyzing the Graham & Dodd net-nets on steroids. But this deserves little or no weight in a TAM analysis, where the emphasis is on acquiring securities on a safe and cheap basis – i.e., the common stock is priced at a big discount from underlying corporate value; the company is well-managed and enjoys super strong finances; and fund managers can see a long-term, highly profitable exit strategy. For TAM, the efficient market does not exist; MCT misleads far more than it informs.

Underlying corporate values are created in four different ways, sometimes related to each other, sometimes not. Briefly the four ways underlying corporate values are created are as follows:

1. The company has free cash flow from operations available to security holders. This is probably rarer than most people think.
2. The company has earnings, with earnings defined as creating wealth while consuming cash. Earnings are the flows that are most common not only for businesses but also for governments. In most instances earnings cannot create long-term value unless it is also combined with access to capital markets in order to finance cash shortfalls. Put otherwise, most of the time a business has to stay creditworthy if its earnings are to be valuable to security holders. MCT postulates that each good investment has to have over its life a positive net cash flow, i.e., a positive Net

Present Value (NPV). This concept is valid for project finance, but not for corporate finance involving going concerns with perpetual lives.
3.   There exist resource conversions. Resource conversions include: changes of control; mergers and acquisitions; tender offers; massive asset redeployments; massive liability restructurings, whether in leveraged buyouts or the reorganization of troubled companies; large scale distributions to stock holders in the form of dividends and/or stock buy- backs; and split ups.
4.   Access to capital markets, either equity or credit markets, on a super-attractive basis is available. One example of such super-attractive access to equity markets revolves around the dot-com bubble prior to the year 2000, when high tech start- ups could go public and get virtually free money. One such example of super-attractive access to credit markets revolves around the availability of long-term, fixed low-interest rate, non-recourse financing for many income-producing real estate properties.

Because there seems to be a dearth of resource conversion opportunities for the Graham & Dodd net-nets, at least as far as changes in control are concerned, and probably limited opportunities for super-attractive access to capital markets, the TAM analysis focuses on forecasting future flows – both cash flows and earnings. These flows are reflected in future NAVs and future distributions to shareholders. If the analyst is close to right about double digit growth in NAV, the holding of the security will tend to be quite profitable, unless the discount from NAV widens very materially. So far, in the twenty-year history of TAM, the TAM analysts seem to have done a pretty good job of buying into the common stocks of companies with growing NAVs, the severe business recessions that occurred during this period notwithstanding.

Looked at from the bottom-up, it is hard to say that OPMI markets reflect realistic values for going-concerns with perpetual lives from any rational point of view. Indeed, at TAM, we believe that without prospects for changes of control, market prices in Japan never have to be anything but a random walk. Thus, in recent years TAM funds have lightened up on their holdings of well-financed Japanese companies, because of the belief that managements and control groups tend to be indifferent to the interests of OPMIs. Therefore, Japan's market prices never have to reflect any rational values because, generally, there are no prospects for changes in control. (As an aside, it seems as if the absence of change of control possibilities combined with the indifference toward OPMI interests have been important contributors to Japan's twenty-year long recession.)

The factors that OPMIs emphasize just do not reflect underlying values for going concerns with perpetual lives. The factors emphasized by most OPMIs seem to encompass the following:

- An extreme short run orientation. Short run market prices are important. Try to pick price bottoms to buy and price tops to sell.

- Emphasize the Primacy of the Income Account, at the expense of paying attention to the qualitative and quantitative aspects of balance sheets.

- Most market activity is undertaken by people with no training, no talent and no time for fundamental analysis, e.g., high frequency traders and day traders. The underlying view is the market knows all – certainly more than I do. Therefore study markets, not companies or the securities they issue.

- Focus on the macro. It is much more important to have views about the economy, general markets and interest rates, than it is to be bottom-up, i.e., focus on analyzing the company and the securities the company issues.

- Be outlook conscious at the expense of determining whether a security is priced at a discount from, or a premium above, underlying value.

Saying the above does not mean that there do not exist OPMI markets that are highly efficient. It just means that TAM does not, as a rule, play in those efficient markets. Efficient markets exist where short-run price swings have great significance and where prices are determined by reference to a very few computer programmable variables. In my view, efficiency dominates in markets characterized by the following:

- Credit instruments without credit risk, e.g., U.S. Treasuries.

- Derivatives, including options, warrants and convertibles.

- Risk arbitrage, with risk arbitrage being defined as situations where there will be relatively determinate workouts in relatively determinate short periods of time, e.g., a publicly announced merger.

For an efficient market to exist, four conditions have to be met:

1. The market participant is ignorant of, or chooses to ignore, fundamental analysis for the medium- to long-term.
2. The securities to be analyzed can be analyzed by reference to a few computer programmable variables.
3. Short-term price movements are of primary importance.
4. External forces impose a strict discipline on the market place. These external forces can be, among others, competition, government regulations, boards of directors, labor unions, attorneys, accountants, and community representatives.

Also, near-term price tends to become important when the market participant finances his, her or its activities with borrowed money. No TAM entity uses borrowings. In the TAM scheme of things, we place much less weight on market prices than is the case in MCT.

Cash bailouts for securities holders come from three sources.

1. Payments by the company – to creditors as interest, repayment of principal and premium. Equity payments are in the form of dividends and share repurchases. If a TAM Fund owns a performing loan providing a double digit yield to maturity, market price is less relevant than owning a non-dividend paying common stock.
2. Sale to a market
3. Obtain elements of control. The value of control is something almost completely ignored in MCT.

Sometimes market price even has a perverse value. Assume one holds a portfolio of performing loans that is expanding in size and whose maturing obligations are always being reinvested in new performing loans. Assume also that the liabilities financing the portfolio consist of non-interest bearing obligations, e.g., life insurance companies and pension plans. If the market value of this portfolio increases, future net investment income will be less than would otherwise be the case, because interest rates will have come down. Concomitantly, if the market value of the portfolio decreases, future net investment income will be greater than would otherwise be the case. One way of looking at this is to state that cash return analysis is sometimes quite different than total return analysis. There seems to be no recognition of the difference in MCT.

One of the things Fund Managements at TAM try hard to do is to avoid permanent impairments to investments. Generally, TAM seems to have done a reasonable job in this respect, with a very few notable exceptions, e.g., MBIA Common Stock.

The TAVF Portfolio of Graham & Dodd net-nets is quite conservative. Certainly returns might be higher if the Fund were willing to take more investment risk. This is not going to be the case. TAVF is not going to be involved in certain areas:

- Equities of companies that are basically in emerging markets
- Equities of companies which borrow heavily
- Companies that do not provide comprehensive, understandable, disclosures
- Start-ups
- Discovery companies

MCT offers as proof of an efficient market the fact that no one outperforms relevant indices consistently. Consistently is a dirty word; it means all the time. TAM is happy if the Funds' absolute returns are OK and if the Funds outperform relevant indices on average, most of the time and over the long run. TAM will never outperform indices consistently.

The principles followed by TAM, as enumerated above, are not restricted to value investing. Emphasizing underlying corporate values are also the tools of choice in distress investing, control investing and credit analysis.

PART 3

PORTFOLIO MANAGEMENT

"Diversification is merely a surrogate, and frequently a very poor surrogate, for knowledge and control."

July 1994

CHAPTER 14

Portfolio Diversification

JULY 1994

Portfolio Diversification

As I have noted in the past, diversification is merely a surrogate, and frequently a very poor surrogate, for knowledge and control. However, Third Avenue Value Fund (TAVF, "The Fund") is required by its fundamental investment policy, and the Internal Revenue Code, to meet certain standards of diversification. Further, the Fund is a passive, non-control investor and, thus, common sense dictates that TAVF pay much more attention to diversification than otherwise would be the case were the Fund involved in control acquisitions, including leveraged buyouts.

Accordingly, TAVF is somewhat diversified. However, TAVF is far less diversified than the vast majority of mutual funds, measured both by the Fund's willingness to concentrate the bulk of its monies in a relatively few issues, as well as the relatively small number of issues owned. Most other funds seem to be managed by "top-down" asset allocators who bring little, or no, knowledge to the nitty-gritty details that affect the companies and securities in which the typical fund has invested. Thus, "top-down" funds approximating TAVF in size tend to invest in the equities of, maybe, 150 to 250 issuers, compared with 63 for TAVF. Other funds tend to spread their investments over a broad range of industry groups (and the turnover among these 150 to 250 names will be frequent). Rarely will these highly diversified funds put as much as 1.5% of their risk assets (i.e., the portions of the portfolio which are not in cash and cash equivalents) into specific securities. Given the amount of knowledge these fund managers bring to individual situations, their broad diversifications probably are prudent for them. But by no stretch would such broad diversification make sense for TAVF, or for other funds which also concentrate on value. This idea of broad diversification reaches its zenith, of course, in index funds where the fund manager's admitted *raison d'être* is that he, or she, knows absolutely nothing about the underlying securities which are either in portfolios or the components of indices.

TAVF, on the other hand, tries to bring detailed, "bottom-up" knowledge about companies and securities to each of its portfolio investments. Inevitably, the Fund is going to be less diversified than "top-down" mutual funds. The Fund is likely to invest the same proportion of its assets in one security as more diversified entities invest in one industry. For example, as of August 15, 1994, the Fund owned in excess of 5% of the outstanding common stocks of four different issuers. Except for mutual funds in the over $1 billion asset size class, it does not seem usual practice for individual mutual funds to accumulate greater than 5% positions in the equities of individual issuers.

The bulk of the monies invested by TAVF during the quarter ended July 31, 1994, were in expanding existing positions.

In terms of the quality of knowledge that goes into investment decisions, it seems to me that it is infinitely easier for TAVF to get comfortable with concentration in a few situations, than is the case for asset allocators. The knowledge the Fund seeks is a lot more tangible, and capable of analysis, than is the case for many others. TAVF, in seeking knowledge, concentrates on acquiring equities in companies which enjoy strong financial positions, as well as promising long-term outlooks; and to acquire those common stocks at prices which represent substantial discounts from private business values. In acquiring credit instruments, the Fund concentrates on strong covenant protections combined with high yields. Unlike others, the Fund has virtually no interest in gathering knowledge about "soft stuff" which might aid in predicting things like the direction of the general market, interest rates, quarterly earnings, dividends, P/E ratios, business cycles, or Wall Street sponsorship. Nor is TAVF interested in anything that smacks of a technical or chartist approach. Indeed, the TAVF emphasis is much more on ascertaining long-term corporate values, rather than trying to estimate the near-term performance of securities prices. It seems relatively easy to use knowledge if one is striving, as TAVF is striving, to do "good enough," defining "good enough" as, say, earning 20% annually compounded on a long-term basis. It seems difficult to use knowledge if a fund manager has to strive to consistently or continuously outperform the market and/or a peer group. Admittedly, if the Fund was required to be managed using the variables and goals of other funds, it probably would be prudent for TAVF to emulate the other diversification strategies (and I would find something else to do as an occupation).

An Additional Thought: Research

I've spent a fair amount of time and effort criticizing the plaintiffs' bar and academic finance. A third group very low on my totem pole: research departments at broker-dealers. TAVF has been making a conscious effort to direct more business, consistent with best execution requirements, to a variety of broker-dealers who give usable research ideas to the Fund. I've asked a number of broker-dealers to send TAVF copies of their research department's written recommendations. At least 80% of such writings, while they may be terrific for market players, are unfit for consumption by value analysts who have a long-term, buy-and-hold, investment orientation. Some years ago, I had decided that I would essentially restrict my limited time for research reading to company documents, Securities and Exchange Commission and other agency filings, as well as things like litigation files. After spending some time now with broker-dealer research reports, I appreciate anew the wisdom of my earlier decision. In a real sense, this is not so much overt criticism of broker-dealer research departments, as it is another way of reiterating what ought to be self-evident: TAVF's investment practices and investment philosophy are quite different from the practices and policies of most other funds.

CHAPTER 15

Risk Arbitrage

OCTOBER 1994

Four-Year Performance and Third Avenue Value Fund's Objectives

It seems fair to state that the Third Avenue Value Fund's ("The Fund", TAVF) analytic *modus operandi*, first and foremost, is to try to avoid investment risk for the bulk of its investments. This means that TAVF acquires interests in situations where I believe there are minimal prospects that there will be fundamental deteriorations in a business, or in the entitlements attaching to the security in which TAVF has invested. Given a sense that this primary objective of avoiding investment risk is more or less achievable, the Fund then is willing to speculate about what the range of investment outcomes might be for a situation over, say, the next two to five years, as long as there seem to be reasonable prospects of TAVF earning either a total return, or a cash return, of better than 20% annually compounded.

While the Fund tries to guard against investment risk, it virtually ignores market risk. Gauging market risk requires one to have views about what the near-term price performance of any individual issue, or any particular market index, might be. Short-term price movements in securities markets, and market prices for non-arbitrage common stocks, are, in my view, a "random walk" to be studied, if at all, by abnormal psychologists, not financial fundamentalists who are passive investors. To pay attention to market risk, purely and simply, most of the time directly conflicts with an analyst's attempts to invest in securities where minimal investment risks are combined with probabilities for above-average long-term returns.

As of the close of the 1994 fiscal year, TAVF completed the first four years of its existence. The Fund's average annual return from inception through fiscal 1994 was 22.71%. To my mind, this was a satisfactory performance, especially against the background that TAVF's expense ratio was quite high in the first two years, and that from 1990 through much of 1993, the amount of merger and acquisition and takeover activity — potential bailout areas for much of the Fund's holdings — appeared to have been abnormally low.

The key question for TAVF shareholders, however, revolves around measuring the probabilities that the Fund will be able to achieve average annual returns of 20% or better over the next three, four and five years. My personal opinion is that it won't be easy, simply because it may be impossible to avoid a major disaster in one or more individual portfolio positions.

If there is any one thing to which TAVF's good 1990 through 1994 performance ought to be attributed, it is the absence of any permanent impairments in the fundamental values of any of the businesses in which the Fund invested, either as a creditor or an equity holder. I've rarely managed investments for a four-year period in the past without having a few disasters in the portfolio.

I've certainly never gone seven, eight or nine years without getting stuck in a few clinkers. Nobody can predict the future. Furthermore, if you operate in the real world, there seems to be a tendency for almost everyone, including TAVF, to relax investment standards on occasion. All good investors, passive investors anyway, seem to run into capital impairment problems from time to time. Warren Buffett, for example, has US Air; Peter Lynch had Crazy Eddie.

The Fund's criteria for investing in equity and equity-type securities bottom on four factors which, if not compromised, ought to go part of the way toward providing insurance against permanent impairments. Yet compromises of investment standards seem to occur sometimes. Briefly, the four factors are as follows:

1. The company in which the Fund is investing should have an extremely strong financial position. This is the single, most important element considered in deciding whether or not TAVF should invest and/or hold. As is pointed out below, the Fund compromises on this factor sometimes, but relatively infrequently.
2. The company should be reasonably well-managed from the stockholder point of view. (Given the trends toward increased management entrenchment and increased insider compensation over the last twenty years, it does not seem to be possible for a passive money manager to invest in a diversified portfolio, say, consisting of at least 10 different issues without compromising this standard.)
3. The company and its securities should be reasonably understandable to me as an outside, passive, minority investor using the public record to make investment decisions. That means, first and foremost, that the disclosures in written documents need to be comprehensive. Second, it means that financial statements published in accordance with Generally Accepted Accounting Principles need to be reliable as objective benchmarks (not truth) which can be used as tools of analysis. As a manager of TAVF, reasonably understandable is a relative term; it is pretty easy for me to have a comprehensive understanding from the public record of, say, financial insurers, money management firms and electric utilities; on the other hand, my understanding of high-tech issuers and basic manufacturers always seems to contain meaningful gaps, no matter how much help I get from non-financial, industry-wise professionals.
4. The price at which the equity is available to the Fund ought to be no more than 50% of what I think the business is worth as a privately owned enterprise, or as a merger/acquisition or takeover candidate. I do not ever consciously compromise this standard.

The permanent impairments to the Fund's portfolio are probably just as likely to come from unpredictable surprises and straight out misanalysis as from having compromised the standards just enumerated. The compromises, however, give rise to "worry situations," characterized by acute angst on my part about particular holdings, even when the Fund does not sell those holdings. I tend to become particularly concerned about those portfolio positions where the underlying issuer lacks a strong financial position. In these cases, there is very little, if any, margin for error in predicting the future.

Risk Arbitrage

Risk arbitrage can be defined as acquiring interests in situations to earn above average returns based on gauging what reasonably determinate workouts will be within reasonably determinate periods of time. There are all kinds of risk arbitrage: currency arbitrage, convertible arbitrage, commodity hedging, derivatives arbitrage, Corporate Events Risk Arbitrage (CERA), etc. TAVF's interest in risk arbitrage is limited to CERA.

CERA, whether it involves mergers and acquisitions, takeovers, liquidations, or reorganizations, requires much the same fundamental analysis as does value investing. Both activities are document driven; the practitioner had better understand well (and read slowly and carefully) the public record. Even interviews of insiders are much more productive if the interviewer has first done his or her homework based on public records. One of the big differences between CERA and value investing is that if you want to be a player in CERA, you need to be prepared to pay up; in value investing you try never to pay up versus fundamental value. The underlying reason for paying up in CERA is that market prices have a much greater tendency toward efficiency than is the case in value investing. Efficiency here might be defined as "the price is right." Excess returns cannot be earned.

All markets tend toward efficiency. A market is defined as an arena in which parties with adverse economic interests reach agreements as to price and other terms which the parties believe are the best achievable under the circumstances. In most markets (e.g., the value investing market, the corporate takeover market, and the market for Inverse Floaters from the point of view of a buy-and-hold investor) the tendencies toward efficiency are so weak that they ought to be all but ignored completely. These markets are characterized by long time horizons and/or very complex sets of variables that are difficult to analyze and weight.

On the other hand, there are stronger tendencies toward efficiency in markets where time horizons are short; and where the investment determinations are governed by a very few variables which are simple, understandable and, perhaps, computer programmable. CERA, therefore, has much more of a tendency toward efficiency than does value investing because first, time horizons are short and relatively determinate; and second, workout values frequently are not that hard to figure out. Value investing is, if you will, a pre-deal business, while CERA is mostly an announced-deal business.

Despite this tendency toward efficiency, and my personal reluctance to pay up, it appears that there may be a fair number of CERA opportunities available to TAVF, in part, because I hope to have on-site an analyst who will spend full time analyzing and reporting on announced deals, whether they are cash tender offers, exchange offers, proposed mergers, or reorganizations.

I doubt that CERA will ever account for a substantial part of the Fund's portfolio, but there ought to be a fair number of low-risk opportunities for TAVF where above average returns can be earned. In great part, these opportunities seem attributable to built-in inefficiencies in CERA markets. So many American passive investments are being managed by top-down investors, such as most mutual funds, who appear ill-equipped to perform any fundamental analysis at all, whether CERA or value, that price inefficiencies just have to go with the territory. Needless to say, TAVF will not consciously invest material amounts in any single CERA deal if it appears to me that such an investment entails the risk of a permanent impairment of capital.

CHAPTER 16

Index Funds and the General Market

JANUARY 1999

In terms of my own money, I have invested rather heavily in Third Avenue Value Fund (TAVF, "The Fund") because I am enthusiastic about the underlying long-term values represented in the Fund's portfolio. On the other hand, the general market scares me because of the lack of sound, underlying values. This view of mine is reflected in a recent article I wrote. A portion of that article is reprinted here.

Index Funds Seem Unusually Dangerous From a Long-Term Point of View

The appreciation in market prices for the common stocks that make up the leading indexes have, in recent years, so far outstripped the growth in book value and earnings for the companies whose common stocks make up the indexes that these market prices seem now to be grossly out of line with corporate reality. Thus, the possibilities for disaster. Here, excellent past performance seems likely to be a harbinger of future under-performance insofar as one believes that over the long term, market prices for passively owned common stocks will have a relationship to underlying corporate fundamentals.

The managers of Third Avenue Funds do not predict the future but rather deal in probabilities. Probabilities are driven by securities prices as they relate to underlying corporate realities. It is our strong belief that the higher the current market prices relative to corporate fundamentals, the greater the investment risk; and the lower current market prices are relative to corporate fundamentals, the less the investment risk. We also believe that for an index, or almost any general aggregate for that matter, corporate fundamentals can be measured by accounting earnings and accounting net asset value per share, i.e., book value.

A principal reason why Third Avenue Fund deals in probabilities, rather than in predictions, is that predictions are so difficult to make. To predict that the prices represented by the S&P 500 Index will crater at a specific time, one has to visualize what the precipitant for such a scenario might be and when that catastrophic event might occur. Third Avenue is not very good at foreseeing precipitants, especially if timing is involved, and we doubt anyone else is much good at it either. Who could really have forecast the timing of the Asian collapse in 1997? Who could really have forecast the timing of sovereign defaults in Russia in 1998, the Mexican Peso devaluation in 1994, the U.S. Savings and Loan debacle in the mid-to-late 1980's, or the plunge in oil prices in 1982 and again in 1998?

The Third Avenue Funds use a balanced approach to analysis, initially measuring the quality of resources in a business, as well as the quantity of resources acquired relative to market prices.

Quality and quantity of resources translate into return on equity. In using financial accounting as a tool to analyze individual companies, no particular number is emphasized by Third Avenue, but rather each accounting number is a function of, modified by, and derived from, all other accounting numbers. Thus, book value is intimately related to earnings, and vice versa. Both are joined at the hip so to speak, in the concept of return on equity, or ROE. R is the earnings figure; E is the book value figure.

Financial accounting in the analysis of individual companies is always subject to adjustment. The most GAAP figures can represent in the analysis of an individual company are objective benchmarks which the analyst uses as a tool to reach opinions about economic reality, either in terms of flows, whether cash or earnings; or asset values, or both. However, financial accounting in the aggregate tends to be highly meaningful. It measures changes over time, the amount of resources in existence and flows, whether cash or earnings. For the aggregates, statistical errors that might exist for individual companies tend to even out.

The Statistical Case Demonstrating That Prices for the S&P 500 Industrial Have Outrun Corporate Reality

Period	Market Price as a Multiple of Book Value	PE Ratio	Book Value	Per Share	ROE*
12/31/1998	6.5x	32.3x	$188.11	$38.09	20.00%
12/31/1997	5.1	18.6	190.12	39.72	21.8
12/31/1995	3.5	18.3	174.33	33.6	22.2
12/31/1990	2.2	19.2	153.01	21.73	14.8
12/31/1987	1.8	14.1	126.82	17.5	13.8
12/31/1982	1.3	11.1	112.46	12.64	11.6

* EPS for the year divided by book value at the end of the prior year

The significance of superlative past performance can be attributed to one of three factors. First, in the case of actively managed funds, it can be evidence of superior skills being brought into play by an active manager. Second, in the case of either actively managed funds or index funds, it can be evidence of superlative growth in underlying corporate fundamentals which growth is reflected in common stock prices. Third, in the case of either actively managed funds or index funds, it can be evidence that increases in common stock prices have outpaced increases in underlying corporate values. The third alternative seems to be the root cause for the excellent performance of the S&P 500 in recent years, as is shown in the following table covering growth rates in market prices relative to growth rates in earnings and book values:

Compound Annual Growth Rates for the S&P 500

Market Prices	EPS	Book Value	
1990-1998	17.90%	7.30%	2.60%
1982-1998	14.5	7.1	3.3

At 6X Book Value For the S&P 500 It Is Hard To Make the Numbers Work

It is hard to justify a 6x multiple of book unless one can postulate that either ROE for the index companies will increase to a number greater than 25%, or that companies in general will be able to issue massive new amounts of common stocks, either for cash or in a merger and acquisition transactions, at prices related to 6x book.

From 1982 through 1998, ROE's for the S&P 500 ranged from a high of 22.2% in 1996, to a low of 10.6% in 1991. The average ROE for the 17-year period was 15.7%. However, for the five years through 1998, the average ROE was 21.0% and in no year was it below 20.0%.

Assuming a market price of 6x Book, PE ratios are as follows based on various ROEs:

Market Price	Book	ROE	EPS	PE Ratio
$6	$1	25%	25¢	24.0x
6	1	20	20	30
6	1	15	15	40
6	1	11	11	54.5

The 6x book value might well be justifiable assuming companies in the S&P 500 could increase their numbers of shares outstanding by 31.5% via the issuance of new shares at 5.25x book. In that instance book value would increase to $2.02 and EPS per share and PE ratios would be as follows at various ROEs:

Market Price	Book	ROE	EPS	PE Ratio
$6	$2.02	25%	51¢	11.8x
6	2.02	20	40	15
6	2.02	15	30	20
6	2.02	11	22	27.3

It seems unrealistic to suppose that, on average, the companies making up the S&P 500 would have such attractive access to capital markets that such a large amount of new equity capital could be raised at those prices. Alternatively, it seems questionable that companies in the aggregate would be able to maintain existing ROEs if massive new amounts of capital were injected into their businesses.

It is always possible that securities pricing for the common stocks that make up the S&P 500 have entered into a new era where greater capitalization rates will be given to earnings, and greater premiums will be assigned to book values, than historically has been the case. These enhanced valuations might persist, or even be improved upon, on a permanent or semi-permanent basis. Such a new era pricing scenario seems to be a possibility, rather than a probability.

In contrast to this statistical picture for the S&P 500, many common stocks, especially well-capitalized small caps, currently seem to be priced at bargain prices relative to long-term earnings prospects and current book values. This type of pricing in markets for passive, minority investments seems to occur frequently at times when the immediate earnings outlooks are poor. The semiconductor equipment stocks Third Avenue Funds are currently acquiring seem to meet these criteria. As a long-term investor, Third Avenue is betting that the probabilities are, for most of these companies, that the next peak in earnings will be well in excess of historic peaks.

Relevant statistics for these issues are as follows:

Issuer	Price 12/31/98	Cash/Total Liabilities %	Market Price as a Multiple of Book Value	PE Ratio Based on Current Price to Past Peak Earnings
ADE Corp.	$13	297%	1.3x	8.8x
AVX Corp.	17	53	1.9	10.8
C.P Clare Corp.	5	26	0.6	5.3
Electroglas, Inc.	12	523	1.3	5.9
FSI Int'l., Inc.	10	85	1.1	8.1
Silicon Valley Grp., Inc.	13	89	0.8	6.3
SpeedFam Int'l., Inc.	17	471	1	10.2

We recommend to investors that they switch holdings in the S&P 500 to Third Avenue Funds or other funds that concentrate on Value Investing. Value investors, by definition, are conscious of the relationship of securities prices to corporate fundamentals. In value investing, asset allocation is driven more by price considerations and less by predicting outlooks.

CHAPTER 17

The Importance of Buying Cheap

OCTOBER 2000

The Importance of Buying Cheap, or Well Below Fair Value

Third Avenue Value Fund (TAVF) seems to have avoided a lot of trouble by being price conscious. The financial world is so complex and unpredictable that a fair amount of our analyses will prove to have been flawed. See USG Common and Repap Common. A dirt-cheap price is an anchor to windward against misperceiving current situations, or being unable to make accurate forecasts.

Over and above flawed analyses, it is important to buy cheap because increasingly, it seems as if activists are ripping off outside security holders, whether creditors or common stockholders, for ever-increasing amounts of wealth. These rip-off activists include corporate managements; lawyers and investment bankers involved with troubled company workouts; investment bankers in merger and acquisition situations; and members of the Plaintiffs' Bar involved with asbestos litigation.

In dollar amount, our largest single holding at October 31 was Silicon Valley Common. On October 2, Silicon Valley announced that it was merging with ASM Lithography Holding, N. V. (ASM) in a common for common exchange as a result of which the former holders of Silicon Valley Common would own a 10% equity interest in the merged company. While the market value of the proposed transaction represented a substantial premium for Silicon Valley Common, the percentage ownership to be received by Silicon Valley Common seems unconscionably low, smacking more of an ASM takeunder than an ASM takeover. In addition, the terms of the merger agreement were markedly in favor of ASM, as for example no walk-away by Silicon Valley if the price of ASM Common craters while the merger is pending; and a bust-up fee of $47 million for ASM if a more attractive offer for Silicon Valley Common stockholders emerges. Still, it is hard for TAVF to argue against a substantial price premium above the pre-announcement market prices. On November 3, the preliminary merger proxy statement was made public. There it was disclosed that the top three members of Silicon Valley management had on October 1 entered into termination and separation agreements. Under these agreements, upon conclusion of the ASM transaction, the three are to receive compensation, mostly in cash, with a net present value of about $20 million. Perhaps, were termination payments lower, there might be more in the deal for the holders of Silicon Valley Common. As far as I can tell, Silicon Valley management is not acting differently than the way a majority of American corporate managements would act in similar circumstances. It just goes with the territory. Incidentally, the Silicon Valley merger transaction fees, mostly payable to lawyers and investment bankers, are estimated at $28 million.

When companies in distress are reorganized, either out of court or in Chapter 11, the company (sometimes known as the "Estate") picks up with minor exceptions, such as U.S. government agencies, all the fees and expenses of all professionals: attorneys, investment bankers, consultants and appraisers not only for the company but also for various classes of creditors and, frequently, the common stockholders. These fees and expenses become priority claims, payable in full before amounts are paid to most pre-reorganization creditors. Professional fees and expenses have grown to such an extent that it tends to be utterly uneconomic to become a general creditor of a small, troubled, company. Thus, TAVF's results as a Hechinger creditor are likely to prove to have been unsatisfactory solely because so much of the Estate is being eaten up by payments to attorneys and investment bankers. Put simply, these payments to attorneys and investment bankers come directly out of the hide of pre-petition creditors.

Payments to investment bankers by the distressed company are particularly galling to me. Over the years, I have been involved in the reorganization of many troubled companies. Most of the time, investment bankers have been much more disruptive than they have been constructive.

In 1993, I was the senior author of a law journal article in which it was suggested that no professionals, other than those representing the company, ought to be paid by the company before the end of a Chapter 11 case. Then, those professionals ought only to be paid if the court finds they had made a "Substantial Contribution" to the case. This idea seems to have no chance whatsoever of being implemented. This is, in fact, how the Plaintiffs' Bar, which takes cases on a contingency basis, is compensated. No one is complaining that the Plaintiffs' Bar does not attract highly skilled and highly motivated practitioners, even though they work on contingencies rather than for fixed fees; and their contingent payments are mostly subject to approvals by courts of law.

Finally, USG would not have the problems outlined above were it not for the Plaintiffs' Bar in asbestos cases, where as a result of asbestos litigation, many lawyers have become very rich.

Note, though, that my statements here are financial commentary, not a statement of social and political philosophy. Indeed, our economy and our markets just would not function if it were not possible for insiders and activists to earn excess returns whether those are people who foster IPO's, mergers and acquisitions, the reorganization of troubled companies, stockholder lawsuits, or the pursuit of redress for otherwise helpless citizens, such as individual asbestos victims. The point here is that it is important to realize that outside passive investors, whether creditors or stockholders, are going to have to pay the freight for these very expensive activist activities. To compensate for this disadvantage, the outsider ought to buy cheap — say, pay no more than 50 cents for each dollar a common stock would be worth were the company a private company or a take-over candidate; or acquire credits on a basis where the yield to maturity is at least 1000 basis points more than could be obtained from a comparable credit where people in the market do not foresee problems.

Buying at such prices is exactly what TAVF tries to do.

The Value Trap Versus the Growth Stock Trap

A number of people have asked me if I am concerned about the "Value Trap," i.e., having the Fund own cheap stocks that just stay cheap forever. After all, the trader's credo is, "A bargain that stays a bargain is not a bargain." I don't think the Value Trap really has any validity for the Third Avenue portfolio of value common stocks. Either portions of the portfolio are always working out, whether in takeovers or general market recognition, or the value analysis was not very valid to begin with.

In any event, it seems to be much more comfortable to be stuck in the "Value Trap" than to be caught in the "Growth Stock Trap." Participants in conventional growth stock situations are bound to be really trapped if: a) general market conditions change such as might be the case if the NASDAQ Composite were selling at, say, 80 times trailing earnings rather than 120 times earnings; or, b) the growth stock investor, or analyst, turns out to have been overoptimistic in forecasts of revenues, cash flows or earnings.

CHAPTER 18

The Moral Hazard Question

OCTOBER 2003

Moral hazard, a term of art, exists where participants in financial processes bear little, or no, risk of loss if things go wrong. The term moral hazard usually refers to the situation in lending by commercial banks where if a money default occurs, the commercial bank can count on being made whole through grants or gifts bestowed by governments, government agencies or quasi-government agencies. Such a no lose situation for the banks gives the banks incentives to be extremely careless in their lending policies, knowing that if there are to be money defaults, the institution will be bailed out by third parties.

Moral hazard, or the lack of downside for participants in financial processes, is pervasive, encompassing many more areas than just bank lending. U.S. bank deposits insured by the FDIC for up to $100,000 become riskless for depositors. The "hot money" put into emerging market currencies in the 1990's — Thailand, Philippines, Russia, Indonesia — were also riskless because the monies could be converted to other currencies and repatriated easily, and without penalty, to other countries merely by zapping a computer key. Unlike what would occur under Chapter 11 in the U.S., hot money creditors to foreign sovereigns are not stopped from pulling out funds through the operation of an "automatic stay."

Activists involved in all financial processes try, if they can, to eliminate risks. If participants in financial processes do not take risks, gross abuses seem certain to occur, and have occurred, with regularity. This is not good for societies or economies. However, most financial processes do serve important social and economic purposes, even when moral hazard exists. These processes ought not to be abolished. Rather, they ought to be structured so that the various participants have "skin in the game" — i.e., something to lose.

Four areas of moral hazard very much affect Third Avenue Value Fund (TAVF). These areas are as follows:

1. Bank loans
2. Class action litigation
3. Executive compensation and entrenchment
4. Compensation paid to lawyers and investment bankers when dealing with troubled companies

While TAVF has done okay in its Japanese investments made from 1997 on, the Fund would have done a lot better had Japanese banks not been so careless in their lending practices. These poor bank lending practices probably were the most significant factor causing the six-year business recession/depression in Japan. The banks seem to have counted on government bailouts when making loans. From a societal point of view, commercial banks, their managements, and their securities holders, especially their common stockholders, ought to be made to suffer the consequences of imprudent lending practices. However, the banks themselves ought not to be made to suffer so much that the underlying economy is harmed, albeit this does not mean that managements shouldn't be fired, and common stockholders wiped out. It is important, though, that the lending institutions survive in one form or the other. In Japan, the banks themselves suffered too much, and until recently, were reluctant to lend at all, exacerbating the deterioration that was taking place in the Japanese economy.

Fortunately, it does not appear as if either the U.S. banking system or the TAVF portfolio of bank common stocks are going to be victimized by huge amounts of bank loans becoming "scheduled items" or "non-performing loans" in the period just ahead. Third Avenue has restricted its investments in depository institutions to the common stocks of extremely well-capitalized regional and community banks, none of which appear to be troubled. Nationally, it appears as if the banking system has never been sounder, at least in areas where I think we at

TAVF are knowledgeable. Corporate lending by banks has never been more conservative, the growth of securitizations has reduced portfolio risk for most banks, and banks in general have learned to grow fee income, a higher quality source of profitability than interest spread income. Admittedly, I am hardly knowledgeable about the investment risks the larger banks are taking in derivatives, and I don't know much about the credit risks in consumer lending, especially in credit card portfolios. But overall I feel comfortable about the banking system in general and about TAVF's policy of buying the common stocks of well-capitalized regional and community banks when they are available at discounts from book value.

If I were to suggest any reforms for the banking system, it would be to reduce the ability of managements of underperforming banks to continue to be entrenched in office, or to get large severance packages if they are forced to leave office.

The problem with class action litigation is that it is controlled by class action lawyers who incur little, or no, downside risk by bringing lawsuits. In general, these lawyers don't have to worry too much about the underlying merits of any one lawsuit because if they have a portfolio of lawsuits, the lawyers are bound to make a very good living indeed. The vast majority of these lawsuits are settled before trial and the lawyers' cash fees, earned on a contingent basis, are usually approved without opposition.

Yet, class action lawsuits are the best protection passive investors such as TAVF have against overreaching by insiders, fiduciaries and professionals such as auditors. Class action lawyers, as private cops, tend to be a lot more alert in protecting stockholder interests than are the Securities and Exchange Commission (SEC), State "Blue Sky" Regulators, and Self-Regulatory Organizations (SROs) such as the New York Stock Exchange and the NASD. This is part and parcel of what goes on in our mixed economy: frequently, but far from always, the private sector (i.e., class action attorneys) are more aggressive and more able than public sector bureaucrats (e.g., the SEC) in obtaining constructive results.

Most of the world operates under the "English System" in protecting, or not protecting, outside passive minority shareholders. Under the "English System," there is no class action possible; each shareholder exercises his or her own rights at his or her own expense. Small shareholders under the "English System" have, as a practical matter, no recourse when there has been corporate wrongdoing. In contrast, in the U.S., theoretically a holder of only 100 shares of Microsoft Common can bring a class action lawsuit on behalf of the outside holders of, say 9 billion shares of Microsoft Common. This ability for suits to be brought on behalf of a class makes legal actions by stockholders economic. Under the "English System," if the plaintiff loses the lawsuit, he probably would be liable for the defendants' costs and expenses. Under the "American System," the losing plaintiff will very, very rarely ever be liable for any of defendants' costs and expenses.

TAVF would much rather operate under the "American System" than under the "English System." For example, at October 31, 2003, the Fund had approximately $162,000,000 invested in Toyota Industries Common Stock ("Industries Common"), which as a Japanese company, grants stockholders rights under the "English System." Toyota Industries is the largest holder of Toyota Motor Common ("Motor Common"), owning about 5% of the issue outstanding. Motor in turn owns about 24% of the outstanding Industries Common. The Fund's investment in Industries is predicated, in great part, on the fact that it has acquired an equity interest in Motor at a 30% to 40% discount based on Industries' common stock price in Tokyo and Motor's common stock price on the New York Stock Exchange. If Motor, for example, ever decided to acquire a greater interest in Industries on the cheap in a manner that would forcibly eliminate TAVF's interest in Industries (which I wouldn't put past Motor), TAVF would, as a practical matter, be without recourse. That would not be the case were Industries incorporated in Delaware.

I think the "American System" overall would work better were U.S. Courts--Federal and State--more willing, and more able, to assess to plaintiffs the defendants' costs and expenses for bringing suits which are deemed to be frivolous. If moral hazard, i.e., the absence of downside risk, is pervasive anywhere, it is pervasive among the top managements of American corporations. As a group, these people are grossly overcompensated, and whether they perform capably or not, they tend to be very much entrenched in office. No entity seems to be in a position to show top managements any downside risk. This is supposed to be the duty of Boards of Directors. Most outside directors seem too busy, and too friendly with top managements, to be much more than rubber stamps.

Yet, a high degree of management entrenchment seems justified both for society as a whole, and for TAVF in particular. Almost all the companies represented in the Fund's common stock portfolio seem to be extremely well managed. The last thing Third Avenue would want is for these top managements to be easily removable from office just because the price of the common stock is depressed. Indeed, that is why TAVF acquired the common stock in the first place: the company seems well managed and the price of the common stock seems depressed.

Let's face it: the market is utterly inefficient when it purports to measure the quality of management by the price of the common stock. Rather, the common stock market seems to measure more management's ability to promote, rather than management's ability to run a business day to day. Promoting common stocks is probably not a good use of management time unless the company is in need of reasonably regular access to capital markets, especially equity markets. TAVF goes out of its way to acquire the common stocks of companies that either don't need access to capital markets, or are so financially strong, that the managements completely control the timing of when the corporation ought to access capital markets.

When all is said and done, there is too much management entrenchment. A good start toward achieving a more equitable management-shareholder balance might revolve around banning the "poison pill." A "poison pill" is a device used by almost all corporations whose common stocks are publicly traded, which dilutes a potential acquirer of control to such an extent that it becomes uneconomic for anyone to engage in a contest for control.

My personal *bete noire* for where moral hazard exists, and seems utterly destructive, is payments to professionals--lawyers and investment bankers--involved in the restructuring of troubled companies, whether under the Bankruptcy Code or out of court.

Payments to professionals are different for troubled companies than for other companies. Once a company might have trouble paying its bills, the tendency is for *ad hoc* creditor committees, and even equity committees, to be formed. These groups hire lawyers and investment bankers, which are paid, almost always very handsomely, by the troubled company. Under Chapter 11 of the Bankruptcy Code, there is a requirement that an Official Committee of Unsecured Creditors be formed, with the Committee's professionals paid by the company seeking relief, i.e., the debtor. Professionals retained by other creditors, as well parties in interest, will be paid by the debtor also. The amount of these administrative costs for professional services are huge, off the charts; and they are paid on a pay-as-you-go basis. These professionals also enjoy a super priority over pre-petition creditors when it comes to getting paid by the debtor. Before Kmart could be reorganized and out of Chapter 11, these professional costs were running at a rate of $10 million to $20 million a month. It is estimated that such costs in Enron (with which thankfully TAVF is not involved) will aggregate approximately $1 billion. These huge costs come out of the hide of creditors. Third Avenue gets involved with troubled companies only as a creditor.

From TAVF's point of view, these administrative costs tend to be so large that it is hard to get involved in any investment in a non-giant troubled company unless the Fund can do so as an adequately secured creditor, or pursuant to a pre-packaged Plan of Reorganization. Even in giant companies, these professionals bring investment risks to TAVF that are frequently unacceptable. As a matter of fact, if one failed in reorganizing Kmart in a relative hurry, there likely would have been nothing left for the creditors. It would all have gone to the lawyers and investment bankers who incidentally had considerable financial incentive to keep Kmart in Chapter 11 rather than to reorganize that company expeditiously.

This "Professionals Problem" traces back to the Bankruptcy Reform Act of 1978 ("The 1978 Act"). Congress in its wisdom decided that a higher caliber of professionals would be attracted to bankruptcy practice if these professionals were paid on a regular basis for services performed. There seems to be no basis for Congress' implicit assumption that attorneys working for hourly rates are more competent, or higher quality, than contingent fee attorneys. Prior to the passage of The 1978 Act, professionals, other than the debtor's professionals, in Chapter X cases were paid basically at the end of a case, and only if they demonstrated to the Bankruptcy Court that they had made a "substantial contribution" to the reorganization.

TAVF, as a creditor, would like very much to go back to the pre-1978 way of paying professionals. It hopefully would contribute much to the reorganization of troubled companies both in court and out of court. In writing to you about class action lawsuits, top management compensation and entrenchment, and professionals' compensation in the reorganization of troubled companies, I highlight some of the problems TAVF faces as a non-control investor. My griping, however, should not overstate the reality that, while elimination of certain moral hazards would help, the Fund still seems to operate in a pretty good investment climate.

CHAPTER 19

Third Avenue Value Fund Compared to Private Equity Funds

OCTOBER 2005

It is interesting to compare an investment in Third Avenue Value Fund (TAVF) Common Stock with an investment as a passive investor in private equity funds seeking leveraged buy-outs. The differences appear to be about as follows:

1. TAVF is riding the coattails of super-good managements with proven track records; e.g., Brookfield Asset Management (formerly known as Brascan Corp.), Forest City Enterprises, Nabors Industries, St. Joe Company and Toyota Industries. Managements running LBO companies are probably a lot more dicey.
2. TAVF's costs to the investor are a lot lower. TAVF had an expense ratio of 1.10% of assets under management for fiscal 2005, while the typical private equity fund charges a management fee of 2% of assets under management plus 20% of realized, and unrealized, profits. This is slightly offset in some cases where private equity funds share fees received, such as home office charges, with passive investors.
3. TAVF tends to get into its investments at materially lower prices than private equity funds. The usual buy trigger for Third Avenue is where the common stocks of well-financed companies are available at prices that represent a meaningful discount from

readily ascertainable net asset values. Private equity funds usually pay substantial premiums above estimates of net asset value.

4. TAVF shareholders are not subject to lock-ups of any sorts (other than a modest redemption fee for shares held for less than 60 days) and TAVF shares can be redeemed daily. Most private equity funds forbid redemptions other than once a year, or quarterly after a one-year holding period.

5. TAVF is not a control investor, by and large. Private equity funds are, by and large, control investors.

6. TAVF does not borrow money. Private equity funds tend to operate with maximum leverage.

7. TAVF shareholders are the beneficiaries of a comprehensive regulatory scheme designed to protect investors. Private equity funds are largely unregulated.

To date, TAVF's longterm returns have been as good, or almost as good, as has been the case for the better-managed private equity funds[1] .

Great Economists Can Learn A Lot from Value Investors

During the quarter, I reread three volumes authored by great economists: *The General Theory of Employment, Interest and Money* by John Maynard Keynes, *The Road to Serfdom* by F. A. Hayek, and *Capitalism and Freedom* by Milton Friedman. I came away with the impression that each was observing the earth with their naked eyes from 80,000 feet up. They missed a lot of details that are part and parcel of every value investor's daily life.

To begin with, the three seem to recognize only three major forces directing the economy: capital (private owners, managers or entrepreneurs), labor and government. In fact, there are myriad other non-governmental forces directing any industrial economy, including, among others, management control persons (separate and apart from private owners); creditors; rating agencies; Boards of Directors; professionals, especially attorneys and accountants; trade associations; and self-regulatory organizations such as the New York Stock Exchange.

For the three great economists, governments perform four functions: control the economy; regulate sectors of the economy; set fiscal policies (budget surpluses or deficits); and set monetary policies (interest rates and the quantity of money). In the 21st century, it seems a lot more productive in determining how the nation's resources are to be allocated by the private sector to look at governments as engaged also in the following activities:

1. Levy taxes, with both tax rates and the specific methods of taxation being important
2. Provide credit
3. Enhance credit
4. Provide subsidies
5. Provide infrastructure frameworks, physical and procedural, including having reliable judicial systems
6. Be a customer
7. Be a competitor
8. Provide public protection via the military, police and other

F.A. Hayek wrote *The Road to Serfdom* in the 1940's. The book was relevant for its time. The gravamen of its arguments was that command economies without a private sector, e.g., the Soviet Union then (and North Korea and Cuba today), just do not work. They deny their populaces not only economic well-being but also freedom. Of course, Professor Hayek was 100% right about this. However, in no way does it follow, as many Hayek disciples seem to believe, that government is, *per se*, bad and unproductive while the private sector is, *per se*, good and productive. In well-run industrial economies, there is a marriage between government and the private sector, each benefiting from the other. Since World War II, there have been a significant number of large command economies that have worked well by utilizing an incentivized private sector. Such economies include Japan after World War II, Singapore and the other Asian Tigers, Sweden and China today. For the value investor, the issue is not government versus the private sector. Rather, it is that, in accordance with Adam Smith's invisible hand, those in control, whoever they are, should be incentivized appropriately. Government has a necessary role in determining how control persons are incentivized; and where the private sector will allocate resources in accordance with the invisible hand so that private control persons can maximize wealth for themselves, and also, by indirection, their constituents who are usually the owners of private enterprises.

Whether one likes it or not, how and where Adam Smith's invisible hand allocates resources through actions by private enterprises will be determined in large part by what government actions are. Should these government reactions be random, or at least in small part, a product of planning? In the U.S. today it seems as if the federal government directs resources mostly by "who has political clout." There is no question but that private enterprise, in its actions, is particularly sensitive to what the federal government does in terms of tax policy, both quantitatively and qualitatively; and what the government does in terms of credit granting and credit enhancing. Control persons in the U.S. private sector are extremely sensitive to, and react very efficiently to, government policies in terms of taxation and in terms of credit granting and credit enhancing. Put in Milton Friedman's context, Adam Smith's invisible hand turns out to be more than random. It will be directed, at least in great part, by the government's tax policies, and the government's credit granting policies. Put otherwise, what government policies contribute is important to the private sector's determination of where the profits are.

Professor Hayek, however, seems to miss the opposite point that a free market situation is probably also doomed to failure if there exist control persons who are not subject to external disciplines imposed by various forces over and above competition: governmental, quasi-governmental and private sector. This is probably more true for financial markets than it is for commercial markets, but the point seems valid for both markets. Put simply, competition by itself, tends not to be a strong enough external discipline to make markets efficient. Where control persons are not subject to meaningful external disciplines, the following seems to occur:

1. Very exorbitant levels of executive compensation, a shortcoming rampant in the U.S. today
2. Poorly financed businesses with strong prospects for money defaults on credit instruments, e.g., look at the insolvencies in recent years of Long-Term Capital Management, Retail Chains and Motion Picture Exhibition companies
3. Speculative bubbles, e.g., the 1998-2000 IPO boom
4. Tendency for industry competition to evolve into monopolies and oligopolies where the companies involved have a large degree of

insulation from competitive forces. TAVF loves to invest in the common stocks of companies which have built a "moat" around their operations, insulating the businesses, at least in part, from pure and perfect competition. Such investments include the common stocks of Toyota Industries, St. Joe, Brookfield Asset Management, Forest City Enterprises, and Nabors Industries. All these companies enjoy oligopolistic characteristics.

5. Corruption: i.e., Enron, WorldCom, Refco.

It ought to be noted, too, that many highly competitive industries happen not to be subject to meaningful price competition. Two such industries are money management and investment banking. In the investment banking arena, there seems to be a universal 7% gross spread involved in bringing most new issues public. Third Avenue has invested heavily in the common stocks of financial institutions where price competition seems minimal, or non-existent; e.g., money managers such as Legg Mason and Nuveen; and broker-dealer financial advisors such as Jefferies Group and Raymond James. A principal disadvantage for TAVF in investing in distressed securities revolves around the rip-off of pre-petition creditors by professionals, mostly lawyers and investment bankers. Competition to obtain professional engagements in matters such as USG and Collins & Aikman is intense. But no professionals in the distressed world, with very minor exceptions, ever seem to compete on price.

Disciplines are imposed on control persons operating in free markets by many, many more entities than just governments and competitors. The great economists mostly fail to recognize the existence of these other forces imposing discipline. Some tend to be harsh disciplinarians — creditors and rating agencies; and some seem to be very weak disciplinarians — passive owners of common stocks and Boards of Directors. These other forces imposing disciplines on control persons include the following:

1. Owners
2. Boards of Directors
3. Creditors — especially banks
4. Rating Agencies
5. Labor Unions
6. Trade Associations

7. Communities
8. Auditors
9. Attorneys

Compared with value investors, great economists from Keynes to Modigliani and Miller seem largely oblivious to the very important role creditworthiness plays in any industrial economy. Indeed, a principal shortcoming of our current monetary and fiscal authorities, especially Alan Greenspan, is that creditworthiness does not seem to be on their radar screen at all. The authorities seem focused on Gross Domestic Product and the control of inflation-deflation. They worry not about creditworthiness, which ought to be the third leg of their analytical stool. Creditworthiness in the U.S. seems to be a mixed bag when looking at the three principal economic entities: Private Businesses, Governments and Consumers. On the one hand, corporations, in general, perhaps including depository institutions, probably have never been more strongly financed. On the other hand, Governments — federal, state and local — and Consumers probably have never been less creditworthy than they are now. I think the TAVF common stock portfolio is fairly well insulated against money defaults from any sector, but I'm not sure.

Milton Friedman is "gung-ho" for free markets, unfettered by government intervention. As he states on p. 22 of *Capitalism and Freedom* , "To the liberal, the appropriate means are free discussion and voluntary co-operation, which implies that any form of coercion is inappropriate." Professor Friedman also states on p. 13, "Fundamentally, there are only two ways of co-ordinating the economic activities of millions. One is control direction involving the use of coercion — the technique of the army and the modern totalitarian state. The other is voluntary co-operation of individuals — the technique of the market place."

Professor Friedman, unfortunately, seems to have no background, or experience, in corporate finance. If he did, he would understand that public corporations just would not work unless, in the relationship between control persons and owners, certain activities would encompass voluntary exchanges while other activities would encompass coercion. So it is also on the national and global levels.

Also, given a background in corporate finance, Professor Friedman would get to understand that there are three general ways for coordinating the economic activities of millions, not two. One is central direction without the existence of a private sector. The second is complete voluntary cooperation without the existence of many coercive external disciplinary forces, whether governmental or private, influencing the marketplace. The third general way is the real world situation where governments and other external forces have an influence on, and frequently direct, the activities that transpire in the market place. Indeed, the various marketplaces in the U.S. seem to be ultra-sensitive to certain directions they get from governments through tax policies, credit granting and regulation.

In public corporations, there are certain activities that are essentially voluntary and others that are essentially coercive from the point of view of non-control securities holders. Voluntary activities, where each person makes his or her own decision whether to buy, sell, or hold, encompass open market trading activities, certain cash tender offers, private purchase and sale transactions and most exchanges of securities, including the out-of-court restructuring of troubled companies. Coercive activities, where each individual security holder is forced to go along with a transaction or event, provided that a requisite majority of other security holders so vote, encompass proxy voting for Boards of Directors; most merger and acquisition transactions including reverse splits and short form mergers; certain cash tender offers; calls of convertible bonds or preferred stocks; the reorganization of troubled companies under Chapter 11 of the Bankruptcy Act; and the liquidation of troubled companies under either Chapter 7 or Chapter 11 of the Bankruptcy Act.

I am as one with Professor Friedman that, other things being equal, it is far preferable to conduct economic activities through voluntary exchange relying on free markets rather than through coercion. But Corporate America would not work at all unless many activities continued to be coercive; security holders may get a right to vote (which vote may be pro forma and meaningless), but the security holders are coerced into going along whether they like it or not once a requisite vote has taken place.

Incidentally, appraisal rights under state law, can be pretty meaningless in the scheme of things in merger and acquisitions, and can hardly be thought of as voluntary. Without some element of coercion, two undesirable things are bound to occur in a free market:

1. Adverse selection, i.e., individuals who believe they are benefited economically by a transaction go along, while those who believe otherwise opt out of the transaction. If this were permitted, there would be no mergers and no Chapter 11 reorganizations, something highly destructive to corporate well-being and the well-being of the general economy.

2. There would be unsolvable hold out problems. For example, voluntary bond exchanges to make a company more creditworthy would frequently be doomed to failure because those who hold out know that because of their hold out, their bond position would be credit enhanced if most of the other bondholders exchange.

Assuming that the goal of an economy ought to be to maximize the average per capita income, and wealth, for its citizens (or residents), then adverse selection and hold-out problems have to modify, in certain areas, reliance solely on voluntary exchanges or the free market. Specifically, there are areas where, because of adverse selection and hold-out problems, the U.S. should not rely wholly on market mechanisms. These areas include the following:

- Medical Care. There is one good measure of how well cared for a population is; to wit, the average age of death. Here, the U.S. performs worse than most industrial economies. This seems a shame because the very best medical care in the world exists in this country for those who can afford it. The country would be much healthier if all its residents had access to decent medical care without adverse selection opt-outs.

- Social Security and Pension Plans. Clearly, the adverse selection problem will loom large if these retirement mechanisms are made wholly, or almost wholly, voluntarily.

- Education. This country seems to be falling behind much of the rest of the industrial world in elementary through high school education, even though the U.S. probably still has the best university system in the world. There seems to be a real problem between allowing each parent to pick the school which their child should attend and the problem of adverse selection. Tough choice; I don't have any easy answers.

Government regulation is not, *per se*, good or bad. There is good regulation and there is bad regulation. An example of good regulation is the Investment Company Act of 1940 as amended. An example of bad regulation is the Sarbanes-Oxley Act of 2002.

It ill behooves any successful money manager in the mutual fund industry to condemn the very strict regulation embodied in the Investment Company Act of 1940. Without strict regulation, I doubt that our industry could have grown as it has grown, and also be as prosperous as it is for money managers. Because of the existence of strict regulation, the outside investor knows that money managers can be trusted. Without that trust, the industry likely would not have grown the way it has grown. Outside investors know that the money managers cannot steal, cannot be involved in self-dealing, are limited in causing the fund to borrow money, fees charged are controlled, and the mutual fund must diversify as a practical matter. All of this occurs for the benefit of shareholders, while still permitting the money manager to prosper mightily from the receipt of management fees. This is an example of good, intelligent regulation. Messrs. Hayek and Friedman probably do not recognize the existence of such beneficial regulation.

On the other hand, Sarbanes-Oxley, (SOX) is an example of stupid, non-productive regulation. It seems to be regulation based on the belief that every company, every Chief Executive Officer, and every Chief Financial Officer, is associated with Enron, WorldCom or Refco. Every company, therefore, should be subject to onerous regulation although such regulation does not seem to do anything, or much at all, about investor protection. The upshot of SOX is that it detracts mightily from the attractiveness of U.S. capital markets. No CEO or CFO likes being subject to liabilities that arise out of SOX. Smaller public companies cannot afford to comply with SOX. Few, or no, foreign companies are going to subject themselves to American jurisdiction unless they absolutely need access to American capital markets trading publicly owned securities. It is likely that Messrs. Friedman and Hayek believe most regulation is SOX-like. I do not. Some regulation is good; some bad. It's all case by case.

The goals desired by economists ought to be more balanced than they appear to be. Monetary and fiscal authorities seem focused only on maximizing periodic Gross Domestic Product (GDP) while avoiding rampant inflation or deflation. I think their goals ought to be broadened and encompass the following:

- Maximize periodic GDP within the context of controlling inflation and deflation, while keeping the principal sectors of the economy creditworthy. Certainly in recent years, the creditworthiness of governments and consumers has deteriorated.

- Maximize periodic GDP within the context of controlling inflation and deflation while providing safety nets for the poorest 25%-33% of the population.

- Maximize periodic GDP within the context of controlling inflation and deflation while enhancing long-term growth of the GDP. In the 21st Century, it seems obvious that long-term growth cannot be enhanced without emphasis on the education and training of the population.

I am no fan of Milton Friedman simply because he seems not to understand the many limitations that have to be placed on free markets if an economy is to function well. Yet, I found his ideas ever so useful when I recently testified about SOX before the SEC Committee on Smaller Public Companies. I recommended to the Committee that small issuers (and also foreign domiciled issuers) be exempt from SOX, provided the issuers present comprehensive disclosures in SEC filed documents, and/or other publicly available documents, about the disadvantages and risks investors would be taking if they chose to hold securities of companies that did not comport with SOX. Given this information, the free market would appraise the merits of SOX through adjusting the prices at which specific securities would sell. Maybe the securities of non-SOX compliers would sell at materially lower prices than the securities of SOX compliers; whether or not this would be the case would be determined in a free market whose participants are well informed. This is pure Friedmanesque-University of Chicago type thinking. I also recommended to the Committee that legislation ought to be enacted under which foreign domiciled issuers could be sued for alleged violations of securities laws only in their home jurisdiction, provided such issuers fully disclosed to investors the disadvantages and risks to such investors of not being protected by U.S. regulation and U.S. class action lawsuits. In fostering these proposals, I am really proposing compromising investor protection in order to enhance the growth prospects for U.S. capital markets, especially against the background that repeal of SOX seems to be a non-starter. Admittedly, it is also true that the adoption of these two proposals would be beneficial to many of the companies whose common stocks are held in the TAVF portfolio. It would also be helpful to the Fund itself as a shareholder of many small companies and many foreign domiciled issuers. For TAVF, it is a real disadvantage that so many of the foreign securities it holds are not traded at all in U.S. markets.

[1] Based upon long-term performance of the Cambridge Associates LLC U.S. Private Equity Index®

CHAPTER 20

Risk from a Third Avenue Point of View

APRIL 2006

Fund management views risk quite differently from the conventional views as embodied in literature such as *Against the Gods— The Remarkable Story of Risk* by Peter L. Bernstein or *Principals of Corporate Finance* by Richard A. Brealey and Stewart C. Meyers. Put simply, at Third Avenue, the word "risk" is meaningless unless an adjective describing the particular uncertainty is placed in front of the word "risk".

For Third Avenue Value Fund (TAVF), there is, *inter alia*, market risk, investment risk, credit risk, failure to match maturities risk, commodity risk, hurricane risk, terrorism risk, etc., etc. There just is no such thing as general risk.

In particular, market risk refers to fluctuations in the prices of securities mostly traded in public markets. Investment risk, on the other hand, refers to probabilities of things going wrong fundamentally with businesses or with the securities issued by those businesses. TAVF strives hard to minimize investment risk. It rather completely ignores market risk. In contrast, Modern Capital Theory (MCT), typified by the writings of Brealey and Meyers, is focused solely on market risk; MCT seems to misdefine "market risk" as all "risk", or to use their underlying concept, they believe that markets are efficient; and all risks that exist are reflected in the market prices of common stocks traded on markets populated by Outside Passive Minority Investors (OPMIs).

The Fund's "Safe and Cheap[1]" approach to common stock investment encompasses consideration of four factors: super strong financial positions; reasonable managements; understandable businesses; and a price that represents a meaningful discount from our estimate of what the security would be worth were the business a private company, or a takeover candidate. Very frequently, and probably most of the time, the nearterm earnings outlook for the common stocks Third Avenue is acquiring is anywhere from clouded to very poor.

If Fund management tried to pay attention to market risk, it would eschew investments in those securities where the near-term earnings outlook was clouded or poor. Rather, management acquires the common stock of well-financed companies when the underlying values, measured over a long term, appear to be good enough. Unlike MCT acolytes, TAVF does not try to estimate what near-term stock price performance might be, nor does TAVF try to predict stock market lows. Given a perception in the general market that there exists a Primacy of the Income Account, it seems to me to be impossible to follow a "safe and cheap" investment approach and at the same time to give any weight at all to attempts to gauge market risk. Market risk for Third Avenue is merely a "random walk", best ignored altogether. The investment in Intel Common during the quarter seems a good example of a situation where the near-term outlook is clouded but the underlying values seem sound.

Thus far, over the fifteen plus years of life of TAVF, ignoring market risks altogether has not been a major problem. While market risk has been a factor for individual securities held by the Fund, it has not been important for the TAVF portfolio as a whole, even though the Third Avenue portfolio seems to be far more concentrated than are the portfolios of other mutual funds of comparable size.

Ignoring market risk can be worrisome for portfolios financed with borrowed money; for portfolios run by managers with a trading mentality; for portfolios run by managers who do not study individual securities in depth; and by managers who believe that the market knows more than they do about any individual security, e.g., believers in MCT. These factors are just not a Third Avenue problem.

There is a view that over the long run, market prices in markets populated by OPMIs will reflect "true value" and, thus, market risk will be equated with investment risk. This is, by and large, an irrelevancy for TAVF. As long as there exists mispricing between OPMI market prices and underlying corporate values, a long-term arbitrage will take place. Insofar as OPMI prices are too low, asset conversion events such as mergers and acquisitions, massive share repurchases, and going-privates will occur. Indeed, over the years, most of Third Avenue's exits from portfolio positions in common stocks have occurred because the companies were taken over or taken private, not because TAVF sold to the OPMI market. In other words, OPMI mispricing is usually a capital gains creating factor in and of itself; and something more significant in the Fund's investment experience than is any long-term tendency for OPMI market prices to approximate underlying investment values.

TAVF tries to deal in probabilities. The principal way that the Fund attempts to put the odds in its favor is by acquiring the common stocks of well-financed companies at prices that represent meaningful discounts from readily ascertainable net asset values. However, favorable odds alone should not trigger an investment if the consequences of a mistake might be draconian for Fund shareholders. Thus, Third Avenue will forego investing, even where the probability of success seems great, if the loss from being wrong might be truly harmful. This approach I call being conscious of odds and consequences. Specifically, in all Fund investments which account for more than 3% of portfolio net assets, e.g., Toyota Industries Common, USG Debentures, Cheung Kong Holdings Common and Brookfield Asset Management Common, I believe that on a reasonable worst case basis, each of these investments will always have material value. If I did not feel this way, the prospects of adverse consequences would make any one of these investments unsuitable for the Fund.

Ignoring market risk will mean that, from time to time, TAVF's performance will be lumpy; the Fund is unlikely to outperform benchmarks consistently. Rather, the goal is to outperform on average, most of the time and over the long run. Measuring investment risk involves the consideration of three factors:

1. Quality of the Issuer
2. Terms of the Issue
3. Price of the Issue

In MCT, only quality of the issuer and terms of the issue are considered because price is assumed to be in equilibrium. Therefore, in MCT there exists a risk/reward ratio — i.e., the more the risk of loss, the greater the possibilities for reward. In the TAVF case, the assumption is that the price is wrong and the Fund tries to acquire common stocks at prices below underlying value. In the Third Avenue scheme of things, there is no risk/reward ratio. For us, the lower the price, the less the risk of loss and the greater the prospects of gain.

[1] "Safe" means the companies have strong finances, competent management, and an understandable business. "Cheap" means that we can buy the securities for significantly less than what a private buyer might pay for control of the business.

CHAPTER 21

Securities Regulation, Disclosure and Third Avenue

OCTOBER 2006

The principal Federal laws covering securities regulation are the Securities Act of 1933, as amended ("the 1933 Act") and the Securities and Exchange Act of 1934, as amended ("the 1934 Act"). The 1933 Act and the 1934 Act have three principal regulatory purposes:

1. Insure the maintenance of free, fair and orderly trading markets.
2. Provide disclosure to Outside, Passive, Minority Investors (OPMIs).
3. Provide oversight of Managements, Directors, Insiders, Control Persons and Professionals.

Disclosure has two principal purposes:

1. Aid and abet the maintenance of free, fair and orderly markets. This function is directed exclusively toward meeting the perceived needs of short-term traders who believe they are vitally affected by near-term fluctuations in market prices.
2. Provide information to long-term buy-and-hold investors such as Third Avenue Value Fund (TAVF, "The Fund").

For short-term traders, what the numbers are, especially earnings per share (EPS) as reported become of paramount importance. A consequence of catering to short-term traders has been that Generally Accepted Accounting Principles (GAAP) has come to be dominated by rigid rules, rather than principles. As a result, GAAP has been made as complicated as the Internal Revenue Code. Such complications are unnecessary for GAAP, whose principal purpose has to be to give OPMIs objective benchmarks, not "truth" or "economic reality", something rigid rules can never do. The Internal Revenue Code, in contrast, has to be complicated because its purpose is to calculate one number – a taxpayer's periodic tax bill.

For buy-and-hold investors (and control persons), the GAAP factor of paramount importance is what the numbers mean, rather than what the numbers are. Here there is rarely a Primacy of the Income Account, i.e., emphasis on EPS. Rather, there is a balanced approach where each element of the accounting cycle – balance sheet, income account, cash reconciliation – is weighted by the user of the financial information. In some cases, there might be a Primacy of the Income Account (e.g., strict going concerns); in some cases there might be a Primacy of NAV (e.g., investment companies); while in most cases there is a Primacy of a Balanced Approach (e.g., everything in the accounting cycle becomes useful for an analysis).

In the current regulatory scheme, there seems to be much too much emphasis on controlling disclosure to meet the perceived needs of short-run traders. There is no question that capital markets are most efficient where the trading markets are free, fair and orderly. However, fulfilling the stated information needs of short-run speculators really does not contribute to the maintenance of free, fair and orderly markets. Rather, the best protection for all participants in OPMI markets is self-protection. Increasingly, disclosure ought to recognize the needs or desires of buy-and-hold investors who are reasonably diligent, reasonably intelligent and reasonably well trained. The best hypothetical standard for disclosure, to my mind, ought to be what is required for making sound judgments by those who are long-term unsecured creditors, holding privately-placed debt instruments; and not the average investor who thinks he, she, or it, are vitally affected by day-to-day, or hour-to-hour, price fluctuations. This is because, at bottom, the average investor cannot be protected unless he, or she, or it, protect themselves. The present emphasis on serving short-run interests seems to be ruining U.S. capital markets for publicly-traded equities.

It ought to be noted, however, that it is hard for TAVF management to complain about the disclosure system. Over the last 40 years, the Securities and Exchange Commission (SEC) has done a magnificent job in improving disclosure for buy-and-hold investors such as TAVF. Disclosure has never been better for the Fund.

One of TAVF's best tools for appraising management is examining the GAAP choices they opt to make when given a choice, e.g., in Exploration and Producing oil companies (E&P), compare the choice between successful efforts accounting and full cost accounting. E&P managements' choices tell TAVF management a lot about how conservative or promotional an E&P management might be. This is an argument against rules and for principles.

The accounting principles that ought to govern GAAP should, in my opinion, encompass the following:

1. Financial statements are prepared under the assumption that the users are well trained, diligent and intelligent.
2. The Company is a stand-alone, never to be substantively consolidated with stockholders, management, or creditors.
3. There exists a modifying convention of conservatism.
4. There is no Primacy of the Income Account. Rather, emphasis has to be placed on a balanced approach without any preconceived notions that the income account is more important than the balance sheet, the cash reconciliation, or footnote disclosures – and vice versa.
5. The goal of GAAP, with the possible exception of mark-to-market investment companies, has to be to provide the user of financial statements with objective benchmarks, not truth. The user's task is to convert objective benchmarks into the user's version of truth.
6. The financial statements, including footnotes, should strive to disclose all material facts that might have negative connotations.

There are certain areas where market participants ought to protect themselves, provided they are given, through regulation, the tools with which to protect themselves. Disclosure is one such area. There are other areas, admittedly, where the only meaningful protection for individuals resides in regulation providing strong, stringent, rules. Such an area, for example, is in the regulation of prescription drugs to assure safety and efficacy. Individuals are in no position to self-protect themselves when it comes to prescription medicines.

In the investing arena, there are federal laws which provide a substantial amount of substantive protection to market participants unwilling, or unable, to self-protect. These laws are embodied in the Investment Advisers Act of 1940, as amended; and, more particularly, the Investment Company Act of 1940, as amended. TAVF is regulated under the Investment Company Act of 1940, as amended, as are all U.S.-based mutual funds.

Third Avenue is harmed by non-productive regulation as embodied both in GAAP, as currently constituted, and the Sarbanes-Oxley Act of 2002 (SOX). Also, frivolous stockholder lawsuits are a problem, especially the class of lawsuits labeled "fraud on the market". As things exist now, no foreign issuer is likely to access U.S. capital markets unless they absolutely need U.S. capital. TAVF invests heavily in foreign securities. Further, many small companies, now publicly traded, are thinking about "going dark", i.e., no longer being subject to regulation by the SEC. Needless to say this environment is not conducive to the well-being of the U.S. economy, which for many years, at least since 1933, has benefited from having the deepest, most efficient, best informed capital markets ever known to mankind.

In retaining strong, efficient capital markets, it remains important that trading markets continue to be free, fair and orderly. It is hard for me, however, to see how requiring traders to self-protect after being given adequate disclosure detracts from efficient markets. If anything, the emphasis on the phony economics embedded in relying on short-run EPS as reported introduces material market inefficiencies. The goal of Federal securities regulation is Investor Protection. I submit that most useful Investor Protection lies in self-protection, and not in precise numbers derived from rigid rules, especially quarterly EPS as reported.

Private Equity Limited Partnerships and Third Avenue

On November 1, 2006, I briefly addressed the Third Avenue Management Value Conference in New York. In those remarks, I compared what TAVF is doing with the bulk of its equity investments to Private Equity Limited Partnerships. My comments, modestly edited, were as follows:

Private Equity Limited Partnerships, such as KKR, Blackstone, Thomas Lee and Carlyle Group are all the rage today. These are entities which acquire control, or elements of control, over a variety of properties or corporations.

A huge amount of Third Avenue's portfolios is in the common stocks of companies performing the same function as Private Equity LPs. These Third Avenue common stock investments include the following: Brookfield Asset Management, Capital Southwest, Cheung Kong Holdings, Forest City Enterprises, Guoco Group, Henderson Land Development, Hutchison Whampoa, Investor AB, Jardine Matheson, RHJ International, Wharf Holdings and Wheelock & Co.

Permit me to compare the differences between Third Avenue's private equity common stock investments with those of the typical Private Equity LP.

1. Third Avenue buys into its private equity investments at prices that represent very substantial discounts from readily ascertainable NAVs. Private Equity LPs obtain control by paying premiums over OPMI market prices. Private Equity LPs most often negotiate deals. Third Avenue pays prices in the open market which are way, way below prices that are paid typically in negotiated deals. However, frequently in the case of Management Buy Outs (MBOs), deals are not negotiated at arm's-length because management becomes part of the buying group. Private equity buyers often can get some very attractive deals in MBOs.
2. The various Third Avenue investments are in companies that are extremely well-financed. Controlled entities of Private Equity LPs tend to be leveraged to the hilt.
3. The Third Avenue Investments tend to be managed primarily for long-term growth. Private Equity LP controlled entities tend to be

managed with the objective of extracting from the operating entities as much cash as possible as soon as possible.

4. Limited Partners (LPs) of Private Equity LP tend to pay much higher promotes to General Partners (GPs) than do Fund shareholders. The Third Avenue expense ratio is 1.1% of Assets Under Management (AUM). Typical LP fees are 2% of AUM plus 20% of gains after, say, a 6% bogey.

5. There is no meaningful lock-up for Third Avenue Funds. Any shareholder can redeem daily, subject only to a small redemption charge for short-run holders. The typical LP can't redeem any investment for at least a year.

6. In terms of corporate governance, Third Avenue shareholders have manifestly more rights and protections than do LPs.

7. Lead Investors in Private Equity LPs get to do "due diligence" on the LP and also negotiate many terms of the arrangements between the GPs and the LPs. Third Avenue Funds relies on the public record, and also interviews with managements and others. Third Avenue owns common stocks. It does not negotiate terms.

My family and I have invested a substantial part of our net worths in Third Avenue. We have almost no investments in Private Equity LPs.

I like it that way.

CHAPTER 22

Characteristics of Long-Term Investing

APRIL 2013

One conservative, but highly productive, approach to long-term common stock investing is to acquire issues which have the following characteristics:

1. The issuer has as especially strong financial position.
2. The common stock is selling at prices that reflect at least a 20% discount from readily ascertainable Net Asset Value (NAV) as of the latest balance sheet date.
3. There is comprehensive disclosure including reliable audited financial statements; and the common stock trades in markets where regulations provide substantial protections for Outside Passive Minority Investors (OPMI).
4. The prospects seem good that over the next three-to-seven years NAV will be increasing by not less than 10% compounded annually after adding back dividends.

Characteristics 1, 2 and 3 are easily ascertainable but Characteristic 4 requires considerable analytic skill.

Concentrating on long-term growth in NAV ought to give OPMIs far greater downside protection than would the conventional approach where the emphasis is on predicting periodic future operating cash flows or earnings (with earnings defined as creating wealth while consuming cash). For perhaps 90% or more of companies whose common stocks are publicly traded, 90% to 95% of the time, NAV or book value will increase in each reporting period. The last time the Dow Jones Industrial Average was over 14,000 was October 2007. Today the Dow Jones Industrial Average's book value is some 70% higher than it was in October 2007. More importantly, the quality of that book value probably has improved dramatically since October 2007. Thus, in order to not suffer large losses, all that has to happen is that discounts from NAV do not widen materially. The "NAV common stocks" with which various Third Avenue Management (TAM) portfolio managers are involved include issues by Brookfield Asset Management, Capital Southwest, Cheung Kong Holdings, Forest City Enterprises, Henderson Land, Investor AB, Lai Sun Garment, Toyota Industries, Wharf Holdings and Wheelock & Company. These common stocks sell at prices relative to NAV ranging from 0.3x NAV to 0.8x NAV. In contrast the common stocks of the companies that make up the Dow Jones Industrial Average and the S&P 500 are selling at close to 3.0x book value (which is closely related to NAV).

Unlike conventional analysis where there is a primacy of the income account and the managements are appraised mostly as operators of going concerns, in our approach managements are appraised not only as operators but also as investors and financiers. If economic times get very bad, and absent social unrest and violence in the streets, astute managements of creditworthy companies will be in a position to make super-attractive acquisition deals just as was the case after the 2008 economic meltdown. Astute managements which made super attractive deals after 2008 include Brookfield Asset Management, Cheung Kong Holdings and Wheelock & Company.

Conventional securities analysis, while helpful for trading purposes, contributes very little toward helping OPMIs understand businesses or the securities they issue. This seems attributable to a gross overemphasis on four factors in conventional security analysis:

1. An emphasis on a primacy of the income account, whether to measure periodic cash flows or periodic earnings. There has been a consequent denigration of what, at least since 2008, has been the most important factor in financial and economic analysis, i.e., corporate creditworthiness.

2. Short termism. Short termism is the only way to go when dealing with "sudden death" securities, i.e., options, derivatives or risk arbitrage but it does nothing to help evaluate a business with a perpetual life.
3. An emphasis on top-down analysis (predicting market levels, interest rates, general business outlooks) versus examining businesses from the bottom up (contract terms, potential future competition, litigation, financing, and refinancing opportunities, changes of control).
4. A belief in equilibrium pricing. The OPMI market price is the right price in an efficient market and will change only as the market absorbs and interprets new information.

While I think that trying to buy growth in NAV at a discount is a highly productive pattern for OPMIs to follow, it is important to recognize a number of shortcomings to the approach:

In 2013, managements of companies with super strong financial positions are sacrificing Return on Equity (ROE) and Return on Investment (ROI) for the safety and opportunism inherent in having a strong financial position.

Strongly financed companies without much, if any, Wall Street sponsorship, are frequently run by dead head managements who don't own any common stock, but this seems a bigger problem for Japan than for the U.S., Canada or China.

The OPMI market seems efficient enough most of the time that large discounts from NAV indicate an absence of catalysts that could result in dramatic near-term price appreciation for a common stock, e.g., a contest for control.

Unlike situations where market participants seek control, or elements of control, the NAV common stocks mentioned in this letter are marketable securities whose prices in the near term will be heavily influenced by market fluctuations in what is basically an irrational market from the point of view of long-term buy and hold investors.

For those interested in further reading, these are some of the concepts used by Third Avenue's investment team, and are discussed in greater detail in my newly published book, *Modern Security Analysis: Understanding Wall Street Fundamentals*.

CHAPTER 23

Thoughts on the Detroit Bailout

JULY 2013

There was an interesting article in the July 22, 2013, issue of *Fortune* entitled "The Party Could Be Over for Stocks." The most interesting part of the article is that it describes precisely what Third Avenue Management does not do when it comes to analyzing equity securities. The *Fortune* analysis seems irrelevant for Third Avenue shareholders.

The gravamen of the article is that the Federal Reserve Board might reduce its $85 billion of monthly bond purchases and end the program entirely by mid-2014. As part of the change in the Fed, the government agency will no longer deploy extraordinary measures that have driven down interest rates over the last five years. Low interest rates resulted in a bull market for equities because the yields on bonds that compete for investors' money stayed so unenticingly low. This bull market was never justifiable based on so-called fundamentals—dividend yields and earnings potential. Also, lower interest rates mean that earnings are not likely to increase. Further, Price/Earnings ratios are currently quite high—the S&P 500 P/E ratio stands at 18.4x for the latest 12-month period and 23.6x for the 10-year average of inflation adjusted earnings.

The article ignores completely three fundamentals that are crucial in any Third Avenue analysis of a common stock: first the credit worthiness of the company issuing the equity; second, the ability of the issuer to grow net asset value (NAV) (or its surrogate book value) over the intermediate to longer term; and, third, the price of the common stock relative to NAV.

While anecdotal, it seems likely that U.S. corporations whose common stocks are publicly traded are more credit-worthy today than has been the case since the 1950s and the 1960s. In part this is an outgrowth of the era of easy money from 2007 to 2013.

NAVs have continually increased. At July 31, 2013, the book value of the companies making up the Dow Jones Industrial Index was 60.7% higher than it had been at December 31, 2007; and the comparable increase for the S&P 500 was 28.4%.

At July 31, 2013, the Dow Jones Industrial Index was selling at 3.0x book value and the S&P 500 was selling at 2.5x book value. In contrast, most securities in the various Third Avenue portfolios are selling at anywhere from 0.6x NAV to 1.0x NAV. Since the companies in Third Avenue's portfolios enjoy Returns on Equity (ROE) comparable to the companies in the S&P 500, the P/E ratios for the Third Avenue companies are much below those of the S&P 500. Third Avenue's P/E ratios are estimated at around 10x, rather than the 18.4x for the S&P 500. Further the Third Avenue companies on average are probably more credit-worthy than the S&P 500 companies, i.e., they enjoy stronger balance sheets. Also, for the Third Avenue companies, I am confident that most of the issuers will increase NAV in most future reporting periods (as has been the case in the past) albeit it may be that such NAV increases will be smaller than had been the case from 2007 to 2013.

At Third Avenue we know how hard it is to predict the future, and we are especially skeptical of anyone's ability (including our own) to make successful macroeconomic predictions. Assuming that conditions are bad economically, but without social unrest and physical violence in the streets, many Third Avenue portfolio companies will be in a position to make super-attractive acquisitions, as was the case after the 2008 Financial Crisis. Such Third Avenue portfolio companies include Brookfield Asset Management, Cheung Kong Holdings, Exor, Investor A/B, Pargesa and Wheelock & Co.

One final comment about the *Fortune* article. It seems doubtful that there is a close relationship between bond yields and dividend returns on common stocks. The correlation certainly exists where the investors are primarily interested in cash return. As far as I can tell, most common stock investors are interested primarily in total return, with cash return being distinctly secondary, and most bond investors do not own common stocks because they need contractually guaranteed interest payments, (e.g., banks and insurance companies).

Motor City Blues

While Third Avenue is not directly involved, our readers might be interested in my take on the Chapter 9 bankruptcy of Detroit.

In the USA, outside of a court proceeding (usually a bankruptcy case), no one can force a creditor to give up a right to a money payment for principal, interest or premium unless that individual creditor consents. Therefore, a voluntary program in Detroit could never have worked— too many hold-outs. Chapter 9 was inevitable.

Creditors in Chapter 11 and Chapter 9 cases can be coerced into accepting a reorganization with either the requisite votes of the impaired classes of creditors, or a cramdown (a reorganization workout ordered by the bankruptcy court without the requisite vote of impaired classes of claimants and parties of interest). True liquidation does not seem to be an option for Detroit. For practical purposes, Chapter 9 is just like Chapter 11, except that the period of exclusivity for the debtor to propose a Plan of Reorganization (POR) lasts forever, and unlike corporate Chapter 11, as part of any reorganization it may be impossible to give ownership interests to pre-petition creditors to satisfy part or all of their claims. Also in Chapter 9, no trustees are likely to be appointed. After all, unlike corporations, Detroit and Michigan are sovereign entities.

The goal of Chapter 11 and Chapter 9 is to make the debtor feasible (i.e., creditworthy) within the context of maximizing present values (PVs) for creditors and also comporting with a rule of absolute priority where no creditors of a class are treated to different values than other members of the class. There are two broad classes of credits in Detroit—Secured and Unsecured. Secured credits ought to include certain municipal bonds which become senior up to the value of the collateral. Pension, retirement and healthcare liabilities seem to be unsecured. This will be vigorously argued for a long time by very able lawyers and investment bankers, all of whom will be paid by Detroit.

To accomplish a successful reorganization, you follow what you would do for a Leveraged Buyout (LBO)—first determine forecasted cash flows, realizations from asset sales and the debtor's dynamics. Then, apply an appropriate capitalization to the above. In an LBO, you leverage up. In a Chapter 9, you deleverage as part of a POR.

To make Detroit feasible on an operational level seems a Herculean, possibly impossible, task. Maybe regional authorities like Port Authority of New York, Metropolitan Transportation Authority, or Bay Area Rapid Transit can be important contributors to a feasible reorganization. No matter the difficulties, reorganization has to take place somehow. Perhaps Detroit and the surrounding region can attract new, productive investments. Detroit seems to enjoy a relatively efficient infrastructure (e.g., a great highway system), lots of land and, probably, sharply reduced labor costs.

For Detroit to obtain a feasible capitalization, provided operations can be stabilized, there are only a few things that can be done to compromise some $18 billion of obligations:

• Reduce principal
• Reduce interest rates and /or cash interest payments
• Alter covenants
• Extend maturities
• Provide credit enhancements

I would bet that as part of a POR the State of Michigan, the private sector and/or Federal agencies will have to provide credit enhancements to Detroit via either dedicating tax revenues to Detroit and/or guarantying obligations. There is ample precedent for this. New York State, through the Municipal Assistance Corporation (MAC), credit enhanced New York City obligations in the 1970s. Credit enhancements, incidentally, could create a lot of investment opportunities for Third Avenue.

Detroit's Chapter 9 will take a long time and be very, very expensive. Detroit, under Chapter 9, will have to pick up all administrative expenses for almost every participant in the reorganization (say, professionals hired by the Committee of Retirees) i.e., lawyers, investment bankers, accountants, actuaries, etc. Detroit will pay them on a priority basis in cash with perhaps minor holdbacks on a pay as you go basis. I can almost guarantee that Administrative costs for Detroit will be at least $500,000,000 and might well be in excess of $1,000,000,000.

CHAPTER 24

On Creditworthiness

JANUARY 2014

Much emphasis is placed on general "debt levels" in the belief that the amounts borrowed by U.S. Federal, State and Local governments are way too excessive. Indeed 74% of recent poll respondents stated that a high priority ought to be given to debt reduction by governments.

It is obvious that this almost universal emphasis on general debt levels is misplaced. Rather the emphasis should be on the creditworthiness of borrowers, specifically what are the borrower's abilities to access capital markets, if needed.

There are two things about borrowing that any rational analyst ought to keep in mind. First, while individual debt instruments mature, aggregate debt for most borrowers almost never gets repaid from the borrower's perspective. Rather for most borrowing entities, debt is refinanced and expanded as the borrower becomes increasingly creditworthy. Second, if a borrower is not creditworthy and can't be made creditworthy, then sooner or later that borrower has to reorganize or liquidate. Reorganization can encompass capital infusions, major asset sales or a recapitalization designed to reduce or extend cash service that the borrower has to pay out for interest, principal retirements and premiums.

Creditworthiness is a function of four factors for feasible borrowing entities – whether corporate or governmental:

- Debt level
- Terms of the Debt
- How productive are the Use of Proceeds received from the borrowings
- How liquid is the borrower

There seems to be a common belief that a government's use of proceeds is always non-productive. Insofar as this is true, it seems to be valid to concentrate attention on the debt level because large debt levels coupled with a lack of productive use of proceeds means that the government entity will not be, or remain, creditworthy. However, there seems to be no evidence that all government expenditures are non-productive. Indeed, in at least three historic areas, the federal government's use of borrowed moneys was unbelievably productive, probably returning to society and the country benefits with a present value hundreds of times greater than the amounts spent. These three areas which come to mind are as follows:

1. The Homestead Act of 1862 which enabled and accelerated the rapid settlement of the U.S. West.
2. The Serviceman's Readjustment Act of 1944 (the GI Bill of Rights) which resulted in the U.S. obtaining a highly educated population and the world's best university system.
3. Research and Development expenditures by the U.S. military after World War II which, among other things, gave the U.S. and the world, the Internet and a highly efficient aviation industry.

The U.S. Government, and its agencies, are creditworthy and seem likely to remain creditworthy for the foreseeable future. In contrast, many states and local governments, including Puerto Rico, a territory, are not creditworthy. Sooner or later many of these entities will have to reorganize, i.e., restructure their debts to reduce or eliminate periodic cash burdens.

Reorganizing governments seems to be many times tougher than reorganizing corporations:

It may be hard for various Third Avenue Funds, managed by Third Avenue Management (TAM), to become involved with much troubled municipal debt unless prices are manifestly lower than they are for troubled corporate debt. For this there are three general reasons:

1. Chapter 9 may not be available to the defaulting debtor.
2. It may be impossible to get rid of incompetent elected officials.
3. It may be hard to issue equity to impaired pre-petition creditors to satisfy part, or all, of their claims.

Many governments including all 50 states and Puerto Rico are not eligible to reorganize under Chapter 9 of Title 11 (the Bankruptcy Code). Access to courts through Chapter 9 provides a structured setting in which the rules for reorganizations are spelled out for local governments and their agencies. Also, post-petition borrowings can be very attractive to lenders if the borrower has been granted Chapter 9 relief.

No municipality can seek Chapter 9 relief without the affirmative consent of the state in which the municipality is located. It seems as if in the vast majority of instances outside Title 11 no creditor in this country can ever be forced to give up his, her or its, rights to money payments without his, her or its consent. In a court proceeding (such as Chapter 11, 7 and 9 of Title 11) this right can be abrogated. Without the ability to coerce creditors to give up their rights to cash payments, huge hold-out problems exist markedly reducing the probabilities of achieving a successful Plan of Reorganization (POR). If Chapter 9 is available to a government or its agencies, individual creditors can be forced to accept a POR which entails the creditor giving up rights to contracted for money payments upon the affirmative vote for the POR by two-thirds in amount and 50% in number, of the votes cast by each impaired class. Alternatively, the reorganization can take place in Chapter 9 after a cram-down ordered by a court of competent jurisdiction, usually a Bankruptcy Court.

Unlike corporate reorganizations, for sovereigns such as municipalities the period of exclusivity lasts forever (Corporations have exclusivity for 210 days after a Chapter 11 filing). Elected government officials most probably can't be removed from office as a result of bankruptcy proceedings.

The ultimate goal of a reorganization is to make the debtor feasible (i.e., creditworthy) within the context of maximizing present values for creditors up to the amount of the creditors' claims in accordance with a rule of absolute priority where no creditors of a class are given preference over other members of the same class, (forgetting certain priorities written into the Bankruptcy Code).

In corporate reorganizations, it is relatively common to issue ownership interests to impaired pre-petition creditors in satisfaction of the present value of their claims. Such equity interests might satisfy some or all of a creditor class's claims. In issuing cash, or new debt which requires cash payments sooner or later, as part of a POR, the debtor has a harder time becoming feasible than if ownership interests were issued in, say, common stock which does not pay a dividend. In the vast majority of governmental reorganizations, it seems not possible to satisfy any portion of creditors' claims by issuing ownership interests either in the form of equity interests or the direct distribution of assets.

The Role of Net Asset Values for Certain TAM Portfolio Companies
Many common stocks in various Third Avenue Portfolios: e.g., Brookfield Asset Management, Dundee Corp. Exor, Henderson Land, Investor A/B, Lai Fung Holdings, Lai Sun Garment, Pargesa, Toyota Industries, Wheelock & Company and a goodly proportion of the issues held by Third Avenue Real Estate Value Fund; are selling at discounts from readily ascertainable Net Asset Values (NAV) of anywhere from 25% to 75%. These are the common stocks of companies which are well-financed and which have had good to excellent records of growth. In contrast to these discounts, the Dow Jones Industrial Average (DJIA) at January 31, 2014, was selling at 2.79 times book value. In other words, certain TAM Portfolio companies can be acquired at, say, 25¢ to 75¢ for each $1.00 of corporate net assets most of which are accounted for under International Financial Reporting Standard (IFRS),while comparable DJIA assets cost $2.79 for each $1.00 of corporate net assets most of which are accounted for under Generally Accepted Accounting Principles (GAAP). This discrepancy makes no economic sense except that the discounts have always existed for the securities named at the start of this paragraph and no catalysts such as changes in control or going private, appear to exist for those companies.

The quality of net assets of the TAM portfolio companies appears to be significantly better than the quality of the net assets of the DJIA portfolio companies. Also NAV, or book values, seem to be significantly more important in analyzing the TAM portfolio companies and their securities than is the case for the DJIA portfolio companies. There are a number of reasons for this superior quality factor:

The TAM portfolio companies appear to be more strongly financed than the DJIA portfolio companies.

The reported NAV's in accounting statements for TAM portfolio companies which are domiciled outside the United States are mostly more realistically stated than are the NAVs for DJIA portfolio companies. Non-US companies which are publicly traded use IFRS in reporting publicly while US companies rely on GAAP. Insofar as portfolio companies own income-producing real estate (as many TAM portfolio companies do), the real estate accounted for under IFRS is carried at an appraised value based on appraisals by independent appraisal firms; under GAAP income producing real estate is carried at depreciated historic cost less impairments.

The assets of TAM portfolio companies are probably more liquid and probably more easily measurable than is the case for the DJIA portfolio companies. A large portion of the TAM portfolio companies' assets consist of income producing real estate, performing loans, Assets Under Management ("AUM"), and marketable securities; assets, that by and large, are measurable, separable and salable. In contrast, most DJIA assets have almost all their value tied-up as an integral, and inseparable, part of going concern operations.

The Price Earnings Ratios (PE) for the TAM portfolio companies are manifestly lower than is the case for the DJIA portfolio companies. Indeed, several of the TAM portfolio companies' which report under IFRS standards, sport PE ratios of 2 to 3 times reported earnings. PE ratios are integrally related to NAV's and are a function of Return on Equity (ROE). The TAM portfolios, of course, have much higher equity values per dollar of market value than do the DJIA portfolio issues. The ROE's for the TAM portfolio companies appears to be comparable to the ROE's for the DJIA portfolio companies. Thus, the TAM portfolio common stocks are characterized by relatively modest PE ratios.

There are problems with an NAV emphasis, in general, and with the TAM portfolios, in particular.

Discounts from NAV, and NAV itself, are pretty much ignored by most market participants, including even disciples of Graham & Dodd (G&D). G&D were believers in the primacy of the income account, even though they did not ignore NAV completely.

There is a tendency for the managements of well-financed companies such as those in the TAM portfolio to be relatively oblivious to the needs and desires of outside minority shareholders. In a way this is understandable since managements, which often own little or no common stock, run companies that need little or no access to capital markets. Historically, this has been a special problem for many well-financed Japanese companies whose common stocks were selling at material discounts from NAV. TAM tries to avoid investing where these types of managements exist. In the TAM portfolios, managements and/or insiders are substantial shareholders.

In this era of ultra-low interest rates, companies with strong financial positions are sacrificing ROE for the safety and opportunism inherent in having a strong financial position. TAM is very prejudiced in favor of opportunistic managements such as those heading Brookfield Asset Management and Wheelock & Company, both of which subsequent to the 2008 economic crisis were able to acquire companies or assets on highly attractive bases.

There is little or no attraction in focusing on NAV for going concerns lacking catalysts if the market participant has a short run goal; i.e., where short-term market performance is the most important consideration. I believe that a vast majority of market participants are short–run oriented.

One major problem with the TAM portfolio is that there appears to be little possibility that there will be changes of control or going-private, two courses of action that could result in immediate, and substantial, market price appreciation for a common stock. Rather in the TAM portfolio, one has to rely on the continued growth of NAVs in an environment where discounts don't widen materially over a longer term period.

However, for virtually all TAM portfolio companies, at least 80% of the time in at least 80% of the cases, NAV seems likely to be larger in each reporting period than it was in the prior period. Historically this has been the case, at least since the end of World War II. While this fact alone does not guaranty good market performance for a TAM portfolio, it at least seems to have promise of putting the odds in TAM's favor where the common stock was acquired at a meaningful discount from NAV.

Having served on an audit committee, as a Director of an NYSE company audited by a member firm of the Big 4, I think a comment about how reliable and protective of minority stockholders I think US audit statements are, appropriate. This is important when investing in companies where financial statements are important for an analysis something that is always the case in credit analysis and also is the case both for TAM portfolio companies and DJIA portfolio companies. (Financial statements are less important when analyzing the common stocks of high tech start-ups or natural resource companies seeking or exploiting new discoveries). Auditors tend to be ultra-strict and conservative when certifying audited financial statements. The auditors will insist that material matters be disclosed by management; and that disclosures be complete and comprehensive within the modifying convention of conservatism. Audits can be relied on by market participants to be comprehensive, reliable and essential tools for most analyses. It seems remote, to me at any rate, that the US companies in which TAM invests, will be subject to all the problems several years back that existed in connection with the Enron financial statements. The last thing a Big 4 Audit firm seems to want is accountant's liability arising out of stockholder class actions or Securities and Exchange Commission proceedings. The last thing TAM portfolio managers and analysts want to do is invest in the common stocks of companies whose financial statements are incomprehensible, or almost so.

PART 4

MODERN SECURITY ANALYSIS

"A Third Avenue analysis focuses on what the numbers mean, rather than what the numbers are."

July 2002

CHAPTER 25

The Unimportance, and the Importance, of Book Value

JULY 2003

There are two separate, and distinct, ways of analyzing a security. The first involves trying to predict the prices at which a common stock will sell in the immediate future, whether that immediate future is tomorrow, next week, next month, three months from now, or a year ahead. The focus here is on the trading environment; in the words of John Maynard Keynes, trying to fathom what will be "the average opinion of the average opinion."

The second approach focuses solely on trying to understand a business and the securities issued by that business, either credit instruments, equities, or both. The Fund uses only this second approach, and TAVF analyses involve concentrating on underlying factors, both qualitative and quantitative. No attempts are made to predict what near-term market prices will be except for the occasional risk arbitrage investment, such as USG Senior Credits. (Risk arbitrage exists where there ought to be a relatively determinate workout in a relatively determinate period of time.)

Most people, including most fund managers, focus strictly on the trading environment. Here, insofar as company results are analyzed, book value (i.e., net asset value per share computed in accordance with Generally Accepted Accounting Principles [GAAP]) is usually ignored in almost all analyses of companies other than financial institutions and regulated utilities. Put simply, there exists in the trading environment a Primacy of the Income Account. Near-term common stock prices are going to be influenced mightily by what reported future income account flows will be, whether those flows are cash flows from operations or earnings from operations computed in accordance with GAAP. (Earnings are defined as those operating activities which result in the creation of wealth for companies and/or stockholders, while the company involved consumes cash). Changes in book value can pretty much be ignored in this trading environment simply because book value is unlikely to influence where a common stock will sell in the immediate future. As Graham, Dodd and Cottle point out in the 1962 edition of *Security Analysis* on Page 217, "There is good reason for not taking the asset-value factor seriously. The average market price of a common stock depends chiefly on the earning power and the dividend payments."

Indeed, for the vast majority of common stocks, Ben Graham looked at book value only as an anchor to windward, a hedge against being wrong about earning power and dividend payments. Ben Graham never seemed to recognize that book value could be one tool to help an analyst forecast future earning power and dividend paying ability. As Graham states on Page 103 of the 1973 edition of *The Intelligent Investor*, we are led "to a conclusion of practical importance to the conservative investor in common stocks. If he is to pay some special attention to the selection of his portfolio, it might be best for him to concentrate on issues selling at reasonably close approximations to their tangible asset value – say, at not more than one-third above that figure."

Thus, it is prudent, valid and appropriate to state that in the trading environment, book value is relatively unimportant, insignificant most of the time compared with flows from operations, whether cash flows or earnings flows. "A Primacy of the Trading Environment" view has been adopted not only by most money managers, but also by most academics, by all television financial commentators and by many securities regulators, including the Securities and Exchange Commission (SEC).

However, if one's goal is to understand a business, the securities issued by that business, and that business' long-term outlook, a balanced approach is needed. Here, there exists no Primacy of the Income Account and certainly no Primacy of the Trading Environment. Where a business and its securities are being analyzed in depth, book value is as equally important, or unimportant, as reported earnings. There exists an accounting cycle, and every accounting number, say earnings per share, is derived from, modified by, and a function of, other accounting numbers, say book value for one. In fact, for most companies, the largest single component of book value is retained earnings, i.e., historic net income not paid out as dividends.

Modern Capital Theory (MCT) describes only the trading environment and misses completely the need for a balanced approach to understand almost any business enterprise. At best, MCT is involved with only half a loaf: 100% weight to flows and 0% weight to the amount of net wealth existing on corporate balance sheets. Neither of the leading texts, *Principles of Corporate Finance* by Brealey and Myers, nor *Corporate Finance* by Ross, Westerfeld and Jaffe, contain more than a passing mention of net asset values, or book values, in their volumes, which together, are almost 2,000 pages long. As Brealey and Myers state on Page 119 of their 7th edition, "Only Cash Flow is Relevant."

The elementary fact of life when it comes to understanding a business is that corporate economic earnings, or cash flows, are valuable only insofar as they either enhance the wealth of a company, both qualitatively and quantitatively, or are available for distribution to securities holders. On the other hand, corporate asset values are valuable only insofar as they can be used in order to enhance future corporate cash flows and economic earnings, both qualitatively and quantitatively, or to enhance returns to corporate securities holders. Economic earnings for a corporation can consist of many things other than earnings, or cash flows, from operations. These other things encompass all the activities which create realized appreciation, unrealized appreciation (which is, of course, generally untaxed and not generally reflected in book value), as well as financing, and refinancing, opportunities.

Most businessmen, and businesses, have as their primary goal the creation of wealth rather than the creation of income. In this sense they are exactly like Outside Passive Minority Investors (OPMIs) who seek to maximize risk-adjusted total returns rather than to maximize income from dividends and interest. Given a choice, most businessmen would prefer to create wealth in the most tax-advantaged manner which means striving for realized appreciation, unrealized appreciation, and financing opportunities, rather than having operating, and therefore taxable, earnings. This desire to create wealth by means other than enjoying operating earnings is mitigated by a number of factors. One, many businesses don't have any choice but to create wealth through successful operations. Two, insofar as wealth is created by having access to capital markets, having more reported earnings from operations tends to stand a company in better stead when raising equity capital at attractive prices (or at all) on Wall Street rather than having less operating earnings. Nonetheless, it should be noted that striving to create wealth through realized appreciation, unrealized appreciation and financing opportunities has a balance sheet (i.e., book value) emphasis, not an income account emphasis.

Almost 65% of the common stocks in the Third Avenue portfolio are of companies which essentially strive to create wealth through means other than having operating, and therefore taxable, earnings. These "primarily asset value emphasis" companies include financial institutions (29.9% of the total portfolio), land development companies (8.9% of the total portfolio) and real estate companies (8.2% of the portfolio). In contrast, only about 35% of the TAVF common stock portfolio are "primarily earnings emphasis companies." It should be noted that very few companies are either pure asset value plays, or pure earnings plays. Most who emphasize building asset values also pay attention to operating earnings, and vice versa.

No one can understand corporate finance in general if their focus is strictly on cash flows from operations. It is just not productive outside of the trading environment to place any reliance on the academic view that has prevailed at least since 1938, that "Investors only get two things out of stock: dividends and the ultimate sales price, which is determined by what future investors expect to receive in dividends." This shibboleth ignores two obvious factors of key importance in corporate finance: wealth creation is the primary goal for most participants in investment processes; and control (not dividends) is the *sine qua non* for acquirers of common stocks who don't happen to be OPMI's.

Book value, and reported earnings, are frequently unimportant in a microanalysis, i.e., when analyzing an individual company. In contrast, book value is almost always extremely important on the macro level, i.e., where one is trying to determine if general market prices are too high or too low. At August 1, 2003, the S&P 500 Stock Index, according to *Barron's*, was trading at 2.82x book value. In contrast, the TAVF portfolio, excluding real estate common stocks, was priced at around 1.5x book value.

TAVF's principal goal in most of its common stock investing is to try to establish positions in well-financed, well-managed companies whose common stocks are selling at substantial discounts from readily ascertainable Net Asset Values (NAV). In determining the readily ascertainable NAV, a Third Avenue analysis always starts out with book value. The book value is then adjusted in an analysis to reflect the Fund's version of economic reality. But book value is always the starting point, even though it is rarely the ending point. For Toyota Industries, the cost basis book value is adjusted to reflect the market value of its portfolio holdings of common stocks of other companies (mostly business affiliates). For St. Joe, book value is adjusted to reflect probable values for undeveloped land. For MBIA, book value is adjusted to reflect the company's equity in unearned premiums, and for Forest City Enterprises, book value is adjusted to reflect the capitalized value of expected future rental income from credit-worthy tenants.

GAAP, as reported, has to be accurate, or truthful for the trading environment with emphasis on Earnings Per Share (EPS) as reported. However, in understanding a business, no one expects GAAP to be accurate or truthful. Rather, it provides the analyst with objective benchmarks derived from that relatively rigid, and therefore frequently unrealistic, set of rules known as GAAP. When trying to understand a business, there is no particular emphasis on any one number, whether that number is EPS or book value. Here the GAAP numbers serve as the one essential objective benchmark which the analyst uses as a tool to assist in determining his or her version of reality.

Toyota Industries serves as a good example of potential differences between GAAP reporting and economic reality. Over half of Toyota Industries' assets consist of portfolio securities of common stocks based on the market prices for those common stocks. Since no one of the portfolio securities constitutes as much as 20% of the common capitalization of that issuer, none of Toyota Industries' share of the undistributed equity in the earnings of these portfolio companies is reflected in Toyota Industries' GAAP earnings. This is in accordance with both U.S. and Japanese GAAP. GAAP rules require that Toyota Industries report as Toyota Industries' earnings only dividends received from Toyota Industries' portfolio of common stocks, since none of Toyota Industries' portfolio positions carry a presumption of influence or control. Viewing the reported earnings on a GAAP basis, Toyota Industries Common sells at around 20x earnings. Viewed on a "look-through" basis, where Toyota Industries picks up as its earnings the earnings of portfolio companies' common stocks which were not paid out as dividends, Toyota Industries Common is selling at around 8 times earnings. Which is more realistic, 20x earnings or 8x earnings or some number in between? That is something for the analyst, the user of financial statements, to decide, not something to be decided upon by the CPAs who prepared the financial statements, or the politicians who dreamed up the Sarbanes-Oxley Act.

Ascertaining the economic NAV of Capital Southwest Corporation, a very low expense ratio business development company, is something best left to analysts, and not to CPAs who prepare financial statements or the politicians who dreamed up the Sarbanes-Oxley Act. At June 30, 2003, Capital Southwest reported that its NAV was $56.12 per share after deducting an allowance of $18.94 per share for deferred taxes on net unrealized appreciation. Those deferred taxes may never become payable, and if they do, Capital Southwest ought to have considerable control over the timing for incurring any actual tax liability. Meanwhile, Capital Southwest has completely free use of the assets offsetting the $18.94 per share "tax liability" just as it has free use of retained earnings. What is the appropriate NAV for Capital Southwest: $56.12 per share, $75.06 per share, or something in between? This analyst opts for something in between.

There are many tools analysts can use to predict future earning power of a company. No one method ever has to be used exclusively to the exclusion of other methods. Graham & Dodd seem to rely mainly on the past earnings record. For predicting the future earnings of many of our common stocks, i.e., MBIA and AMBAC, the past earnings record may well be prologue. Equally important in forecasting for these companies, however, is to estimate future Returns on Equity (ROE). Here "R" equals earnings, but guess what, "E" equals book value. Thus, book value is very often a key tool in the business world for estimating future earnings.

The Fund's investments in the common stocks of well capitalized regional, or community, depository institutions, serves as a good example of how TAVF uses "E," i.e., book value, to forecast future earnings and exit strategies. Third Avenue acquired around 10% of the outstanding common stock of Woronoco Bancorporation at about 80% of book value about 3 years ago. The theory behind the Woronoco investment was that the bank, a recently converted mutual, ought to enjoy an annual ROE of at least 10% going forward (non-troubled banks normally have ROEs of 8% to 20%), and that in five years, Woronoco could be taken over at two times book value because it operates in an industry where takeovers at better prices than two times book value are fairly common. If this 10% annual ROE, and two times book value exit were to occur, the Internal Rate of Return (IRR) to TAVF on the investment would be 32%. Actually, Woronoco's ROE has been better than 10% in recent years, and Woronoco Common is performing better than we had forecast when TAVF acquired its Woronoco position.

High book value frequently has negative connotations. Other than OPMIs who are not on margin, no one, and certainly no corporation, can own or control assets without assuming material obligations in connection with such control or ownership. Assuming obligations means assuming costs and liabilities, whether for licenses, storage, property taxes, environmental matters, employee protection, etc. If the assets are not earnings assets, the corporation will suffer far greater losses than would be the case were those non-productive assets to be shed. This highly realistic negative thought does not seem to pertain to TAVF. First and foremost, in looking at book value, the Fund concentrates much more on the quality of book value than it does on the quantity of book value. Put simply, if the candidate for inclusion in the TAVF portfolio is not extremely well financed, TAVF is unlikely to own that company's common stock.

Mitigating the negatives that can attach to high book values are three factors. First, a high book value might create tax advantages for U.S. Corporations. The sale of assets used in a trade or business (Section 1231 Assets) at a loss generally creates an ordinary loss that the corporation can apply to offset current year taxable income, if any, thereby reducing current year tax liability. Any excess losses may be carried back in order to get a refund for income taxes paid in the two prior years, and then if losses remain, a 20-year carry-forward is created as a potential offset to income taxes on future earnings. Also in legal cases, say statutory appraisal proceedings in certain states, the courts may attribute a separate value to NAV. Third, other things being equal, the more retained earnings a business has, the more dividend paying ability the company will have. For most companies, a majority of book value consists of retained earnings. The sine qua non for a company to have dividend paying ability, however, tends more to be a function of adequate finances rather than large amounts of retained earnings. For TAVF, our common stock portfolio is invested in the issues of companies which enjoy great financial strength, and where the price of the common stock is much closer to the amount of retained earnings than is the case for general market common stocks. I think there exists a lot of dividend paying ability in the TAVF portfolio, especially when related to the market prices for the Fund's portfolio securities.

Tangible book value has become less and less important as a measure of NAV than had been the case before, say 1960. In the old days, hard assets–receivables, inventory, property, plant and equipment–constituted a lot more of corporate America than is now the case. These hard assets have become less important as intangibles, like intellectual property and franchises, have become more important. Also, increasingly, the U.S. economy has become a service economy rather than a manufacturing economy. Again, this hardly seems a key factor for the Fund since Third Avenue has almost no investments in the common stocks of old economy, U.S. manufacturing companies.

Any entry on the asset side, or the liability side, of the balance sheet can serve as an objective benchmark for the analyst striving to understand a business. In contrast, in the trading environment, certain balance sheet entries can be ignored because, given the Primacy of the Income Account, managements are appraised strictly as operators of going concerns. Thus, it makes sense in a trading environment to eliminate from an analysis consideration of Purchase Goodwill. Positive Purchase Goodwill refers to the premium over fair value paid by a corporation for another business when pooling of interests accounting was not used. (Pooling of Interests GAAP accounting was eliminated for mergers initiated after June 30, 2001). In striving to understand a business, managements are appraised not only as operators, but also as "resource converters" engaged in mergers and acquisitions, liquidations, spin-offs and diversifications; and also in financing and refinancing the liability side of the balance sheet. Purchase goodwill acts as an objective benchmark helping the analyst decide on management skills in the "resource conversion" area. Third Avenue knows well that there are very few strict going concerns; most businesses will not go as long as five years without engaging in major "resource conversion" activities. TAVF normally will not acquire common stock interests in serial acquirers (i.e., WorldCom or Tyco International) unless the corporate management has shown exceptional skill over the years in the acquisition arena. Two such managements would appear to be the people running Nabors Industries and Quanta Services.

In the years after World War II, there had been a set of Pervasive Principles governing GAAP. These Pervasive Principles have now been all but forgotten. One of the old Pervasive Principles of GAAP was that financial statements were prepared under the assumption that the user of the financial statements was intelligent enough, and well trained enough, so that he, or she, could understand the uses and limitations of financial statements. This Pervasive Principle has now been completely eliminated for those operating in the trading environment. For them, financial statements are now supposed to be accurate and are supposed to tell them the truth, especially about one number, reported EPS. The goal of GAAP today, which seems to be impossible to fulfill, is to make GAAP useful for the "average investor." GAAP tends to be complex in an understanding of the business environment. In this business environment, it seems likely that GAAP can be useful only to "the reasonably diligent, reasonably well trained, investor or creditor." The "average investor" is going to be hopelessly lost. Only in the business approach is the old Pervasive Principle understood, that any accounting number, book value or reported EPS is useful only insofar as it gives the analyst objective benchmarks, not the truth. It is the analyst's job to take these objective benchmarks and use them as tools to help him or her determine his or her version of what economic truth might be.

In the book, *Value Investing — From Graham to Buffett and Beyond*, by Greenwald, Kahn, Sonkin and Van Biema, there are discussions of NAV. An important point in the book revolves around the view that if the market price of a common stock is well above the reproduction value of assets, the company and the industry, in the normal course of events, will draw new competition which will result in diminished returns unless the company can build a moat to insulate itself from new competition (i.e., Coca-Cola, Gillette and WD-40). From a strict operating point of view, this observation seems quite valid. From a corporate management point of view, though, it seems to be incomplete. In the hands of a reasonably competent management, an overpriced common stock tends to be an important asset with which to create future wealth by issuing that common stock in public offerings, and in merger and acquisition transactions.

With the TAVF emphasis on understanding the business and using a balanced approach where reported earnings and book value tend to be given even weights, the Fund's analytic activities tend to be a lot less competitive than is the case for those analysts concentrating on the trading environment.

Without a balanced approach which involves an examination of the balance sheet, the income accounts and the footnotes to audited financial statements, it becomes virtually impossible for an analyst to start to answer a key question he or she almost always has to ask: "What don't I know that I should know?" An analyst can't even contemplate that question if the approach to the analysis revolves around placing almost sole reliance on the Primacy of the Income Account. Things the analyst trying to understand a business will want to know that can't be gotten from the income account include, among others, measures of corporate financial strength; contingencies, risks and uncertainties; key contracts; pension plans; out-of-the-ordinary financing arrangements; representations, warranties and indemnities; and certain transactions with control persons.

There does exist a trade-off within corporate managements between striving to improve ROE, and striving to enhance corporate feasibility, i.e., corporate financial strength. TAVF, in its investments, opts for managements more interested in feasibility than enhanced ROE, for better or worse.

In summary, if you are to operate in a trading environment, book value tends to be unimportant. However, if you are to operate in an understanding-the-business environment, book value is just as important, or unimportant, as reported EPS; they are both made of the same stuff. For TAVF, book value tends to be very important as the starting point for most analyses. It is rarely the finishing point.

CHAPTER 26

Third Avenue Approach to Valuation

APRIL 1998

The Third Avenue Value Fund ("The Fund", TAVF) acquired an initial position in Toyoda Common during the quarter at an average price in U.S. dollars of $17.18 per share. Toyoda analytically consists of three elements: manufacturing operations, an investment in Toyota Motors Corporation Common Stock ("Toyota Motors Common"), and investments in other marketable securities:

	(000 and per share)			
	(U.S. $)		Per Toyoda Share 315,000 Shares (a)	
Operating businesses valued at 6x and 8x operating income - latest audit	$1,555,477	2,073,968		
Less non-convertible funded debt	225,600	225,600		
Value of operating business, net	1,329,246	1,848,368	$4.22	$5.87
192,735 shares Toyota Motors Common valued at market of $26	5,010,850	5,010,850	15.91	15.91
Remaining Portfolio of Marketable Securities valued at market 4/30/98	1,991,607	1,991,607	6.32	6.32
Net Asset Value ("NAV") appraising Toyoda as a closed-end investment company			$26.45	$28.10
Discount from NAV at market price of $17.54 for Toyoda Common			33.7%	37.6%

(a) approximate number of common shares outstanding on an all converted basis after share repurchases

For TAVF, Toyoda Common is a very attractive value purchase at its current price, which is about equal to the Fund's cost. TAVF has bought into a high quality business at a substantial discount from NAV. I have long thought that Toyota Motors was just about the best automotive company in the world. It, too, is extremely well-financed and seems to have decent, long-term growth prospects not only as an automotive manufacturer with a worldwide presence, but also as a promising participant in the telecommunications, housing and finance industries. I am not quite sure of what the Fund's ultimate exit strategy for Toyoda Common might be, but it could include market appreciation if Toyoda remains in its current form, and/or appreciation arising out of a Toyoda resource conversion if, say, Toyoda is ever merged with Toyota Motors or if Toyoda's portfolio, including Toyota Motors Common, is ever spun off as a separate investment company to Toyoda's shareholders. The largest Toyoda shareholder is Toyota Motors, which holds an approximate 22% common stock interest in Toyoda on an all-converted basis. Toyoda is the largest holder of Toyota Motors Common, owning about 5% of the outstanding issue.Toyoda had founded Toyota Motors in 1933. The two companies became separate corporate entities in 1937. The relationship between Toyoda and Toyota Motors has remained close ever since. Approximately 51% of Toyoda revenues in the fiscal year ended March 31, 1997, were in the production of automobiles, castings and engines for Toyota Motors, another 23% were in the production of industrial equipment, notably forklifts, marketed under the Toyota name, and another 23% of revenues were in air conditioning compressors for automobiles. Further, most of Toyoda's remaining investment portfolio, other than the investment in Toyota Motors Common, consists of the common stocks of other Toyota Motors' affiliates.

The principal drawback for the Toyoda investment to Third Avenue is that the public disclosures are not as comprehensive (at least in the English language) or as timely as they ought to be and as they would be were Toyoda a filing company with the U.S. Securities and Exchange Commission. Other analysts will find much else wrong with Toyoda Common.

It ought to be instructive in giving TAVF shareholders insight into the Fund's investment approach to examine not only how we, at Third Avenue, look at Toyoda Common but also how other analysts and money managers probably would view Toyoda Common. This comparative examination, of course, results in overgeneralizations about other analytic approaches since there will always be differences among individual analysts in assessing any specific security. Nonetheless, the exercise ought to be helpful. Other, non-TAVF, approaches include the following:

- Control Investors
- Risk Arbitrage
- Academic Finance as embodied in the Efficient Market Hypothesis (EMH) and Efficient Portfolio Theory (EPT)
- Graham and Dodd Fundamentalism
- Broker-Dealer Research Departments and Conventional Money Managers

Most control investors, say Ron Perelman, Richard Rainwater and Larry Tisch, probably would agree with TAVF that Toyoda is an attractive common stock, price-wise. They probably would use pretty much the same analytic techniques as the Fund to determine that Toyoda Common was an attractive security at its current price. However, control investors probably would have no interest in Toyoda Common because it does not seem to be a "doable deal"; no elements of control seem available to anyone outside the Toyota family of companies. Toyoda Common seems like a lot of other common stocks control analysts look at. It tends to be not that hard to find "attractive securities" among publicly-traded common stocks from a control point of view. It tends to be a bitch, though, to find issues which are not only "attractive securities" but also "doable deals."

Risk Arbitrageurs would have no interest in Toyoda Common now. Risk arbitrage exists where there are opportunities for profits from situations where there are relatively determinant values to be realized in relatively determinant periods of time. A risk arbitrage situation would exist, for example, if Toyoda and Toyota Motors announced now that they intended to merge. In that instance, risk arbitrageurs might acquire Toyoda Common at prices of, say, 24 or 27. Markets, especially risk arbitrage, markets, tend enough toward efficiency so that one cannot engage in risk arbitrage, unless one is willing to pay up compared with pricing that is attractive for TAVF. Within the risk arbitrage community, what Third Avenue does is known as "pre-deal" investing. However, what Third Avenue is doing in Toyoda Common may really be "pre-pre-deal" investing since, aside from a modest common stock buy-back program, there seem to be no indications that Toyoda management contemplates having the company undertake any activities outside of the ordinary course of business for the foreseeable future.

Academics would be unconscious of the business characteristics underlying Toyoda Common. This is not what they do. If asked to explain why Toyoda Common, as a marketable security, sells at such a substantial discount from the value of Toyoda's net assets, which are also measured largely by the market values of its portfolio securities, the likely explanation would revolve around something called "investor expectations." The primary thrust of most academic analyses would be to measure the past total return performance of the fund holding Toyoda Common, versus indexes or other funds with the same investment style. Academics also might be interested in asset allocation — how much of a fund's assets ought to be in Japanese securities or automotive securities. If Toyoda Common were to be valued independent of its market price, that value would be determined by forecasts of discounted cash flows.

Some Academics might be aware of the efficient market arbitrage inherent in the principal characteristics affecting Toyoda, to wit, the Company enjoys an exceptionally strong financial position; Toyoda Common sells at a low price compared with underlying values; and Japanese interest rates are ultra-low currently. For example, Toyoda, theoretically, could borrow on a long-term basis the equivalent of about $1,125,000,000 at 3% and use the proceeds to acquire via a Cash Tender Offer 50,000,000 Toyoda Common at $22.50 per share, equal to a premium over current market of about 28%. The net interest cost to Toyoda for the borrowing, after eliminating the dividends on the 50,000,000 shares of Toyoda Common to be acquired would be less than $28 million per year before taking account of possible tax savings from substituting interest charges for dividend payments. Partly because such a transaction would result in increasing Toyoda's pro-forma earnings per share and Toyoda's pro forma NAV per share, and partly because such a transaction would indicate that Toyoda management is employing its resources more aggressively, TAVF would conclude that the Cash Tender Offer would likely result in an improved market price for Toyoda Common after the conclusion of the Cash Tender Offer over what the market price would otherwise be. Most Academics, in contrast, would likely conclude that the benefits of such a theoretical buy-back are already reflected in the existing market price of Toyoda Common.

In an important sense, Graham and Dodd might be just like TAVF in finding Toyoda Common attractive because it is priced below the per share value of its net current assets, including investments at market value, after deducting all book liabilities short term and long term, except for deferred income taxes on the unrealized appreciation of portfolio securities. However, outside of these "net-net" considerations, Graham and Dodd would tend to emphasize a whole gamut of factors pretty much ignored by TAVF. Graham and Dodd probably would place great weight on Toyoda's earnings record over the past five years; its present dividend rate and dividend policy; and the immediate outlook for the Japanese economy, the Japanese Stock Market, and the worldwide automotive industry. For Graham and Dodd, the perceived exit strategy for Toyoda Common would be sale in the stock market as reported earnings increase. Graham and Dodd probably would weight much less heavily than TAVF possible exit strategies occasioned by resource conversion events, such as mergers and acquisitions, spin-offs or massive share repurchases.

The primary objective of Broker-Dealer Research Department Analysts and Conventional Money Managers is to estimate the price, or range of prices, at which Toyoda Common (or any equity security) might trade in markets for passive investments over the next 30 days to, say, one year. The probable approach would emphasize top-down considerations (rather than TAVF's bottom-up). Factors that Research Departments and Conventional Money Managers probably would emphasize encompass the following:

1. Outlook for the Japanese Stock Market with the outlook for the Japanese economy a principal variable in determining a market outlook
2. Outlook for the worldwide automotive industry in the period just ahead
3. Earnings outlooks for the next year for Toyoda and Toyota Motors
4. Is Toyoda Common selling at a lower price earnings ratio than comparably situated issues?
5. Is the fact that Toyoda Common trades at a discount from "net-net" asset value unique? (A fair number of Japanese equities seem to be trading currently at prices less than net-net asset value.)
6. Is there any resource conversion catalyst in evidence that might cause the Toyoda common NAV discount to narrow or disappear over the next year or so?
7. Is Toyoda Common trading near the lows of recent years? (It is trading about in the middle of its five-year price range.)

Probably, neither the Research Department Analyst nor the Conventional Money Manager would have any interest in Toyoda Common, unless they thought there was a rational basis for expecting near-term price appreciation in Toyoda Common. Many of these analysts might conclude that Toyoda Common was a good way to participate in a Japanese Stock Market rebound. But they would be unlikely to become bullish about Toyoda Common, unless they first foresaw a Japanese Stock Market rebound.

I, personally, am very comfortable with the TAVF approach to analysis as embodied in the reasoning behind the Fund's investment in Toyoda Common. While the Fund seems quite different than others in its analytic approach, TAVF has no magic formula. There are things to be said in favor of the approaches followed by Risk Arbitrageurs, Academia, Graham and Dodd, and Conventional Money Managers, especially if one's portfolio management bottoms on having concerns about near-term market performance for individual securities. Many of these near-term concerns are quite legitimate in connection with the management of other portfolios. They just don't seem to have any relevance for the management of the TAVF portfolio.

CHAPTER 27

Corporate Valuation

JULY 1997

The Third Avenue Value Approach to Corporate Valuation

The Third Avenue investment approach seems quite distinct from that of most other mutual funds; even others who, like the Fund, claim to be buy-and-hold value investors. In a nutshell, TAVF emphasizes the primacy of a Resource Conversion Approach ("Resource Conversion") in most valuations of equity securities. Almost all other money managers emphasize the primacy of a Going Concern Approach ("Going Concern") in most corporate and securities valuations. The key factor for Third Avenue in a Resource Conversion analysis is the quality and quantity of resources existing in a business at the time of analysis; i.e., a "what is" approach focusing on an adjusted balance sheet. The key factor for a Going Concern analyst is an estimate of future flows, whether those flows are cash or earnings; i.e., a "what will be" approach focusing on estimated income accounts.

Going Concern is the bedrock for business valuations in just about all literature about finance, including Generally Accepted Accounting Principles (GAAP), academic finance as embodied in the Efficient Market Hypothesis (EMH), and fundamental analysis as embodied in the writings of Benjamin Graham and David Dodd, their predecessors and their successors (collectively, "G&D"). The best analysts embracing Going Concern, for example G&D, do not ignore Resource Conversion (just as TAVF does not ignore Going Concern in its corporate valuations). G&D's connection to Resource Conversion seem to come mostly in the context of being aware of liquidating values. G&D point to the attraction of acquiring common stocks at prices below liquidating value, especially prices below net, net current assets. Net, net current assets refers to net current asset value after deducting all GAAP liabilities, both short term and long term.

The least sophisticated analysts, e.g., EMH, believe that Resource Conversion is the exclusive value determinant anytime values can be measured by trading prices in markers populated by Outside Passive Minority Investors (OPMIs). In all other cases, Going Concern is the value determinant. Thus, for academics a Resource Conversion emphasis for corporate valuations is adopted by requiring that performing loans held in corporate portfolios be valued at market. In general, EMH operates on the assumption that financial results for all corporations other than investment companies are to be measured strictly by Going Concern standards; while portfolio results for an investor in those corporations' securities are to be measured strictly by Resource Conversion standards. This academic approach is not helpful at all for a Third Avenue type corporate analysis.

The underlying force driving Going Concern is the strict going concern assumption. Corporations are seen in Going Concern as devoted essentially to the same day-to-day operations they have always conducted within the same industries in which they have always operated; managed and controlled as they always have been managed and controlled; and financed pretty much as they always have been financed. Up until the early 1990's this strict going concern assumption accurately described the environment existing in the electric utility industry. It never described accurately most U.S. corporations whose securities are publicly traded. The strict going concern assumption no longer seems appropriate even for electric utilities.

Certain conclusions follow logically if one grants the strict going concern assumption. First, among buy-and-hold fundamentalists there is a primacy of the income account, and a consequent denigration of the balance sheet for corporate valuation purposes. (Further, among traders not engaged in risk arbitrage, i.e., situations where there will be relatively determinant workouts in relatively determinant periods of time, the income account is supreme; short-term movements in common stock prices, after all, are likely to be heavily influenced by changes in reported earnings and not influenced at all by changes in book values). Further, G&D point out that the past earnings record of a corporation usually is the best tool for estimating earnings for the years just ahead over a business cycle or growth phase. If one grants the strict going concern assumption, G&D are absolutely right about the relative importance of the past earnings record as a tool for predicting future earnings.

Third Avenue believes that the strict going concern approach is utterly unrealistic. Most companies whose securities are publicly traded will always combine elements of the going concern and elements revolving around the conversion of corporate resources to other uses, other ownership, other control and other financing or refinancing. In the Fund's view, few U.S. corporations are going to go for as long as five years without being involved in resource conversion activities-mergers and acquisitions; changes of control; management buyouts; massive share repurchases; major financings, refinancings or reorganizations; sales of assets in bulk; spin-offs; investing in new ventures in other industries; and corporate liquidations. G&D describe these resource conversion activities as non-recurring events. For TAVF, there is nothing non-recurring about them.

Both going concern considerations and resource conversion considerations are important in most corporate valuations. Indeed, in most situations going concern considerations and resource conversion considerations are related intimately to each other, derived from, modified by, and a function of, each other. The current sales value of an asset is determined frequently by what it is believed that asset can be caused to earn. Much of the "what is" value for many, if not most corporations probably was created by past going-concern prosperity. Third Avenue, in its valuation approach, does not subscribe to a primacy of Resource Conversion over Going Concern in its evaluation of equity securities because of a view that Resource Conversion is more important or more commonplace necessarily in the overall economic scheme of things. Rather, the Fund subscribes to a primacy of Resource Conversion because it seems to provide the Fund with superior tools of analysis for the types of buy-and-hold investments of interest to Third Avenue. Emphasizing Resource Conversion makes it easier for the Fund to identify publicly-traded securities that meet the Fund's twin objectives for an investment — "safe" and "cheap."

People who focus on Going Concern tend to believe that value creation is a function of just one factor — estimated free cash flows appropriately capitalized: EMH; or estimated earnings appropriately capitalized: G&D. For Third Avenue, corporate values are derived from one, or more, of four, separate, but often related, sources:

> 1. Free cash flow from operations. A minority of going concerns generate excess cash flows from operations which become available to service a company's capitalization. TAVF holds substantial positions in the common stocks of companies engaged in money management, an industry with a strong tendency to produce free cash flows. While no corporation would undertake a specific project unless it were believed that the project, as a stand-alone, would produce cash flows with a positive net present value, it seems probable that most profitable going concerns actually do not create free cash flows, but rather create earnings because the nature of good going concern operations is to expand by acquiring large amounts of assets that have to be financed by obtaining outside capital

> or

> 2. Earnings from operations. Earnings are defined as the creation of wealth while consuming cash. This seems to be what the vast majority of prosperous going concerns do, and all growing economies do. In general, since earnings result in the consumption of cash, earnings cannot have any independent value unless they are also combined with access to capital markets, whether such access is to credit markets, equity markets, or both

> and/or

> 3. Conversion of assets to higher uses and/or other ownership or control; and/or the financing of asset acquisitions or the refinancing of liabilities. These activities sometimes take the form of Mergers and Acquisitions (M&A), contests for control, Leveraged Buyouts (LBOs), the restructuring of troubled companies, and acquiring

securities in bulk through cash tender offers, exchange offers, and the use of corporate proxy machinery. The vast majority of equity securities held by Third Avenue were acquired at prices which we believed represented substantial discounts from an adjusted Net Asset Value (NAV). The long-term exit strategies for such investments include a multiplicity of Resource Conversion and Going Concern possibilities encompassing redeploying existing surplus assets to uses with higher returns than are currently being realized (Tokio ADRs and Carver Federal Bank Common Stock); having new ownership which would pay substantial premiums over NAV to acquire these companies (depository institutions might acquire regional broker/dealers and financial insurance companies); use the existing asset base to create large, new NAVs (Forest City Enterprises, Tejon Ranch and St. Joe Paper); or use the existing asset base to realize markedly improved earnings and Return on Equity (ROE) during the next up cycle for a growth industry (semiconductor equipment common stocks, Cummins Engine, or Tecumseh Products).

and

4. Have access to capital markets on a super attractive basis. It seems probable that more corporate wealth, and, certainly wealth for financiers, is created by this route than any other. Groups accessing capital markets on a super-attractive basis include those financing many M&As as well as LBOs; and those taking advantage of the pricing available relatively frequently in the market for IPOs. Third Avenue tries to select equity securities for its portfolio which have been issued by companies which will be attractive acquisition candidates for others at prices well above those existing in OPMI markets such as the New York Stock Exchange and NASDAQ. The Fund believes that most acquirers of control positions analyze the same way Third Avenue analyzes — there exists for them a primacy of Resource Conversion and like the Fund an emphasis on the quality of NAV rather than the quantity of NAV. Further, Third Avenue also invests from time to time in private

placements at prices close to NAV where the exit strategy, after a few years of growth in NAV, is to sell a new issue of common stock in an IPO at a substantial premium price above that future NAV. This is the analysis behind TAVF's investment during the quarter in CGA Units.

As I have pointed out in previous letters, each investment the Fund makes has something wrong with it, and we spend a lot of time trying to figure out what is wrong and worrying about it. We make investment commitments when, in our judgment, what is right seems to outweigh strongly, what is wrong. One of the more important areas where there are trade-offs between right and wrong is in the differences that arise when emphasizing Resource Conversion and de-emphasizing Going Concern. Frequently, what is right for Resource Conversion is wrong for Going Concern, and vice versa. Here are a few examples:

Japanese nonlife insurers   Viewed as investment trusts whose principal assets are performing loans and passive investments in marketable common stocks, these well-financed issuers seem inordinately attractive from a Resource Conversion point of view since they are trading at discounts from an adjusted NAV of anywhere from 30% to 70% if one does not deduct a potential liability for income taxes on unrealized gains. Viewed from a Going Concern point of view, however, these issues hardly appear attractive at all selling at 20 times or more reported earnings. The outlook for existing operations is very clouded since for the first time, this sheltered industry is going to face real competition, especially price competition, concomitant with the "Big Bang" reforms taking place as part of the deregulation of financial institutions in Japan.

Retailing Industry   From a Resource Conversion point of view, retail inventories are a current asset convertible into cash within twelve months. From a Going Concern point of view, retail inventories are an illiquid fixed asset of the worst sort. If a retail business, say Sears, is to remain a going concern it will have to keep its aggregate level of inventories relatively constant or even expanding. These assets are subject to fashion swings, markdowns, shrinkage and obsolescence. Third Avenue's positions in retail equities are small. In our view, common sense here dictates that a Going Concern analysis ought to take precedence over a Resource Conversion analysis. Put otherwise, TAVF is not particularly enchanted with the G&D approach toward favoring companies that happen to be in retailing because these common stocks are trading at prices below GAAP net, net current assets; most of the time that type of pricing for retail equities impresses us as "cheap" but not "safe."

Forest City Common   As a Resource Conversion, the company's huge portfolio of income producing real estate properties, carried for GAAP purposes as a fixed asset, is very much a current asset, probably salable at close to appraisal values "over the phone." Third Avenue acquired its interests in Forest City essentially because those interests were available at steep discounts from what we thought the appraised values of the income producing properties were. The Resource Conversion analysis, though, was incomplete. As a practical matter, Forest City has many Going Concern attributes, one of which is that the best properties are not for sale and that as a going concern Forest City will dedicate cash flows from its successful properties to support cash drains from its poorer projects. Also, as a Going Concern investment builder, Forest City has been super successful in creating Resource Conversion values over the years. Hopefully, Forest City cash flows will continue to be devoted to Going Concern value creation.

Fixed Income Portfolios of Performing Loans   The TAVF portfolio is growing in size and the Fund has no interest-bearing debt in its capitalization. The same is true for the investment portfolios of the various U.S.-based insurance companies in whose common stocks TAVF has invested. All of these insurance company portfolios are invested essentially in performing loans. Viewed as a Resource Conversion, the various portfolio values are mostly carried at market value, i.e., marked to market. If interest rates rise, the market value of the portfolios go down. Viewed as a Going Concern, though, as interest rates go up, future investment income increases more than would otherwise be the case as new funds, as well as maturing funds, are invested at interest rates that provide increased returns. If interest rates do rise, I think the insurance companies probably will be benefited more by the Going Concern effect, than they will be harmed by the Resource Conversion effect. (There seems to be a knee-jerk reaction in the general market that higher interest rates are bearish universally; that is just what that general sentiment is — knee-jerk reaction. Some companies would be helped by higher interest rates, some harmed, albeit most of the Fund's equity portfolio where the underlying companies are cash-rich probably will be helped).

While the Fund does not ignore Going Concern in the analysis of securities, there is no question that Third Avenue places primary emphasis on Resource Conversion. This emphasis results in certain advantages and disadvantages. The advantages for the Fund in emphasizing Resource Conversion seem to be about as follows:

- It is a relatively non-competitive activity. Most money managers seem to concentrate on forecasting earnings or cash flows.

- The businesses are easier to analyze. TAVF does not get involved in common stocks, unless the businesses are extremely well financed and we can understand what they do. This is our basic criteria for "safe." As to "cheap," TAVF tries not to pay more than 50 cents for each $1 dollar we think the company is worth as a private company or a takeover candidate. The Fund uses certain preliminary "rules of thumb" to ascertain "cheap" when acquiring common stocks:

> **Small Cap High Tech** Usually pay no more than an 80% premium over book value on the theory that this is the "normative" price a first stage venture capitalist would pay if the venture capitalist were financing the enterprise de novo. As compared with venture capitalists, Third Avenue is creating positions in companies which are already public and which are cash-rich. On the other hand, the Fund has no elements of control over the companies in which it invests and Third Avenue research has to rely more on the public record and less on "due diligence" investigations involving insider information. Because public records tend to be so good, the Fund probably has an information advantage compared with many venture capitalists financing many privately owned businesses.

Financial Institutions: Buy at a discount from adjusted book values (insurance companies); at a discount from stated book values (depository institutions); or at a discount from tangible book values plus 2% to 3% of assets under management (broker/dealers and other money managers).

Real Estate Companies: Buy at a discount from appraisal values.

Insofar as long-term, future earnings are to be forecast, estimating returns that might be earned on a realistic asset base is probably as good, or better, a tool than is a corporation's past earnings record, albeit one is not a substitute for the other. The analyst ought to use both tools a good deal of the time.Aside from those times when a corporation, or its control shareholders, are seeking access to equity markets, usually an occasional occurrence, American business seems to be run much more with a Resource Conversion emphasis than with a Going Concern emphasis. This is certainly true for virtually all privately owned companies not seeking to go public, and is probably true, also, for most of the better run public companies. Most corporations, where managements do not have their eye wholly on OPMI stock prices, seek to create wealth in the most income tax efficient manner. The most inefficient tax way to create wealth is to have reportable operating earnings, a Going Concern emphasis; while the most efficient tax way to create wealth is to have unrealized (and, therefore mostly unreported) appreciation of asset values, a Resource Conversion emphasis.

Aside from those times when a corporation, or its control shareholders, are seeking access to equity markets, usually an occasional occurrence, American business seems to be run much more with a Resource Conversion emphasis than with a Going Concern emphasis. This is certainly true for virtually all privately owned companies not seeking to go public, and is probably true, also, for most of the better run public companies. Most corporations, where managements do not have their eye wholly on OPMI stock prices, seek to create wealth in the most income tax efficient manner. The most inefficient tax way to create wealth is to have reportable operating earnings, a Going Concern emphasis; while the most efficient tax way to create wealth is to have unrealized (and, therefore mostly unreported) appreciation of asset values, a Resource Conversion emphasis.There is a high level of comfort for a buy-and-hold OPMI investor such as Third Avenue, when investing in the equities of companies which enjoy strong financial positions. Not only does the cushion of a strong balance sheet make buy-and-hold investments feasible, but insofar as these strong financial positions are not dissipated, it makes it relatively easy for Third Avenue to average down when stock prices plummet.

There is a high level of comfort for a buy-and-hold OPMI investor such as Third Avenue, when investing in the equities of companies which enjoy strong financial positions. Not only does the cushion of a strong balance sheet make buy-and-hold investments feasible, but insofar as these strong financial positions are not dissipated, it makes it relatively easy for Third Avenue to average down when stock prices plummet.

We believe that Third Avenue is less likely to be victimized by securities frauds and securities promoters than are other investors. The Fund will have a fair number of unsatisfactory investments because sometimes we misanalyze and because the future is mostly unpredictable. Losses, though, because of management or control group malfeasance or outright fraud are probably a lot less likely for the Fund than for many other institutional investors, who rely on insider forecasts of the future and insider statements unsupported by public records as the principal weapons in their analytical arsenal.

Third Avenue's emphasis on Resource Conversion carries a number of disadvantages. These seem to be about as follows:

- While trying to avoid investment risk, Third Avenue, in almost all its purchases, assumes a lot of market risk, i.e., the risk that stock prices in OPMI markets will plunge. In almost all investments by the Fund the immediate earnings outlook is anywhere from poor to uncertain (see the Japanese non-life insurers). Certainly the immediate earnings outlook is almost never good. The OPMI market seems efficient enough so that there exists a trade-off — Third Avenue's investment criteria are met because the prospects are poor for those factors of the most immediate importance to participants in the OPMI market. The Fund is pretty much stuck with buying what is unpopular when it is unpopular.

- The managements the Fund deals with tend to be very conservative, non-promotional types, frequently indifferent to what Wall Street thinks or does. There is a certain "efficiency" in this because these management groups, by and large, are not seeking near-term access to equity markets.

- The Fund ignores factors that are important in the management of many portfolios; e.g., dividend payouts and marketability of individual securities.

- Resource Conversion seems largely unrelated to, or the antithesis of, certain short-term measures important to other analysts; Return on Assets, ROE, or Economic Value Added (EVA). Indeed, TAVF rejects, as a tool of analysis, any system which assumes that there exists a substantive consolidation between the interests of the corporation, itself, and the interests of those OPMIs who emphasize short run prices in securities markets. EVA bottoms on an assumption of a substantive consolidation between the company and short run OPMIs.

- Using Resource Conversion there seem to be a much more limited pool of eligible investments than exists under Going Concern.

- Resource Conversion is unsuitable as an investing technique where the money manager is operating with borrowed money or is otherwise heavily influenced by daily marks to market. Resource Conversion is also unsuitable for traders who treat securities investing as one more casino game.

- To be successful at Resource Conversion, it seems to take not only a fair amount of training in fundamental corporate valuation but also a fair amount of knowledge about securities law and regulation, financial accounting and income taxation; say, enough knowledge in these areas to be an intelligent client in dealing with full-time securities law, accounting or income tax professionals.

- Resource Conversion is not particularly relevant for portfolios, or portions of portfolios, investing in credit instruments without credit risk for the purposes of either obtaining assured streams of cash income or speculating on changes in interest rates. As a final comment, it ought to be noted that TAVF does not invest as if it were in competition with other mutual funds. Rather our goal is to minimize investment, but not market, risk while earning, on average, and over the long term, a compound annual rate of return of 20% regardless of what other funds, or the general market, have as rates of return. For TAVF to continue to have this type of long-term return, we are going to have to be both good and lucky. The benefits of Resource Conversion notwithstanding, it won't be easy.

CHAPTER 28

Role of Accounting in Security Analysis

JULY 1999

Corporate reporting of "the numbers" has become so important, and so publicized, it might be helpful to Third Avenue Value Fund (TAVF) stockholders if I commented briefly about how the Fund's management uses, and thinks, about financial statements prepared in accordance with Generally Accepted Accounting Principles, or GAAP. TAVF is quite different from most others in how the Fund makes use of financial information.

First, financial statements are always of utmost importance in the TAVF scheme of things. This, perhaps, may be the most significant reason why Third Avenue has never been involved with pure play Internet issues. Here, corporate numbers don't seem to count at all. The only important thing seems to be to gauge short-term investor psychology — something to which TAVF management pays scant attention.

GAAP figures can serve two different roles for outside passive minority investors. First, an accounting number — usually earnings per share — is a tool to be used to help predict the price at which a common stock will sell in markets just ahead. Alternatively, all accounting numbers — the whole bookkeeping cycle — are tools to be used to give an investor objective benchmarks, clues to aid him, or her, in understanding a business and its dynamics.

The vast majority of analysts seem to view GAAP only in its first role, as a tool to be used to help predict the price at which a common stock will sell in the period just ahead. The regulators, whether governmental as embodied in the Securities and Exchange Commission, or private as embodied in the Financial Accounting Standards Board, seem to share the same view wholeheartedly. Estimating the market impact of accounting numbers is what counts for them. Thus, there is a primacy of the income account. There has to be as accurate a statement as possible of quarterly reports of income from operations; Earnings Before Interest, Taxes, Depreciation and Amortization (EBITDA); and Earnings Per Share (EPS). The focus is on an income account, or flow, number with full attention paid to what the numbers are, as reported, rather than what the numbers mean.

Third Avenue belongs to the second school in its use of GAAP. TAVF believes that financial accounts are essential tools giving analysts objective benchmarks, clues that will aid in understanding a business and its dynamics. In equity analysis, accounting cannot, and should not, be expected to tell real world Truths. Rather, the limiting assumptions of GAAP — for example, depreciation is based on original cost rather than current value — means that what the numbers are, are not what economic truth is. Additionally, if one wants to understand a business and its dynamics, one has to focus on a considerably greater number of factors than merely flows — whether income from operations, EBITDA or EPS. Equally important, and usually more important than flows, in a TAVF analysis is the quality of resources existing in a business and the quantity of resources (relative to the price being paid for a common stock) existing in a business. Quality of resources and quantity of resources are essentially balance sheet, rather than flow, considerations.

Further, in a TAVF analysis, there is no primacy of anything such as earnings, but rather a realization that any number within the whole "ball of wax" can be important. Every accounting number is a function of, derived from, and modified by other accounting numbers. The analytical techniques used by Third Avenue, while different from those that seem to be used by most money managers, seem to be quite similar to those used by most investors in control, or interested in obtaining control, of companies.

Against this background, it seems productive to examine a couple of controversies existing in the accounting profession today: 1) how to expense the issuance of common stocks in acquisitions or the issuance of common stock equivalents, such as options to executive and employees; and 2) how to account for corporate acquisitions — purchase accounting vs. pooling of interest accounting.

In a TAVF analysis, a company is a stand-alone for accounting purposes and its books and records affect what exists in the company and what is happening to the company. As far as the Fund is concerned, corporate accounting, per se, should not, in any way, be related to common stock prices of particular corporations. There is a great hue and cry in the financial world stating that companies ought to charge as an expense against the income account the market value of securities, such as executive stock options, issued as management compensation. This charge against the income account should equal charges for cash payments to management, such as for salaries and bonuses.

This point of view seems to be arrant nonsense for the purpose of any fundamental analysis, especially because the company ought to be viewed as a stand-alone separate and apart from its shareholders. Obviously, the effects on a company are quite different when the company has to make a cash payment (or distribute other assets) compared with when a company issues new common stock or common stock equivalents. The payment of cash by a company diminishes the company's assets quantitatively and perhaps qualitatively as well. In contrast, the issuance of new common stock, where a company pays no dividends, does not affect the company directly but, rather, results in a dilution of ownership. Dilution of ownership is a stockholder problem, not a company problem. Ownership dilution can only have a cost to the company if it results in the issuer having less attractive access to capital markets than would otherwise be the case. Potentially less attractive access to capital markets is a difficult thing to measure for a company.

In contrast — the cost of cash outlays is easy to measure for a company. Measurement of the true cost of stock options is not something that ought to be part of GAAP, in part because measurement is so difficult. The true cost to a company of stock options ought to be estimated by security analysts, not determined by accountants. In connection with the issuance of stock options, their cost probably ought not to be measured by the imputed market value of the stock option, whether the one who measures such cost is an analyst or an accountant. The market value of the stock option to the recipient may well reflect the value of that option to the recipient. The value of a benefit to an optionee, however, has no necessary relationship to the cost to the company to bestow that benefit. It's as if an employee receives an item of inventory from the company which cost the company $10 and has a retail selling price of $50; and, therefore, the company's income account is charged $50, the value of the inventory item to the recipient rather than the company's $10 cost.

In purchase accounting, the acquiring company is deemed, for valuation purposes, to have paid a cash consideration for the acquired entity even though the consideration paid can consist of cash, debt securities and equity securities. The premium, as so measured paid over an adjusted book value of the net assets acquired, is deemed to be purchase goodwill. Purchase goodwill is amortized in not over 40 years (soon to be reduced to 20 years) by periodic charges to the acquiring company's income account. Pooling can take place when certain requirements are met, among which are that an acquisition include only exchanges of common stocks for common stocks between, or among, merging companies. In a pooling, old accounts are consolidated as they appear on each entity's books and no purchase goodwill is created. Pooling accounting is soon to be banned.

From a TAVF point of view, both purchase accounting and pooling accounting have merit. If the analyst wants clues only as to how to appraise an entity as a strict going concern engaged in day-to-day operations, pooling tends to fill the bill. On the other hand, if managements are to be appraised as investors as well as operators, purchase accounting gives additional clues, to wit, the amount of premium paid over an adjusted book value. Either approach to an analysis can be legitimate. Neither purchase nor pooling ought to be expected to tell economic Truth. That is for the analyst to determine for himself or herself using the clues provided by purchase or pooling, as well as financial accounting in general. It seems as if the accounting profession has now got it right in solving the purchase vs. pooling controversy. Commencing next year, only purchase accounting will be used, but companies will report two results — one with a periodic charge for goodwill deducted as an expense and one without any expense deduction for goodwill. The authorities, in connection with this issue, and other pronouncements as well, seem to be waking up to the GAAP fact of life that there is no "holy grail," i.e., that there never can exist just one number, presumably EPS, that reflects a universal *Truth*.

It is not that quarterly earnings or EPS are ever unimportant for TAVF. They are important when they provide clues that a permanent impairment of capital may be taking place. Permanent impairments are much more likely to occur for companies which are poorly financed. These are just the sorts of companies in whose equities Third Avenue does not invest.

In terms of what the numbers mean rather than what the numbers are, it may be constructive to examine what the numbers may mean for Tejon and Toyoda. Basically what Tejon management seems to be creating in its real estate activities is unrealized appreciation. Unrealized appreciation for assets, other than marketable securities, is never reflected in financial statements. Therefore, the reported earnings figures for Tejon, which is well-financed, do not mean a lot. One has to look well beyond them to understand the Tejon business and its dynamics.

A number of brokerage house analyses of Toyoda focus on the fact that Toyoda Common sells at over 50 times reported earnings; none seem to focus on the Toyoda net asset value as measured by market prices for its huge securities portfolio. In these brokerage house analyses, what the earnings number is, and is projected to be in the period ahead seem to be key. Not one of these analyses picked up the fact that the Toyoda income account and EPS reflects only dividends received from the common stocks of portfolio companies, including Toyota Common. If Toyoda used "look through" accounting where, besides dividends, the Toyoda income account also included Toyoda's equity in the undistributed earnings attributable to the common stocks of portfolio companies, then the PE ratio would be materially more modest than 50 times earnings. Also, Toyoda reflects in its income account its share of losses being incurred in the Sony LCD venture.

Assuming that the Sony LCD venture is promising, a reasonable analyst might conclude that it makes better business sense to capitalize, rather than expense, those losses for purposes of a valuation analysis.

CHAPTER 29

Fair Disclosure

JULY 2001

This letter seems an opportune place to discuss three issues very much in the news nowadays: The Role of Financial Accounting in Security Analysis; Security Analysts and Conflicts of Interest; and SEC Regulation FD — Fair Disclosure. Needless to say, my positions tend to differ from the conventional wisdom on the three issues by about 180 degrees in each case. The issues seem important, not so much because they might affect Third Avenue Value Fund (TAVF) on a day-to-day basis (they won't), but rather because of possible impacts on the integrity of U.S. Capital Markets — the best of mankind.

The Role of Financial Accounting in Security Analysis

In the TAVF scheme of things, financial accounting is useful, indeed essential, because it is the only tool which provides the objective benchmarks that a security analyst can use in trying to determine corporate values and corporate dynamics. For the Fund there is no belief that accounting should be expected to describe Truth: rather, financial accounting gives results derived in accordance with a relatively rigid system: Generally Accepted Accounting Principles (GAAP). Many of the underlying assumptions of GAAP have to be unrealistic, as for example, property values are based on historic cost less periodic depreciation charges, rather than estimated market values for properties. For TAVF, there is no *a priori* reason why any one accounting number, say earnings per share, has to be more important than any other accounting number, say book value. Indeed, every accounting number is derived from, modified by, and a function of, all other accounting numbers. For the Fund, what the numbers *mean* tends to be much more important than what the numbers *are*.

In contrast, conventional security analysis, at least equity analysis, looks to have financial accounting reflect *Truth*, i.e., describe some sort of economic reality. Moreover, just one set of accounting figures is deemed to be important: earnings from operations or its derivatives; EBITDA, cash flow from operations, or earnings per share. In conventional security analysis what the numbers are tends to be far more important than what the numbers mean. Insofar as one labors under the assumption that the goal of security analysis ought to be predicting what the price performance of a publicly-traded common stock will be in the immediate future, conventional security analysis seems to be applying an appropriate emphasis to a primacy of the income account approach, as reported for GAAP purposes. It seems obvious that earnings as reported tends to be a key factor influencing short-term fluctuations in the prices of publicly-traded common stocks, even though those reported earnings give little, or no, clues as to what underlying values may be.

Most analysts, whether money managers or employed in research departments of broker-dealers, seem to believe that their primary job is to forecast near-term earnings results as reported, say for the next 3 months to 12 months. These analysts tend to put "buy" or "strong buy" recommendations on the common stocks of companies likely to report improved earnings soon. If the immediate profits outlook is glum, conventional analysts would rather not take a position in the security, not at least until they perceive that a bottom is near. In contrast, at TAVF, we are striving to identify underlying long-term values for companies and the securities they issue. For most of the common stocks the Fund acquires, the near-term earnings outlook at the time of acquisition is poor. The Fund buys at the time the near-term outlook is poor provided the company is well capitalized, if our analysis indicates that the common shares are available at a low price earnings ratio relative to long-term future earning power and/or are selling at a substantial discount from an adjusted, and measurable, net asset value. Thus, the difference between the ways TAVF uses financial accounting and the way most conventional equity analysts use financial accounting, seems understandable. It's the difference between a long-term balanced approach with emphasis on what the numbers mean (the Fund) vs. a short term, primacy of earnings approach with emphasis on what the numbers are (conventional analysts).

The stock option controversy serves as a good example of how conventional security analysts are unable to use GAAP to determine the Truth. On one side, the granting of stock options to executives are not a charge against the GAAP income account at the time of grant, albeit details of the options are fully described in footnotes to financials. Many conventional analysts want to alter GAAP so that the income account is charged with the market value of stock options granted to executives. Thus, assuming an executive received options on 2,000,000 shares of common stock with a value as determined by the Black-Scholes formula, of $2 per option, then GAAP should be altered so that operating income would be charged with a $4 million expense, the same as would be the case if, in lieu of options, the executive were paid $4 million cash.

The conventional proposals to alter the GAAP treatment of stock options tend to be ludicrous. First, there is no necessary correlation between the value of a benefit to a recipient — the executive — and the cost to an issuer — the company — to grant that benefit. What is the proper charge against income when a retail sales employee acquires a sweater with a retail price tag of $100 which cost the company $20 at a 60% employee discount, or for $40? The value of the sweater to the recipient is $100; no one would argue that the cost to the company is anything other than $20.

In fact, the cost to the company from issuing the executive stock option, which has a value to the executive of about $4 million, is the present value of the diminution, if any, in the company's future ability to access capital markets for new equity. This is something hard to measure. There may be other company costs, but I haven't figured out what they might be.

Issuing executive options often results in diluting the common capitalization outstanding. But common stock dilution in those instances where no cash dividends are paid is a stockholder problem, not a company problem insofar as it does not detract from a company's ability to access capital markets.

A good part of the problem for conventional security analysts, and virtually all academics, is that they fail to view the company as a stand-alone. Rather, they implicitly assume that there exists a substantive consolidation between the interests of the company and the interests of its stockholders. Most of the time, substantive consolidation is an unrealistic economic assumption. Indeed, in credit analysis, whether for performing loans or distressed credits, the company is almost always analyzed as either a stand-alone, or a stand-alone with parent-subsidiary relationships. The stockholder just doesn't figure in most of the time.

There are macro problems involved with designing GAAP to meet the perceived needs of conventional equity analysts for Truth determined on a short run basis with emphasis on the primacy of the income account. To begin with filling those perceived needs probably is an impossible task. More importantly though, trying to fulfill those needs has unnecessarily made GAAP just about as complex as the Internal Revenue Code. The Internal Revenue Code has to be complex because it leads to just one number — a taxpayer's tax bill. GAAP on the other hand need only give the analysts objective benchmarks. From the available information, I can figure out for my analytic purposes, what the true costs of executive stock options to a company might be. I don't need a Certified Public Accountant to do it for me, even assuming the CPA could.

Security Analysts and Conflicts of Interest

There is now a general sense of rebellion against security analysts, who during the period prior to April 2000, were putting out strong buy recommendations for dot com common stocks, telecom common stocks, and other issues of companies whose only apparent real asset was an ability to sell new issues to the public at ridiculous prices. Many analysts are perceived to have had conflicts of interest because, among other things, the investment banking departments of the broker-dealers employing these analysts, benefited because the recommendations were essential if the investment bankers were to keep, or develop, relationships with present or potential issuers. There is validity to this view of conflicts of interest. However, it overlooks the main point of what went on during this period of speculative excess. The main point is that many, if not most, analysts, by and large, were incompetent. They drank the Kool-Aid. Put otherwise, I bet the same trillion of dollars would have been lost by the investing public even if there had been no conflicts of interest.

Many analysts are very smart and also very well informed. However, except for the extremely rare genius and skilled risk arbitrageurs (risk arbitrage exists where there are relatively determinate workouts in relatively determinate periods of time — e.g., announced merger transactions), it seems as if no one person, or group, can outperform a market, or index, by trying to predict short-term swings in security prices. It seems apparent that you can't beat the market by trying to beat the market consistently.

During the period of speculative excess, it was very hard for conventional analysts to not recommend dot com, telecom and similar common stocks, no matter what the price. If the analyst failed to outperform his peers, or benchmarks consistently, not only might his or her compensation level been in question but even his or her job. These analysts were in no position to pay attention to "safe and cheap" even if it was on their radar screens. It had little, or nothing, to do with conflicts of interest.

At present the major broker-dealers are implementing programs to assure that security analysts give out advice that is objective. Who do you want your investment advice from? Someone who is objective or someone who has their money where their mouth is? At Third Avenue, you don't get objectivity; you get managers who are investing on the same terms as any other TAVF stockholder.

The macro issue here is that so much ought to be done to raise the standards of security analysis practice so that in equity analysis, there is a de-emphasis on the importance of outperforming benchmarks consistently in the stock market. There's much to be learned from credit analysis where the analyst has to look mostly to the resources in the business and the performance of the business in order to gauge the quality of the security being analyzed. In credit analysis there tends to be little attention paid to market psychology, i.e., what will a bigger fool pay me for the security I hold regardless of that security's underlying merit or the security's price.

SEC Regulation FC — Fair Disclosure

Regulation FD is now under attack. FD requires issuers to make disclosures available to everyone in the market at the same time, rather than leaking disclosures to a select few. Many people want FD repealed. The issue really does not have anything to do with the Fund. Ever since TAVF has been in existence, Third Avenue has almost always been the last to know. TAVF does not operate with needs to obtain superior, i.e., early, disclosure. Rather, Fund operations revolve around using the available disclosures in a superior manner.

Yet, I think Regulation FD, which has been in existence only since October 2000, is very important as one guarantor of market integrity from a macro point of view. One of the United States' most valuable assets is that its capital markets are perceived as the best, deepest, most informed, most honest capital markets that have ever existed. This is a perception that should be nurtured carefully. Trading markets have to be viewed as fair. It can be said today that the U.S. does not really have a trade deficit but rather that the U.S. is exporting participations in its magnificent capital markets.

That confidence in U.S. markets might cease to exist if trading markets came to be viewed as unfair and disorderly. Regulation of securities, especially by the SEC, covers three principal functions:

1. The maintenance of fair and orderly markets
2. Providing disclosure
3. Oversight of fiduciaries, and quasifiduciaries.

Of the three, the first seems to be most important. Regulation FD goes a long way toward preserving the perception that the public trading markets are fair and orderly. Regulation FD should not be repealed.

CHAPTER 30

How Third Avenue uses Accounting Disclosures

JULY 2002

Increasingly, the Inmates Seem to Be Running the Insane Asylum

Washington politicians, corporate executives and securities analysts at times seem to be driven by a herd mentality. They frequently seem to be lemmings. Look at the dot com bubble before it burst in early 2000. Look at the extremely ill-advised "airline bailout" approved almost unanimously and in a hurry by Congress in the fall of 2001. That wasn't an airline bailout; it was a temporary bailout of airline creditors. Look at the current stampede by corporate executives to account for stock options as a corporate expense. Stock options are not, in the vast majority of instances, a corporate expense; they are a stockholder expense. In my view, the most egregious malpractice of the herd today is to have everyone dump on public accountants. The vast majority of problems with financial accounting today have nothing to do with the preparers of financial statements, the public accountants. Rather, the problems lie with the users of financial statements, equity analysts appraising publicly-traded securities, who have little or no willingness or ability to use appropriately the vast amount of information imparted to them by financial statements prepared in accordance with Generally Accepted Accounting Principles (GAAP). These analysts, and their cohorts in the media, in the Plaintiffs' Bar and in the political arena, are the inmates who, increasingly, are determining what financial disclosures ought to be. They, indeed, seem to be running the insane asylum.

It ought to be instructive to Third Avenue Value Fund (TAVF) shareholders to compare how Third Avenue uses accounting disclosures with how the great majority of securities analysts in research departments use accounting disclosures. While the TAVF approach may appear to be aberrational compared with Wall Street convention and with the precepts that make up almost all of the academic literature, the Third Avenue approach seems to me to be the majority, mainstream approach in the U.S. economy. The TAVF approach is the same as that followed by private companies not seeking access to public markets for equities; businessmen seeking favorable tax attributes so that they can create wealth on a tax-sheltered basis; most creditors; and all investors who seek in the management of their own portfolios to maximize total return, rather than just invest for interest income and dividend income. Interest income and dividend income in investor portfolios is the precise equivalent of revenue from recurring operations for going concern corporations.

How Third Avenue Uses Accounting Disclosures

The TAVF objectives are to ascertain what a business and its securities might really be worth to a control buyer, and what the range of dynamics might be for the corporation over the long term. Short-term considerations are always ignored with the exception of risk arbitrage situations. Risk arbitrage situations exist only where there are relatively determinate workouts in relatively determinate periods of time, e.g., when there is an announced corporate merger.

Managements are appraised looking at three interrelated factors. Managements are appraised as operators of going concerns; as investors employing and redeploying the assets of a business; and as financiers obtaining the necessary capital to conduct company activities. Of the three interrelated activities, appraising management as investors, not as operators, is probably the most important single factor in a Fund analysis. A majority of the TAVF common stock investments are in companies acquired at substantial discounts from

Fund management's estimates of net asset value (NAV), where Fund management believes that prospects are good that NAV will be steadily increased over the long term. In many instances, those increases in NAV will come from places such as enhanced land values or securities market price appreciation, rather than going concern income from operations. At July 31, 2002, common stock investments in NAV driven (rather than earnings driven) companies accounted for 54% of the Fund's common stock portfolio. Principal industry groups containing NAV companies were real estate, insurance, depository institutions, business development and Japanese issuers whose principal assets were portfolios of marketable securities.

In appraising managements as investors, there is no such thing as non-recurring charges or expenses. Non-recurring charges are the method used in GAAP accounting to record past investment mistakes.

In a TAVF appraisal, no one accounting number is ever all-important. Rather it is realized that every accounting number is derived from, modified by, and a function of, all the other numbers that comprise the accounting cycle. Most analyses are complicated, and different numbers — operating income, cash flow from operations, comprehensive income, book value, revenues, inventory turnover, capitalization ratios, returns on equity — are given different weights dependent on context.

In a TAVF analysis, one size never fits all. Depository institutions are analyzed differently than high tech companies, which are analyzed differently than real estate companies, and distress credits seem, in great part, to be off into a different world.

What is expected of GAAP accounting in a TAVF analysis is that it provides to the analyst objective benchmarks, which the analyst can then use to determine truth and accuracy. As a matter of fact, GAAP is usually the only source of numerical objective benchmarks for the analyst. Outside of mark-to-market accounting for investment companies, it is utterly ludicrous to expect GAAP to reflect truth and accuracy for all contexts. Like the Internal Revenue Code, GAAP is based on a relatively rigid set of unrealistic assumptions — e.g., depreciation of property, plant and equipment is based on historic cost; and most debt obligations of a company are carried at the face amount of the debt obligation, rather than marked to current market. Any system of accounting has to have shortcomings that cause it to be unrealistic in one, or more, contexts. Cash accounting has shortcomings in that it fails to reflect a company's accrual, or wealth creation, experience during a period. Accrual accounting has shortcomings in that it fails to reflect a company's cash experience during a period. Nonetheless, both cash accounting and accrual accounting are important. As a general rule, the common stock analyst might want to give overriding weight to cash accounting for companies whose financial positions are quite weak, while emphasizing accrual accounting for companies sitting with huge amounts of surplus cash.

A TAVF analysis focuses on what the numbers mean, rather than what the numbers are. Disclosure is what counts, not how things are disclosed, e.g., in the case of stock options, it is important that the term of options be disclosed in footnotes to GAAP audits. It is not important that the value of options (no matter how inaccurately value is determined) be deducted from accounting net income. Knowing the details of an item such as stock options enables the TAVF analyst to either adjust financial statements, adjust the price the analyst might be willing to pay for a security, or both.

For TAVF, financial disclosures have never been more comprehensive, more meaningful and more useful than is currently the case. This remains true even though, in general, accounting fraud *à la* WorldCom seems to have increased materially in recent years. Given the Fund's *modus operandi* though, where few common stocks are acquired if the company does not enjoy an extremely strong position, it seems to me that the Fund remains far less likely in its common stock portfolio to be victimized by accounting frauds than will be conventional equity analysts.

GAAP accounting by Toyota Industries and GAAP accounting for debt on the balance sheets serve as two examples of how GAAP provides the Third Avenue analyst with objective benchmarks and how the Third Avenue analyst uses those objective benchmarks to get at his or her version of truth and accuracy.

Assuming that Toyota Industries' going concern operations are valued at 6 to 7 times operating income, the assets dedicated to these operations, after deducting all non-convertible funded debt, constitute between 8% and 12% of Toyota Industries' assets. 60% to 63% of assets are in Toyota Industries' holdings of Toyota Motor Common Stock valued at market, and 28% to 29% of assets are in the market value of common stocks of other companies, most of which, like Toyota Industries, are also affiliates of Toyota Motor. In reporting earnings in accordance with GAAP, Toyota Industries includes in its earnings only dividends received from portfolio companies. Looked at this way, Toyota Industries Common is selling at around 21 times latest 12-month earnings. However, if Toyota Industries' income account is adjusted to pick up, as additional earnings, the Company's equity in the undistributed earnings (i.e., earnings not paid out as dividends) of Toyota Motor and the other portfolio companies, then Toyota Industries Common is selling at only 8.5 times latest 12-month earnings. Which is the more realistic reflection of Toyota Industries' performance — as reported under GAAP, or as adjusted to reflect the equity in the retained earnings of business affiliates? I would think that the adjusted earnings figure probably is more realistic, but this is far from certain. Were I the CEO or CFO of Toyota Industries and was I asked to swear that the earnings as reported were true and accurate, I might decline to sign. However, it is doubtful that including the equity in the undistributed earnings of affiliates is 100% accurate either. Toyota Industries has no control over the uses to which these undistributed earnings might be put. Here, truth lies in the analyst's interpretation of results, not in GAAP reports. Under GAAP, the presumption is that the undistributed earnings of affiliates would be included in earnings if Toyota Industries owned 20% or more of the outstanding common stock of the affiliate. 20% is a relatively rigid rule, which does not necessarily describe economic reality. The Third Avenue analyst, though, really does not have to make a decision about which of the two ways to report earnings is really proper. He or she need only decide at which price, if any, the analyst would recommend buying Toyota Industries Common. In fact, at TAVF we give much more weight to the fact that Toyota Industries Common sells at a 35%-40% discount from NAV than to the price to earnings ratios for Toyota Industries Common.

Whether debt obligations ought to be viewed as valued at the amount of claim, or at market prices, depends on who is doing the analysis and for what purposes. Regardless of the amount at which the debt obligation is carried on the company's balance sheet for GAAP purposes, if the company lacks the financial wherewithal to acquire debt obligations at discounts from the creditors' claims, then from the points of view of the corporation itself and its common stockholders, the debt ought to be valued at the amount of claim, i.e., principal amount plus accrued interest. In bankruptcy, there exists a "rule of absolute priority." Senior debt has to be paid in full under the rule before the corporation can give any value to junior securities, including the common stocks owned by OPMIs. On the other hand, from the point of view of a distressed bond buyer seeking to reorganize the company, the market price of the debt obligation (particularly as a percentage of claim) becomes the key number. However, what the key number really is has to be decided by the analyst, not the accountant preparing the numbers in accordance with GAAP. GAAP will follow a set of rigid rules about recording debt. The Third Avenue analyst will determine economic reality for his or her purposes.

How Most Conventional Analysts Seem to Use Accounting Disclosures

The conventional analyst's objectives seem to revolve around estimating what the market price for securities trading in an OPMI market will likely be in the weeks, months or years ahead. Put in conventional language, what is the target price?

Managements are appraised solely as operators of strict going concerns. Thus, one number becomes all-important whether it is reported, recurring earnings from operations, cash flow from operations, revenues, or Earnings Per Share (EPS) from normal recurring operations. Thus, there exists a primacy of the income account. Balance sheet considerations — both quantitative and qualitative — are denigrated.

One size tends to fit all. There tends to be one "magic" number which is the key to analyzing any company, whether that "magic" number is Discounted Cash Flow (DCF), EPS or Earnings Before Interest, Taxes, Depreciation and Amortization (EBITDA).

GAAP ought to reflect economic reality, i.e., give a true and accurate account of operating results for a period. What the numbers are becomes more important than what the numbers mean. Thus it becomes highly important that the value of options be reflected in reported net income, even if the details are contained in the footnotes.

This approach, combining a primacy of the income account plus reliance on numbers as reported without adjustment, seems the most appropriate approach insofar as the objective of an analysis is to predict what might happen to common stock prices in OPMI markets over the near term. Market players, most of the time, are focused on income numbers, not balance sheet numbers. Immediate market prices tend to react to earnings numbers as reported.

For the economy as a whole though, I think this current emphasis on reporting operating earnings accurately and truthfully is dangerous. First, there is no way reported numbers are going to really be truthful and accurate in all contexts no matter how many Chief Executive Officers and Chief Financial Officers so attest as they were required to do from August 14, 2002 forward. Setting the standards under which executives have to attest to the truth and accuracy of financial statements seems certain to give the Plaintiffs' Bar license to pursue frivolous lawsuits. Society is better served when the Plaintiffs' Bar is instead incentivized to take action against meaningful wrongdoing by corporate insiders, as for example the alleged stealing by the controlling shareholders of Adelphia Communications.

GAAP cannot be made to reflect economic reality. GAAP can only provide objective benchmarks. To try to get GAAP to be more than that results in making GAAP so complex that its usefulness for people trained to use it becomes impaired. The Internal Revenue Code has to be very complicated because it is designed not to reflect reality, but to determine one number, the taxpayer's tax bill. GAAP ought to be designed to give trained users objective benchmarks. This doesn't seem unduly complicated.

As I've stated in past letters, GAAP can be most useful insofar as it provides disclosure against the following background:

1. The Company should be viewed as a stand-alone, separate and apart from its common stockholders and management. In other

words, it does not make a lot of sense to have what is a stockholder expense, stock options, reflected as a company expense.

2. The underlying assumption ought to be that the user of the financial statements will be a reasonably intelligent person who understands what the complete accounting cycle is.

3. GAAP financial statements ought to, first and foremost, fill the needs and desires of creditors, not shortrun stock market speculators.

A Plauge Upon Almost All Their Houses

The shareholders of TAVF are Fund management's constituency. Therefore, it is important that Fund management look at things primarily from the point of view of that constituency — broadly speaking, OPMIs — while remaining cognizant of the points of view of other constituencies within the financial community.

It is apparent, to me at least, that there has been an inexorable trend in the last 10 or 15 years toward having OPMIs in particular, and corporations in general, increasingly ripped off not only by corporate managements but also by the Plaintiffs' Bar, by Bankruptcy Attorneys, by Defense Attorneys and by Investment Bankers. (Please note that public accountants are specifically excluded from this list of underperformers and overreachers.) Ameliorating the rip off problem probably will require various reforms that go well beyond the recently enacted Sarbanes-Oxley Act of 2002. Sarbanes-Oxley is a good start. However, many of the most desirable reforms will be fiercely resisted by politically powerful constituencies, e.g., corporate executives. Many of these desirable reforms could result in adverse, unintended consequences, e.g., strengthening the Plaintiffs' Bar.

There seems to be an inherent conflict between Plaintiffs' lawyers, bankruptcy attorneys and investment bankers, on the one hand, and the clients these professionals are supposed to represent, on the other hand. Put bluntly, which comes first for these professionals, their fees or their clients' best interests? My observation is that many bankruptcy lawyers and many investment bankers not only tend to be hugely overcompensated, but also tend to prolong Chapter 11 cases unnecessarily in order to milk the estate for fees. For many plaintiffs' attorneys prosecuting securities class or derivative actions, most of which are settled out-of-court, it is fees first and fuller restitution to clients a distant second.

As far as the Bankruptcy Code is concerned, OPMIs would be well served if payments to professionals were returned to what existed before the passage of the Bankruptcy Reform Act of 1978. Pre the 1978 Act, lawyers and investment bankers were paid generally only at the end of a case, and only if they demonstrated to the court that they had made a "substantial contribution." Nowadays, it is pay-as-you-bill for the professionals, plus "success" fees. A principal reason for the 1978 change was the belief that highly qualified professionals would not take cases if they had to work for contingent fees. What utter nonsense. For better or worse, it is hard to find more competent professionals than plaintiffs' attorneys. All of them work for contingent fees.

Like it or not, the principal cop enforcing laws against corporate fraud and management excesses will continue to be the Plaintiffs' Bar. It won't be the Securities and Exchange Commission (SEC), State Attorneys General, or State "Blue Sky" Commissions. Sarbanes-Oxley gave minor breaks to attorneys suing on behalf of OPMIs. But resistance to expanding the powers available to the Plaintiffs' Bar probably will continue to be highly effective. For example, the New York Stock Exchange (NYSE) on June 6, 2002 put out a booklet under the auspices of the NYSE's "Corporate Accountability and Listing Standards Committee" on recommendations to enhance corporate governance for the benefit of OPMIs. There the Committee states, "we wish to explicitly note — that we have rejected and that we strongly urge policy makers to avoid — repealing or weakening the Private Securities Litigation Reform Act." There is, in my view, a good degree of merit to the Committee's position but it ill becomes a group claiming to be working in the best interests of OPMIs to go out of its way to propose what is, in effect, protection for corporate insiders against OPMI lawsuits. It should be noted that there are considerable counter pressures, or trade-offs, so that the things done to protect OPMIs from overreaching by corporate insiders will continue to be limited, Sarbanes-Oxley and pronouncements by the Bush Administration notwithstanding. The underlying problem is that every financial and legal practice is not only subject to abuse, but will be abused.

Stockholder lawsuits tend to result in abuse and seem to cause much waste. But look at the alternative. OPMIs are mostly raped in other western countries such as Germany and England where the minority stockholders lack access to the courts. See the terrific article on the front page of the August 16th issue of *The Wall Street Journal* entitled, "Toothless Watchdogs — Outside the U.S., Executives Face Little Legal Peril."

I have very mixed feelings about contingency fee lawyers. From an OPMI point of view, those taking securities cases seem to do more good than harm, especially when one looks at the alternative, the so called "English System" where OPMIs are effectively denied access to judicial redress. Those contingency fee lawyers going after tobacco companies are my absolute heroes. My father, a heavy smoker, died of lung cancer at age 62. I hate contingent fee lawyers trying asbestos cases. They are a clear and present danger to Corporate America all the while the vast majority of their clients show no symptoms of any disease. Admittedly, TAVF is among the largest creditors of USG Corporation, an asbestos-tainted issuer.

In terms of corporate governance, management entrenchment, which has grown like wildfire in the past 20 years, is one area where there ought to be reforms. No one, but no one, is making any proposals that would make it easier for managements to be removed from office by stockholders. Instead, stockholder rights in this regard have been abdicated to Boards of Directors, almost all of who seem to be compliant management tools. Given that OPMI stock market prices change so capriciously, society is probably best served if a modicum of entrenchment in office exists. But as things exist now, whether for solvent companies or most issuers in Chapter 11, managements are either bullet-proofed in office, or are extremely well rewarded with severance parachutes if they leave office. In my view, OPMIs and society would be well served if the NYSE and NASD refused to list the common stocks of companies with overbearing provisions for management entrenchment. These provisions include "poison pills," blank check preferreds, super voting common stocks, staggered elections for Boards of Directors, super majority voting provisions, preventing stockholders from convening special meetings, and having the company itself finance all of management's expenditures where there is a contest for control. Relief, if any, on this score would have to come from Self-Regulatory Organizations (SROs), the NYSE and NASD. Not much seems possible at the state level. The SEC has no jurisdiction over corporate governance. But don't hold your breath waiting for reforms in the area of management entrenchment.

The problem of corporate governance, it ought to be noted though, is not a TAVF problem. Most of the managements of most of the companies in which TAVF has invested seem to be doing a magnificent job for which they are either fairly, or modestly, compensated. Only a few companies represented in the portfolio seem to be run by managements which are overcompensated, underperformers, do really stupid things from the stockholder point of view, or pay no more than minimal attention to the needs and desires of OPMIs. Portfolio companies on this negative list, in my opinion, include Aquila, Electroglas, Head Insurance, ICSL, Kmart, MONY Group and Toyota Industries. None of the managements seem so bad though that the Fund should be exiting its positions wholesale at these prices. The toughest thing we do at TAVF is appraising managements. Sometimes we are wrong.

Despite all my carping about how OPMIs in this country are being increasingly ripped off by managements and professionals, the U.S. public and private markets still remain the fairest, best, most efficient, capital markets that have ever existed. This is especially true for the private placement credit markets where the quality of analysis tends to be much, much better than it is for public equity markets. Third Avenue ought to continue to be able to invest reasonably comfortably going forward, the growing amount of rip-offs of OPMIs notwithstanding.

Along these lines, the eminent economist, Lester Thurow, had an Op-Ed piece in *The New York Times* during the quarter. The title of the Op-Ed article said it all — "Government Can't Make The Market Fair." I agree. The solution to this problem for OPMIs is to buy in at prices far, far lower than is usually available in negotiated transactions or in purchasing control. Buying in at such prices is exactly what TAVF tries to do.

CHAPTER 31

Proposed Elimination of Double Taxation on Corporate Dividends

JANUARY 2003

The central focuses of Third Avenue Value Fund (TAVF) in making investment decisions revolve around understanding the characteristics of securities and how corporations function: why they do what they do. This entails a concentration on corporate finance, strictly from the bottom up.

In contrast, economists such as R. Glenn Hubbard, Chairman of the Council of Economic Advisers and the principal proponent of dividend tax relief, and Alan Greenspan, Chairman of the Federal Reserve Board, are essentially top-down economists. Their concentrations are on factors such as the general economy, the behavior of markets, and the general level of prices.

It seems to me that a lack of concentration on bottom-up corporate fundamentals, and probably a lack of training in corporate finance, can lead Professor Hubbard and others like him to recommend courses of action that can be quite harmful to the country (even when the proposals might result in net benefits to the stockholders of the Third Avenue portfolio companies over the long term).

One such proposed action is President Bush's proposal to amend the Internal Revenue Code so that corporate dividends derived from corporate earnings on which taxes have been paid by the corporation would be non-taxable to the recipient shareholder-taxpayer. Further, a shareholder would increase his cost basis for common stock held insofar as a corporation retains earnings on which corporate taxes have been paid.

Three results seem sure to follow if the Bush proposal is ever adopted:

1. Businesses will not receive any material incentives to increase their investments in productive assets.
2. Governments, both Federal and State, will be deprived of much needed revenues.
3. The Internal Revenue Code will become materially more complicated than it already is at a time when strong arguments ought to be made for tax code simplification.

Third Avenue analyzes any company as a stand-alone, not substantively consolidated with its shareholders. This idea of the company as a stand-alone used to be, but no longer is, a "pervasive principle" governing Generally Accepted Accounting Principles (GAAP). The stand-alone concept, however, pervades almost all credit analysis. If each entity filing a tax return is viewed as substantively consolidated with another taxpaying entity, then every taxpayer is subject to double taxation, triple taxation, quadruple taxation, or n times taxation. This "extra" taxation phenomenon is hardly limited to shareholder recipients of certain corporate dividends. A wage earner, for example, pays income tax on the earnings received. This after-tax income is again subject to sales taxes, real estate property taxes, state income taxes, and city personal property taxes. Indeed, if the wage earner purchases an automobile, the price paid by the wage earner-taxpayer includes the cost of taxes paid by the automobile dealer, the automobile transporter and the automobile manufacturer.

Insofar as one desires a fair tax system, each taxpayer ought to be viewed as a stand-alone, filing his, her, its, or a joint return. The tax rate applicable to that taxpayer ought to reflect the appropriate rates relevant to that taxpayer's circumstances. There seems to be no way in the U.S. economy that double, triple or quadruple taxation can ever be eliminated. There does not appear to be any reasonable basis for picking out corporate dividends for such tax-exempt largesse.

Corporations that generate cash, or taxable earnings, can use the amounts so generated in only three ways:

1. Expand the asset base.
2. Pay creditors.
3. Make distributions to shareholders either via dividend payments or repurchasing shares.

With one exception, and I believe the exception is a minor one, making cash distributions to shareholders has to be a residual use of cash. Meeting the needs of the business to maintain or increase the asset base and servicing creditors has to take priority over paying out cash to shareholders. The one exception to this exists insofar as making distributions to shareholders might give the company better access to capital markets, especially equity markets, than would otherwise be the case.

The vast majority of equity financing for American industry is done by having companies retain earnings, not by marketing add-on issues of common and preferred stocks, either publicly or privately. We examined the changes in Net Worth Statements for each of the 30 companies whose common stocks made up the Dow Jones Industrial Average for 2000 and 2001. Except for the exercise of stock options, in each case the increases in net worth were attributable to increases in retained earnings, i.e., net income minus cash distributed to shareholders via dividends and share repurchases. The sale of add-on issues of common stocks was a non-factor.

The best way, and frequently the only practical way, for a company to reduce its debt load is to increase net worth through retaining earnings at a time increases in assets are minimal. Cash payments to shareholders reduce net worth. It is common, indeed, for loan indentures and bank loan agreements to contain provisions forbidding, or restricting, cash payment to shareholders.

The principal reason companies do equity financing by retaining earnings is that public markets are so capricious; and it tends to be difficult to market equity privately if the purchasers of such equity do not receive elements of control over the corporation. Sound managements would not be very sound if they managed as if they could control the timing of the sale of add-on issues of common stock publicly and if they managed in the belief that they could predict future stock market prices. Selling add-on issues of common stock is a very dicey game for most managements whose companies are not benefiting from the presence of speculative bubbles such as existed in 1998 and 1999. Selling add-on issues of common stock is also quite expensive for most companies and/or their shareholders. Access to capital markets tends to be a lot more rational for credit markets than it is for equity markets, even though there can be times when credit markets are completely closed as, for example, when commercial banks won't lend.

The exception I refer to above is what I call the "electric utility exception." This exception, while still present, seems to have become less the rule even for electric utilities. Integrated electric utilities were an extremely capital intensive industry (before the 1990's growth of Independent Power Producers), where a company had to incur capital expenditures of $5 to $7 to produce $1 of annual revenue. Operating income was relatively stable and predictable, tending to grow modestly year-by-year. And the industry was a real growth industry with demand increasing in each year after World War II at rates of 2% to 7% per annum. Against this background, companies followed a policy of paying 70% to 80% of earnings as dividends; and then marketed add-on issues of common stock every 18 months to 2 years. The high dividends attracted investors interested in income and tended to assure companies that they would be able to market add-on issues of common stock at prices above book value. Marketing add-on issues above book value with regularity made it possible for the companies to report modestly increasing earnings per share year by year. This electric utility exception seems to be becoming rarer and rarer. It never was a good example of how most companies in American industry ever financed. It certainly is not a base case today, but rather a relatively rare exception.

Bush Administration officials estimate that the proposed dividend tax relief will boost common stock prices by 5%-10%. But the Bush Administration is, I suspect, just like the rest of us, or at least like me. I really don't have a clue as to what will happen to general stock market prices. Neither, in my opinion, does anyone else. Market levels will, of course, be determined by myriad factors, a goodly portion of which cannot be foreseen.

There seems little reason to believe that dividend tax relief will give companies better access to capital markets than would otherwise be the case. The relief will have no particular effect on credit markets, other than to discourage lenders from lending if they think that the cash amounts being paid to shareholders is imprudent. The only sure effect it will have on other markets is that there ought to be a switch in mezzanine finance structures. Increasing amounts of Preferred Stocks ought to be marketed and there ought to be a material diminution in the amount of Subordinated Debentures marketed.

Insofar as dividend tax relief results in a revenue shortfall for governments, government deficits will increase. Budget deficits, whether for governments or corporations, mean that cash outflows exceed cash inflows. The shortfall is met by accessing capital markets; governments issue government debt while corporations issue claims and securities, including bank loans and common stocks. There is nothing wrong per se with budget deficits viewed in vacuo. Rather, it is the use of proceeds that counts the most. For example, the U.S. Government incurred deficits in the 1940's and 1950's to finance the GI Bill of Rights. A long-term consequence of the GI Bill is that the country ended up with a well-educated populace and a university system that is the envy of the rest of the world. On the other hand, if the deficits are used to finance losses and non-productive activities, the entity incurring the deficits, even the U.S. Government, will, sooner or later, suffer from diminished credit worthiness. I'll leave it to each TAVF shareholder to decide for himself, or herself, whether the use of proceeds arising out of the expected 2003 government deficits will, on balance, be productive or non-productive.

One thing should be obvious though. There is no *a priori* reason to assume that expenditures by governments are less productive for society and the economy than expenditures by taxpayers are. Some are; some aren't. Government expenditures to keep open unnecessary military bases seem a lot less productive than expenditures by private citizens for good housing. Government expenditures for education or airline safety seem a lot more productive than expenditures by private citizens to own, lease, or operate giant SUVs; or to give annual compensations of tens of millions of dollars (and sometimes hundreds of millions of dollars) to well entrenched Chief Executive Officers of underperforming companies.

While final rules have yet to be promulgated, it seems likely that dividend tax relief, if enacted, will result in administrative and enforcement nightmares for the Internal Revenue Service. Every deal person in the U.S. is probably salivating over the resource conversion possibilities inherent in allowing corporations down the road to become involved in things like cash out mergers and management buyouts where a substantial portion of the cash to be paid out would be tax-free to many recipients. For companies managed by their principal owners, there may well be dramatic shifts in whether payouts to owners are structured as compensation or as dividends.

With one exception, I would doubt that there would be any dramatic shifts in corporate capitalizations toward less debt and more equity because of dividend tax relief. For the vast majority of investors, TAVF included, credit worthiness is a far more important consideration than after-tax returns when investing for income. Few senior creditors seem likely to sacrifice safety for enhanced after-tax return. Credit instruments give holders a legally enforceable, contractual right to receive cash in the form of interest, principal and premium, if any. Equities do not give holders any legally enforceable contract rights to receive cash payments except that cash payments cannot be made to common stocks unless required payments are first made to cumulative preferred stocks, or redemption prices when due are paid on redeemable preferred stocks. Banks, insurance companies and finance companies are just not going to switch their portfolios to equities (assuming regulators or rating agencies would permit them to do so). These institutions will continue to be credit quality conscious first and foremost, as will individual holders of investment grade, tax-free, municipal obligations.

The one major change in corporate capitalizations likely to result from the enactment of dividend tax relief is in the area of mezzanine finance, a relatively small component of most corporate balance sheets. Here, there is likely to be a massive switch away from Subordinated Debentures to Preferred Stocks. While holders of Subordinated Debentures do enjoy a legally enforceable contractual right to cash payments, as a practical matter, having that enforceable right usually is akin to having the right to commit suicide because a Subordinate's rights to cash payments virtually always are subrogated to the senior debts' rights to priority payments. The vast majority of Subordinates are not very creditworthy to begin with.

Even now, in a going concern context but not a reorganization context, Preferred Stocks tend to have a *de facto* seniority over Subordinates in many instances. In many cases, holders of Preferreds are better off accumulating dividend arrearages than are holders of Subordinates who will never succeed in exercising their legal rights to cash payments. Preferred Stocks, as a class, would certainly become structurally senior to Subordinates insofar as Preferreds acquired elements of control, e.g., if the Preferreds became entitled to elect a majority of the Board of Directors if four quarterly dividends were passed. To my knowledge, with the exception of closed-end investment companies registered under the Investment Company Act of 1940, as amended, there are no publicly-traded Preferreds which have anywhere near such strong covenants. If dividend tax relief is enacted, smart financiers are likely to try to structure Preferreds where the "dividends" are entitled to an interest deduction at the corporate level but which pay to the security holder a tax exempt dividend. There would be attempts to make these instruments as creditworthy, in form or substance, as a senior loan, or even a secured loan. Perhaps combined tax bills of corporations and their preferred shareholders will be minimized via the issuance of exchangeable securities. Doing these things will, of course, further complicate the Rules and Regulations that are part and parcel of the Internal Revenue Code in that the Internal Revenue Service might have to do something about Senior Loans, masquerading in effect, as Preferred Stocks strictly for tax-shelter purposes.

It seems possible that an attractive business might develop for financial insurers willing to enhance the creditworthiness of Preferred Stocks. If so, the premium charged by the insurers ought to be a lot higher than when insurers credit enhance Senior Loans because the losses seem likely to be manifestly larger in the case of Preferred Stocks. If such a market ever develops, four companies whose equities Third Avenue owns — Ambac, American Capital Access, MBIA, and Radian — ought to benefit.

If a company is viewed as a stand-alone, issuing add-on issues of common stock on which no cash dividend is paid, either in public offerings or mergers, has, for the company, a zero cost of capital. There is, of course, a cost of capital in this instance but the cost belongs to the shareholders, not the company. In that case, shareholders have to either put up new money or see their percentage ownership reduced. Where the company is committed to paying a common stock dividend, the cost of capital for the company when add-on shares are issued is the present value of the future dividend requirements. It is nonsensical to say that making dividends tax-free will reduce the cost of capital for a company. For that minority of companies who finance the way electric utility companies used to finance, there very well could be a reduction in the net cost of equity capital for the company. However, this seems unlikely to hold true for the vast majority of companies.

Individual companies, no doubt, will continue to follow disparate policies in the future just as they have in the past. For example, IBM seems to have been very successful during most of the 1990's in following the policy of borrowing heavily, i.e., incurring deficits, and using the proceeds to buy-in its own common stock.

If enacted, the dividend tax relief proposal probably will be quite helpful for Third Avenue over the long term. Companies with dividend-paying ability might be worth a premium. First and foremost, companies with dividend paying ability are those with strong financial positions, i.e., cash on the asset side and enjoying substantial "surplus-surplus" (a relative absence of liabilities) on the obligation side. These are the types of common stocks in which the Fund invests. Further, the largest potential beneficiaries from dividend tax relief might be those who own common stocks selling at a discount from, or a small premium over, the amount of tax paid earnings retained after year 2000. It seems as if a major portion of book value for most companies consists of tax paid retained earnings. The TAVF portfolio is currently priced at around 1 times book value while the Standard & Poor's Industrial Index is priced at around 4.6 times book value. The Fund may not realize on this proximity to book value advantage for several years. Third Avenue, however, remains with the advantage that its portfolio companies' strong financial positions result in businesses with much above average dividend paying ability.

Regardless of whether or not dividend tax relief is enacted, I remain convinced that the TAVF portfolio is an attractive one.

CHAPTER 32

Reforming Generally Accepted Accounting Principles

JULY 2004

A radical change in thinking seems needed if GAAP are to be made more sensible, and even more useful as an analytical tool. Given its present direction, GAAP increasingly impose unneeded and counter-productive burdens on American corporations, American management and American capital markets. GAAP, first and foremost, ought to be geared toward meeting the needs and desires of creditors rather than the needs and desires of short run stock market speculators, who are vitally interested in day-to-day stock market price fluctuations. Currently, GAAP are directed increasingly toward meeting the needs and desires of short run stock market speculators. This is accomplished by setting up increasingly rigid sets of rules designed to meet an impossible goal: have periodic statements of cash flows from operations, earnings and earnings per share be as accurate (or truthful) as possible.

If GAAP were geared to the needs of creditors, there would be a tremendous change in emphasis away from focusing on reported earnings per share. GAAP would, in a sense, go back to the standards in existence prior to the 1970's:

1. The company whose financial statements are being audited would be viewed as a stand-alone, an entity separate and apart from its stockholders and its management.

2. GAAP would be governed by the modifying convention of conservatism rather than be a system striving for accuracy and for truth.
3. There would be no Primacy of the Income Account. Balance sheets would be equally important and there would be general recognition that each accounting number is derived from, modified by, and a function of, all other accounting numbers.
4. Financial statements would be prepared under the assumption that the users of such financial statements are reasonably intelligent, reasonably diligent, and are people who understand not only the uses, but also the limitations, of GAAP.
5. Comporting with underlying principles would become far more important than specific GAAP rules.
6. The analyst, i.e., the user of GAAP, would understand that the most GAAP can give him, or her, are objective benchmarks which the analyst then uses as a tool to determine his, or her, version of economic truth and economic reality. Only very rarely (e.g., the pricing of marketable securities by mutual funds) does GAAP reflect an economic truth or economic reality.
7. It is extremely important in GAAP that material facts be disclosed in a conservative, consistent and reconcilable manner. How, and where, such material disclosures are made would become, by and large, unimportant.

Third Avenue has always analyzed equities from this creditor point of view. The underlying criteria for a common stock investment has been, and is, that the issue, after thorough analysis, appears to be "safe and cheap." Safe for the Fund comes before cheap; in other words, safe has a first priority. Safe means that the company, in which TAVF is a long-term equity investor, is unlikely to suffer a permanent impairment in underlying value, while its common stock is held by the Fund. This approach to equity investing is similar to how creditors analyze credit investments. Creditors seek to determine whether a performing loan will remain a performing loan over the lifetime of the loan.

One good argument against the Fund's approach is that many companies which need access to capital markets, especially equity markets, have to strive to maximize the trend of earnings per share as reported, or current earnings per share as reported, and to some extent also emphasize dividends. This, however, seems to have little, or nothing, to do with the TAVF portfolio. The Fund tries to restrict its common stock investments to companies with super strong financial positions who either do not have to access capital markets, or else pretty much control the timing of when they will access capital markets over, say, a five-year period.

The Company as a Stand-Alone — Full Disclosure vs. Where Disclosed

The current controversy over stock options, i.e., whether options ought to be expensed using the "fair value method" — FASB 123; or whether options ought to be expensed using the "intrinsic value method" — APB 25, sheds much light on the bad direction in which GAAP seem to be headed.

First, stock options are a stockholder problem, not a company problem. Stock options cause dilution of the existing ownership. Viewing the company as a stand-alone, the cost to the company of issuing stock options equals the present value of the net cash drain from future cash payments to the common stock to be issued on the exercise of options; and also the present value of the probabilities that the company might have less access to capital markets because of the stock options. Both of these "costs" seem difficult to measure.

From a creditor's point of view there can be, and there usually is, a world of difference in the credit-worthiness of an issuer, if the issuer on the one hand, pays out, say, $200 million per annum in cash for executive compensation, or, on the other hand, issues stock options on a non-dividend-paying common stock with a "fair value" of $200 million.

As to that "fair value" of $200 million for stock options, it is a pretty ludicrous number if the company is viewed as a stand-alone. There seems no rationale whatsoever for equating the value of a non-cash benefit to a recipient (i.e., a corporate executive receiving a stock option) to the real cost to the company to bestow that benefit. It seems doubtful that the real cost to the company for issuing the stock option benefit is measurable, while the value of the benefit to the recipient of the benefit does seem measurable by "fair value" techniques. Why saddle the company with such a fictitious cost from a company perspective where the company is a stand-alone?

Fitch Ratings published an interesting article on April 20, 2004 in which it recognized that stock options were basically a stockholder problem, not a creditor problem; but then went on to state, "Because of their dilutive effect, many companies have a high propensity to repurchase shares issued upon exercise of employee stock options. In this context, from a bondholder perspective, employee options have a true cash cost and can be thought of as a form of deferred compensation, which has the effect of reducing available cash to service debt and increasing leverage."

Fitch Ratings seems to be involved in overkill. First, most companies issuing stock options probably don't have stock repurchase programs. Second, any company making cash distributions to shareholders for any reason — whether such cash distributions are in the form of dividends or share repurchases — "has the effect of reducing available cash to service debt and increasing leverage." Indeed, from a creditor point of view, cash distributions to shareholders are helpful only insofar as they enhance the debtor's access to capital markets. Third, share repurchases are strictly voluntary and thus do not have as adverse a credit impact as does required cash payments to creditors for interest, principal, or premium. Finally, some share repurchases can be beneficial to creditors and companies if the common stock being repurchased pays an ultra-high cash dividend.

The FASB 123 vs. APB 25 dispute is strictly about form over substance. Companies using APB 25, the "intrinsic value method," are required under GAAP in financial statement footnotes to disclose the far greater expense of "the fair value method" as contained in FASB 123. The whole dispute revolves around whether disclosure of an ephemeral "expense" ought to be made in the income account or in the footnotes to the financial statements. The question for the serious investor who is not a short run stock market speculator is, "Who cares?" except that in an overall appraisal of management by a trained analyst, information about management attitudes can be gleaned from looking at management opting either for FASB 123 or APB 25.

The Modifying Convention of Conservatism

When I was in graduate school, I studied under a great economist, Oskar Morgenstern, who used to say, *"Everything is unpredictable, especially the future."* Given the uncertain nature of the world as described by Professor Morgenstern, and given that the maximum creditors can expect out of investments is that performing loans will remain performing loans through maturity, it is wise that creditors would want to view GAAP through the prism of the modifying convention of conservatism. The modifying convention means that there will be a plethora of choices under GAAP. Those choices which are chosen ought to be those that, other things being equal, understate profitability and understate asset values as computed in accordance with GAAP. It is the analyst's job to adjust those understated, objective GAAP figures to the analyst's version of economic reality.

Admittedly, it is sometimes hard to state what is conservative and what is not. The most glaring cases probably occur where the analyst has to decide on whether the company ought to be analyzed as a "going concern" or an "investment vehicle." Two examples should suffice to demonstrate the point.

Many financial institutions – insurance companies and pension plans — have their assets invested mostly, or almost exclusively, in fixed income, interest-bearing loans and bonds. However, the liabilities making up the right hand side of the balance sheet are not interest rate sensitive. For a property and casualty insurance company, those liabilities are reserves for losses, while for pension plans and life companies, those liabilities are estimates of the amount and timing of future payments to be made to beneficiaries.

Suppose interest rates increase sharply. Viewing these institutions as investment vehicles, the market value of their fixed income assets will decline, reducing Net Asset Value (NAV). However, viewing these institutions as going concerns, future profitability will be greater than would otherwise be the case as the entities reinvest maturing credits at higher interest rates and as newly inflowing funds are invested at these higher interest rates. TAVF has a large portfolio of insurance stocks.

Net, net, I think the odds are that the going concern benefits from higher interest rates will outweigh the investment vehicle negatives associated with higher interest rates for these insurance companies.

Accounting classifications under GAAP are rigid and never can be wholly realistic because of the going concern-investment vehicle dichotomy. Two of our largest portfolio positions — Kmart Holding Common Stock and Forest City Enterprises Common Stock — bring home the dichotomy.

At April 28, 2004, Kmart carried as a current asset $3.4 billion of merchandise inventory. Viewed as an investment vehicle, that merchandise inventory was indeed a current asset, something that, item by item, would be converted to cash over the next twelve months. Viewed as a going concern, however, that merchandise inventory is indeed a fixed asset, something that, in the aggregate, has to stay in existence, or even be enlarged, if Kmart is to continue as an ongoing operation.

At April 30, 2004, Forest City Enterprises carried as a fixed asset (PP&E) a figure of $5.2 billion for real estate, net. Viewed as an investment vehicle, most of those real estate assets — office buildings and multi-use complexes rented on long-term leases to high quality tenants — were, indeed current assets, readily saleable (or refinanceable), building by building, without interfering at all with Forest City as an ongoing operation. Viewed as a going concern, these long-term assets are the major source of Forest City's operating cash flow and net income.

Whether Kmart's merchandise inventories ought to be reclassified as a fixed asset, and whether Forest City's PP&E ought to be reclassified as a current asset, is something for the analyst to decide. The GAAP classification seems all right to me. But then again, I only expect it to provide objective benchmarks, not reflect economic reality.

Another dichotomy which results in GAAP giving users objective benchmarks rather than realistic numbers is the split between making important the cash experience on the one hand and making important the wealth creation experience on the other. Accrual accounting gives the user tools to use in estimating future wealth creation. For example, the Fund is invested in the common stock of Encana Corporation, a company that has been a huge cash consumer as it discovers, develops, and acquires natural gas reserves in North America. The GAAP emphasis here is on Encana's wealth creation experience, not its cash creation experience. The same can be said for TAVF's investments in the common stocks of Tejon Ranch and The St. Joe Co., two wealth creators which consume cash. Cash accounting, on the other hand, shows flow results and short changes the wealth creation experience. In the case of investment builders where the Fund owns common stocks, say, Brascan, Catellus and Forest City, it is pretty easy to ascertain cash flow from operations, but difficult, using GAAP, to ascertain the periodic wealth creation which is occurring and is such an important component in the appraisal of these securities.

CIT Corporation (CIT), a going concern with a perpetual life, is an example of a company involved in creating wealth on a permanent basis rather than being a business creating cash flows from operations on a periodic basis. As CIT prospers, funds generated, coupled with increased borrowings and increased net worth, are used to increase CIT's principal earnings asset — receivables; and are not used primarily either to increase CIT's cash holdings or to increase cash distributions to shareholders. As the amount of creditworthy receivables expand, and net worth expands, CIT creates wealth by consuming cash (i.e., converting cash to more and more receivables). It should be noted, though, that for CIT to prosper, its existing receivables portfolio, receivable by receivable, has to be cash flow positive after accounting for the cost of money, i.e., the receivables portfolio has to have a Net Present Value (NPV) greater than unity. That CIT's existing fixed-in-size asset base is cash flow positive can be viewed as a form of "project finance" where the analysis takes place individual asset by individual asset. That CIT is continually consuming cash as it expands its receivables base can be viewed as "corporate finance" where the analysis recognizes that the enterprise's modus operandi is to grow by consuming cash, which cash is invested in earnings assets and which cash is generated in part by having CIT access the capital markets, especially credit markets, periodically.

Primacy of the Income Account Exists Only for Short Run Stock Market Speculators

A majority of the Fund's equity investments are in the common stocks of companies that are extremely well capitalized and which have been acquired at prices that represent meaningful discounts from readily ascertainable NAVs. Obviously, for TAVF there is no Primacy of the Income Account.

Less obvious is the observation that the Fund's investment style is a lot more mainstream than is that of the short run stock market speculators who emphasize the importance of periodic earnings per share as reported. First, TAVF tends to analyze the way creditors analyze, and of course, the amount of money invested in credit instruments of all types in our economy dwarfs the amount of funds invested in equities. Second, most people involved with investments are net worth conscious in the management of their own affairs rather than net income conscious. Their approach is "what is my portfolio worth and what is my total return," rather than "what can I expect in the way of dividends and interest." Most private companies, given a choice, seek to enhance NAV by means other than having reported operating income, which is taxable at maximum rates.

For many companies, there is no choice but to create wealth, i.e., NAV, by having operating income: NAV and operating income are each intimately related to each other. Nonetheless, this relationship hardly justifies a view that there exists a primacy of the income account for anyone other than a short run stock market speculator who has a vital interest in what each day's closing price for a marketable security might be.

In fact, corporate and securities holders' wealth is created in four separate, but interrelated, ways. To emphasize any one, or two, of the four to the exclusion of the others is to misunderstand corporate finance. And the present trend of GAAP is to overemphasize two factors — cash flow from operations and reported earnings — with a consequent de-emphasis of other factors that are at least equally important. The four factors involved in corporate wealth creation are as follows:

1. Free cash flow from operations available for the common stock. This seems a relative rarity in the corporate world.
2. Earnings where earnings are defined as creating wealth while consuming cash. This is what most prosperous businesses seem to do. Earnings may be of limited, or no, value unless also combined with access to capital markets to finance cash shortfalls.
3. Asset redeployment and liability financing and refinancing. These activities include mergers and acquisitions, contests for control, diversification, the purchase and sale of businesses, the reorganization of troubled companies, liquidations, and spin-offs.
4. Access to capital markets on a super attractive basis. Probably more wealth has been created through this venue than any other, ranging from the ability of real estate entities to finance on a long-term, fixed, low interest rate, non-recourse basis to venture capitalists selling common stock into an IPO bubble.

On April 27, 2004, an interesting advertisement appeared in *The Wall Street Journal* put out by the Association for Investment Management and Research (AIMR). The advertisement to encourage the fair value method of expensing stock options illustrates some of what is wrong with mainstream security analysis. For example, the ad states, "Investors Want Earnings to Reflect Reality." In fact, investors really want full disclosure and objective benchmarks. Also the ad states, "Financial statements exist to help investors make informed investment decisions." That statement is just plain wrong from either a public policy point of view or a creditor's point of view. Financial statements exist to fulfill the needs and desires of many constituencies: managements, creditors, governments, customers, etc.

A number of academic texts seem off base also. For example, in *Financial Reporting and Analysis* by Revsine, Collins and Johnson 2nd edition, it is stated on page 12, "Investors who follow a fundamental analysis approach estimate the value of a security by assessing the amount, timing and uncertainty of future cash flows that will accrue to the company issuing the security." That statement is news to me and I've been a fundamental analyst for over 50 years. I do want to predict future cash flows and earnings, but also future wealth creation from whatever source. It is just plain wrong to state that current earnings and past earnings records are better tools for predicting future cash flows and earnings (not to mention future wealth creation in the form of realized or unrealized capital gains) than are the present assets in a business measured qualitatively and quantitatively. As a matter of fact, sensible, good predictors use all three: current earnings, past earnings and the current balance sheet.

Investor Protection and the Securities Law

The basic thrust of certain Federal Securities Laws — the Securities Act of 1933 and the Securities Exchange Act of 1934 — in the disclosure area was to provide full disclosures of all material facts to Outside Passive Minority Investors (OPMIs). How the OPMIs used that full disclosure information was up to them and there was the implicit conclusion that if the OPMI was not reasonably intelligent and reasonably diligent, the OPMI could and should suffer the consequences. As things developed, though, this became insufficient at least as far as GAAP are concerned. A theory grew up that not only should GAAP reflect reality without adjustment, but also the form of presentation became important. It was no longer good enough to disclose all material facts, but rather where the disclosures were made became highly important, by, say, requiring that an "expense" be charged to the income account rather than presenting the facts in footnotes (see the Stock Option Controversy). To me, this change in emphasis really does nothing to enhance Investor Protection.

In 1940, the U.S. enacted the Investment Advisors Act and the Investment Company Act. The Investment Company Act regulated mutual funds. For the first time, there was a statute providing substantive protections for OPMIs; they no longer had to be on their own, disclosure-wise, in using the full disclosure information provided. Rather, they could rely on professional advisers, the managers of investment companies.

Put simply, if an OPMI does not want to go to the trouble of being reasonably intelligent and reasonably diligent, the OPMI can hire well-qualified money managers who are closely regulated. In the mutual fund area, there seem to be a good-sized number of qualified managers over and above the managers of the several Third Avenue

Funds. Such managers include those managing funds at, among others, First Eagle, Gabelli, Longleaf, Mutual Shares, Royce and Tweedy Browne.

Principles, Not Rules

Given that in a creditor type approach, the investor seeks objective benchmarks rather than reality or truth, it becomes unimportant that there exist volumes and volumes of specific rules. Rather, GAAP should be governed by general principles – the Company is a Stand-alone; there exists a Modifying Convention of Conservatism; there exists a Balanced Approach where any accounting member can be important rather than a Primacy of the Income Account Approach; and where the object of financial statements is to provide the user full disclosure, consistency and reconcilability. Full disclosure for TAVF purposes seems to mean that the GAAP figures and footnotes be such so that the analyst can figure out what documents are material, and that GAAP statements provide the user a good road map to follow in seeking to do "due diligence." Due diligence seems to mean "reasonable care under the circumstances."

Interestingly, other types of accounting systems have to be governed by rules. The prime example of a complex system of rules is the United States Internal Revenue Code (IRC). Under the IRC, or any tax code, there has to be a precise definition of what taxable income is; and thus the system probably has to be relatively complicated, governed by myriad rules, because its objective is to derive just one number — what the taxpayer's tax bill will be. This is just not the case for GAAP, where it can never provide more than objective benchmarks to be used as tools of analysis by users.

The United States has the best, most efficient, most honest, and deepest capital markets that have ever existed in the history of mankind. We ought to guard this national asset carefully. In our haste to satisfy the perceived needs of OPMIs, the U.S. is denigrating the quality, and depth, of U.S. capital markets. Already, and because of the Sarbanes-Oxley abomination, no foreign issuer who does not need to raise capital in the U.S. will subject their companies, and their executives, to U.S. jurisdiction. Thus, Toyota Industries, one of our largest common stock holdings, is unlikely to ever issue American Depository Receipts (ADRs). That is the Fund's loss and the American capital market's loss.

No modern economy can function well unless its financial institutions — both private and governmental — follow sound lending practices. A plethora of bad loans in an economy always leads to economic depressions, or worse, as witness the 10-12 year business depression in Japan; the economic crisis in Texas during the 1980's as bad energy loans had to be worked out; the savings and loan crisis in the U.S. in the late 1980's and early 1990's; and problems in Russia and Indonesia, among others, in the late 1990's. It would seem impossible, at least in the corporate arena, to have an economy follow sound lending practices unless the lenders are able to rely on audited financial statements, or the equivalent thereof, which provide good objective benchmarks, modified by a conservative bias. Thus, reliable GAAP remain essential not only to creditors, but also to the well-functioning of the U.S. economy. Put simply, corporate creditors couldn't operate without GAAP to rely upon.

The vast majority of equity investment in the U.S. takes place through having corporations retain earnings rather than pay profits out to shareholders. Equity markets, by and large, are just too capricious, and expenses for corporate common stock offerings too great, for most corporate managements to rely much, if at all, on marketing equity issues on a reasonably regular basis in order to obtain needed or desired equity capital for companies. Having said that, it probably still remains true that the more diligent and intelligent, equity investors are as a group, the more efficiently the nation's resources will be channeled. I, for one, doubt very much that short run stock market speculators in their buy-sell-hold decisions do much to enhance the quality of the channeling of resources in the economy. To me, the standards used by creditors result in a more productive channeling of resources. This is yet another reason GAAP ought to be directed primarily toward meeting the needs and desires of creditors.

From the points of view of creditors and value analysts who seek objective benchmarks from GAAP rather than "the truth," GAAP, in particular, and disclosure, in general, have never before been as complete, as comprehensible, and as useful, as they are now. This currently favorable disclosure situation seems to have been part of an inexorable trend which I think dates back to the Securities Acts Amendments of 1964. Specifically, for Third Avenue, this means that I, as the manager, can be, and am, quite comfortable with the Fund's portfolio because the quantity and quality of disclosures now available are so good. This high quality situation could have been achieved just as well if GAAP had been directed toward filling the needs and desires of creditors rather than stock market speculators. Concentrating on the perceived needs and desires of stock market speculators, it seems to me, has placed unnecessary, and counter-productive, burdens on American corporations, American corporate management and American capital markets.

CHAPTER 33

So What Are Earnings, Anyway?

JULY 2006

Put bluntly, and in summary fashion, earnings are one of three things:

1. The flow numbers – whether cash or accrual – as reported under Generally Accepted Accounting Principles (GAAP). These earnings numbers, as reported, are by far the most important numbers for market participants who are, or believe they are, affected vitally by day-to-day, or short run, price fluctuations for individual securities. For these participants, GAAP are supposed to reflect economic reality. In contrast, as reported GAAP are relevant to Third Avenue Value Fund (TAVF) only as objective benchmarks. For example, book value computed in accordance with GAAP has no necessary equality with net asset value (NAV). NAV is Fund management's estimate of true net worth. However, GAAP book values frequently are objective benchmarks, enabling an analyst to more accurately estimate NAV.
2. The flow numbers – whether cash or accrual – as adjusted by the market participant to reflect that market participant's version of economic reality. For these participants, GAAP is an objective benchmark, not "truth" or "economic reality".
3. Wealth creation, or increases in NAV – whether those increases come from flows, realized appreciation, unrealized appreciation or combinations thereof.

The first definition of earnings is largely irrelevant for TAVF. The second and third definitions are what the Fund is involved with. However, the greatest weight and importance lies with the third definition of earnings, i.e., increasing the NAVs of the companies whose common stocks make up the bulk of the Third Avenue equity portfolio after adding back dividends paid during an interim.

Ernest Jones, in his three volume biography of Sigmund Freud, describes Freud's genius as an abhorrence of looking at other people as irrational or "off the wall". Rather Freud sought to understand the underlying reasons for why people acted the way they acted, and why they thought the way they did. Were Freud to be describing the 1998 to 2000 high tech bubble, he probably would have described it as "Rational Overexuberance" rather than "Irrational Exuberance". And so it is with the question of, "So what are earnings anyway?"

Earnings for TAVF purposes are something quite different from what earnings are deemed to be in conventional, plain vanilla, market analysis. Rather, both the Fund and the conventional analysts tend to be rational; they just approach the problem from different places. The fact is that in conventional security analysis, predicting market prices over the very near term is crucially important. In contrast, TAVF ignores near-term market prices for individual securities. Third Avenue tries to buy long-term value safely and cheaply; and allows market prices of individual securities in the portfolio to take care of themselves. The Fund strives to avoid investment risk on a long-term basis, i.e., something going wrong with the business or the securities issued by that business.

Unlike TAVF, many market participants are, in fact, affected vitally by day-to-day price fluctuations in markets for individual securities. For these people, it is important to predict near-term target prices. For them, therefore, there actually does exist a "Primacy of the Income Account" and a need for GAAP to tell them the truth. After all, it seems quite valid to conclude that market prices for most securities will be influenced more by earnings as reported under GAAP than by any other single factor. These market sensitive participants include margin buyers; people and institutions relatively uninformed about the securities and companies in which they are interested; participants holding junior securities – subordinates, preferreds, common stocks and options – in companies that are not well financed; and participants who have to strive to outperform benchmarks consistently (such as many research department analysts who want to keep their jobs and get promoted). There are also market participants involved with both near-term predictions and fundamental analysis — to wit, short sellers and risk arbitrageurs (risk arbitrage is defined as investing in situations where there are reasonably determinate workouts in reasonably determinate periods of time). "The fact is that in conventional security analysis, predicting market prices over the very near term is crucially important. In contrast, TAVF ignores near-term market prices for individual securities. Third Avenue tries to buy long-term value safely and cheaply; and allows market prices of individual securities in the portfolio to take care of themselves."

The basic problem is that this market-sensitive group seems to be the only group that is studied by academics. This group also seems to be the primary concern of securities regulators. However, this group seems to be a small factor in the overall economy, and may even be a minority on Wall Street. Most value investors, control investors, distress investors and venture capital promoters think, and act, more like TAVF than like market participants affected vitally by near-term securities price fluctuations. Like TAVF, most sophisticated market participants look at market prices not as something you predict, but rather something of which you take advantage.

Stealing from Sigmund Freud, it is not that some financial participants are irrational and others are rational. Rather, almost all participants tend toward rationality. It is just that what is rational for those affected by immediate market price impacts, tend to be irrational from the point of view of those involved with long-term fundamentals. Those involved with immediate market impact are involved with market risk, i.e., securities price fluctuations, while those focusing on underlying fundamentals are involved with investment risk. For most fundamentalists, like TAVF, market risk, both for individual securities as well as for macro factors affecting general markets, are things that can be ignored safely.

Also, if a company is not well financed, as a general rule it may be rational to emphasize quarterly reported earnings, and other short-term considerations, more than is the case for well-financed companies. Where a company is poorly financed, a poor quarterly report can often contribute to a permanent impairment of capital where the issuers are either denied any access at all to capital markets, or can access such markets only at an ultra-high cost. This is not a problem for the types of companies whose common stocks constitute the TAVF portfolio.

While Fund management attempts to buy deep value based on fundamental analysis and does not have any views as to how individual securities in the portfolio might perform in periods just ahead, TAVF is quite sensitive to how the overall portfolio performs. Fund management's goal is to have Fund NAV increase more than any benchmarks most of the time, on average, and over the long term. No effort, however, is made to outperform consistently, i.e., all the time. The TAVF idea is that if the portfolio consists of securities that are "safe and cheap[1]" on a value basis, market prices will take care of insuring good performance most of the time. For the NAV investments at discount prices, long-term performance ought to be good enough if the issuer can continue to increase NAV, or if the company engages in resource conversion activities such as getting taken over, liquidating assets, or buying back common stock on a massive scale.

In value investing, common stock assessments are made along a continuum with weights given to appropriate variables. The basic variables revolve around whether principal emphasis in an analysis should be on operating earnings and cash flows and/or whether principal emphasis should be on looking at the company as an investment vehicle where greatest weight is given to NAV. In pure investment vehicles, such as mutual funds striving for total return, most market participants assign 100% weight to NAV and ignore earnings rather completely. Assume Company A is a strict going concern operating in its traditional lines of business, managed as it has been for years and/or financed pretty much the way it has always been financed. Also, Company A is unlikely to be a takeover candidate or to engage in mergers and acquisitions; contests for control; spin-offs or liquidations. Against this background, principal weight for a Company A analysis ought to be given to a Primacy of the Income Account, albeit NAV would never be ignored. On the other hand, assume Company B is realistically an investment vehicle where management's basic goal is wealth creation frequently attained by means other than having taxable earnings. A large part of Company B's *modus operandi* is to engage in massive asset redeployments, including acquisitions and going into new lines of business, massive liability and net worth redeployments (including common stock repurchases), management changes and taking advantage of attractive pricing in capital markets. Against this background, principal weight for a Company B analysis ought to be given to NAV, albeit income and cash flow from operations would never be ignored.

At July 31, 2006, fully 85.4% in market value of the TAVF common stock portfolio were in securities where, at the time of purchase, primary weight was given to NAV. These securities were issues of extremely well-financed companies and were selling at material discounts from readily ascertainable NAVs. Fund management forecasts, in most cases, were that there were good prospects that NAV plus dividend payouts over the long term would increase at a compound annual rate of much better than 10%. For TAVF, in these cases, earnings were clearly defined by looking, not at the income account, but at the prospects for future increases in NAV, whether such increases came from operating profits, realized appreciation or unrealized appreciation. At July 31, 2006, only 14.6% of the TAVF common stock portfolio were in issues, where at the time of purchase, primary emphasis was given to operating income flows – whether income flows, or cash flows. These companies, too, were extremely well financed. In looking at the past flows and prospective future flows, the only reliance on GAAP were as objective benchmarks, not something that would tell Fund management "the truth". So here, even when there was a Primacy of the Income Account, TAVF was different from most conventional analysis in that in looking at the income account, TAVF management cared about what the numbers meant, rather than believing that GAAP numbers, as reported, reflected some sort of reality.

The Fund's concentration on investing in the common stocks of financially strong firms based on pricing that represents discounts from NAVs results in material differences from other funds in portfolio management. Fund management, like other market participants, tries to predict the future. Like other market participants though, Fund management is frequently wrong in its predictions. However, in the TAVF case, the consequences of unpleasant surprises tend to be a lot less draconian than had the investments been made in poorly-financed companies based on predictions of future flows from operations. In common stocks, buying "what is" in well-financed companies seems to carry a lot less investment risk than buying based on forecasts of future operating results, where not much attention is paid to present financial strength. Thus, TAVF has considerably less need to diversify broadly than does the average mutual fund. As a consequence, TAVF is able to concentrate its investments much more than other mutual funds. At July 31, 2006, the ten largest common stock positions accounted for slightly over 50% of the Third Avenue equity portfolio. Each of the 10 was an NAV issue. Also, the nature of NAV investing is buy and hold. TAVF will have an annual turnover rate of, say, 10% to 15%. In contrast, the average mutual fund has a turnover rate in excess of 100%.

Concentrating on a NAV approach seems to be much more mainstream than is Wall Street's obsession with the Primacy of the Income Account. Most investors and most companies are interested in wealth creation rather than ordinary, and therefore, taxable income. Indeed, I never have heard from a TAVF stockholder about the Fund's net income; I do hear a lot about NAV.Corporations

Corporations have, for analytical purposes, four (often, but not always, interrelated) ways to create wealth:

1. Cash flow from operations available for common shareholders. This seems to be relatively uncommon since most companies in their overall activities seem to be cash consumers rather than cash generators. Academics write quite correctly about projects needing to have a positive Net Present Value (NPV) in order for a project to make economic sense. The present value of the cash inflows from the project has to exceed the present value of the cash outflows. However, this refers to project finance, not corporate finance.
2. Earnings, with earnings defined as consuming cash while creating wealth. This is what most corporations do. For most businesses, earnings cannot have a positive value unless also combined with access to capital markets to fund cash shortfalls.
3. Resource conversion – creating wealth through asset redeployments (including mergers and acquisitions, liquidations); liability redeployments; and management changes.

4. Have access to capital markets – both credit markets and equity markets – on a super attractive basis. Probably more fortunes have been built because of super-attractive access to capital markets than any other way.

Emphasis on Primacy of the Income Account made more sense in the old days when most businesses were strict going concerns, concentrating on one or two spheres of operations, managed as the business had always been managed, and financed the way the business had always been financed. Nowadays, almost no strict going concerns exist. Over any five-year period, virtually all businesses will undergo massive resource conversions ranging from mergers to major refinancings. NAV is now a lot more important in corporate analysis than it had been in the days of strict going concerns. A strict going concern approach tends to be more important when analyzing old line American manufacturing companies. TAVF tends not to invest in the common stocks of such issuers. All of the Third Avenue NAV holdings are in the common stocks of real estate companies, financial institutions and businesses holding large portfolios of either marketable common stocks or performing loans.

As you might expect, the Fund's NAV emphasis is not without specific investment risks. Given today's pricing, the bulk of TAVF's NAV investments are being made in East Asia – Japan, Hong Kong, South Korea and Singapore, where the various companies also have interests in projects located in the People's Republic of China. One troubling factor is that in East Asia, outside passive minority investors such as TAVF just do not get close to the same investor protections as are present in the U.S. Also, there probably is less political stability in East Asia than there is in this country. Neither of these disadvantages, however, have been "show stoppers".

A real problem for TAVF shareholders revolves around the draconian income tax disadvantages for U.S. citizens and residents from owning the common stocks of certain foreign issuers selling at discounts from readily ascertainable NAVs. For U.S. income tax purposes, certain of these issuers are classified as Passive Foreign Investment Companies (PFICs). For practical purposes, this means that each year, Fund shareholders are subject to ordinary income tax on the annual unrealized common stock appreciation of the PFICs. To date, most foreign issuers in which TAVF holds investments have not been deemed to be PFICs. Hopefully it will stay that way, but one cannot be sure. The PFIC problem arises for TAVF because the U.S. income tax legislation was drafted so poorly.

It is interesting to contrast the TAVF style of investing with that used on behalf of limited partners in private equity funds involved with Leveraged Buyouts (LBO). LBO participants pay premium prices, i.e., control premiums, which are then offset by the availability of attractive senior finance coupled with prospects for asset redeployments plus constructive management changes. TAVF, on the other hand, buys in at non-control discounts, hopefully very steep discounts, and then leaves things on the corporate level as is, not seeking any asset redeployment, liability redeployment or management changes. Of course, expenses for TAVF shareholders are much more modest than is the case for limited partners in private equity funds. Third Avenue's expense ratio is around 1.10%. In contrast, the typical private equity fund will charge a management fee of, say, 2%, and also allocate 20% of profits from operations, realized gains and unrealized appreciation to the general partner after the limited partners receive a priority return of, say, 6% to 10%.

As far as I can tell, there ought to continue to be available many attractive situations selling at discounts from NAV. For one thing, in conventional security analysis, many believe that there ought to be a "normal holding company discount" of around 20%. The vast army of believers in the Efficient Market Hypothesis seem convinced that NAV discounts don't exist, and never have.

I daresay that in my lifetime, most participants in the non-control investment community will continue to believe in the Primacy of the Income Account, and will treat almost all companies as strict going concerns creating value only from operations. This seems to be the case even though, increasingly, most companies seem to have become basically investment vehicles rather than merely operating entities. If so, there are likely to continue to be opportunities for TAVF to invest in the common stocks of well-financed companies at prices that reflect meaningful discounts from NAVs.

Within the Fund's NAV portfolio, two sectors have not been increasing NAV, at least, at a 10% compound annual rate. One sector is Japanese non-life insurance companies, and the other is Mutual Holding Companies (MHC), i.e., certain small U.S. community banks. If interest rates increase materially in Japan, I think the non-life insurance companies would have a good chance of exceeding a 10% return on NAV. The MHCs are held by TAVF mostly because they appear to be attractive acquisition candidates. Academics, whether efficient market theorists or behaviorists, spend much effort in postulating how information impacts markets. The underlying problem academics seem to have is that they think of material information in terms of impacts on day traders. The fact is that what is material information for Third Avenue are things that are quite different from what is material information for day traders. One suggestion is that academics be required to spend two to three hours a day for six months reading Forms 10-K, Forms 10-Q, Forms 8-K, and Proxy Statements before making pronouncements about what information is and how information impacts markets.

Insofar as TAVF keeps expanding in size as new moneys come into the Fund, or in any event, the Fund does not shrink because of redemptions, there is little pressure on the Fund to sell securities in the portfolio. Insofar as NAV companies show promise that NAV will continue to grow over the long term; and the common stock does not appear to be grossly overpriced, Third Avenue will not sell the issue. Time has proven that in following the Fund's "safe and cheap" approach, the analytic discipline works much better on the buy side than the sell side. In other words, absent compelling reasons to sell, most of the common stocks in the TAVF portfolio are very, very, long-term holdings.

In NAV investing, scant attention is paid to top down factors such as predicting Gross Domestic Product, interest rates, the Dow Jones Averages, federal deficits or balances of payments. Rather, the emphasis is on bottom-up "nitty gritty". It is assumed that the NAV investor ought to do okay long term as long as there exists political stability and an absence of violence in the streets. This has been the case for value investing since World War II. The Fund is betting that the environment of the last 60 years, where macro factors have been relatively unimportant for value investors, will continue.

One of the huge advantages of being a long-term investor in well-financed companies is that the strong finances give reasonably competent managements opportunities to be opportunistic, something probably unavailable to most managements when they are forced to be supplicants to creditors.

TAVF, in its analyses, uses GAAP as an objective benchmark, adjusting the numbers to reflect an economic reality. For example, over half of Toyota Industries' assets are invested in securities, principally a larger than 5% interest in Toyota Motor Common. Only dividends received from its portfolio holdings are reflected in Toyota Industries' income account, so that on a GAAP basis, Toyota Industries Common is selling at over 27 times earnings. However, if the Toyota Industries' GAAP income account is adjusted to pick up Toyota Industries' share of the portfolio companies' retained earnings (i.e., earnings not distributed as dividends), then Toyota Industries Common is selling at less than 10 times earnings. Forest City Enterprises creates great amounts of cash flow without it being reflected in a GAAP income account. Say Forest City finances one of its office buildings with a $100 million, 15-year issue of a non-recourse, mortgage loan. The building, well maintained, tends to increase in value over time insofar as high quality, long-term leases are entered into. Say in seven years, the loan is paid down to $80 million and Forest City refinances with a new non-recourse mortgage for $120 million. Forest City on this transaction gains $40 million of new cash without any effect on its income account.

The U.S. securities laws as enforced by the Securities and Exchange Commission (SEC) are designed to provide Investor Protection. The laws seem to have three principal functions:

1. Maintain free, fair and orderly trading markets;
2. Provide disclosure; and
3. Provide some oversight of professionals such as broker-dealers, accountants, corporate executives and other insiders.

TAVF is interested particularly in the disclosure area where over the past forty years, the SEC has done a magnificent job of improving disclosure to outsiders. Going forward, however, I think it is increasingly important that the authorities recognize that the best investor protection in the disclosure area is Self Protection. Make disclosures available. If participants – say day traders – don't want to use that information, that is their business. Disclosure requirements ought to be based on the view that disclosure is geared toward a reasonably intelligent, reasonably diligent, long-term investor – say someone akin to a long-term, unsecured, private placement creditor. From GAAP, such an investor needs objective benchmarks, not truth. Adopting such an attitude might be a boom for American Capital Markets, which seem to be losing out to foreign markets at a rapid rate. [1] "Safe" means the companies have strong finances, competent management, and an understandable business. "Cheap" means that we can buy the securities for significantly less than what a private buyer might pay for control of the business.

CHAPTER 34

Conventional Security Analysts

JANUARY 2012

The Third Avenue Management (TAM) investment team approaches security analysis from a different perspective than most conventional security analysts. In fact, the Third Avenue approach has more in common with corporate finance than it does with the conventional approach. The conventional approach is accepted as basic tenets by Modern Capital Theory (MCT), in Graham and Dodd valuations (G&D) and, to some extent, in Generally Accepted Accounting Principles (GAAP). The differences between conventional security analysis and other financial analysis bottom on conventional security analysis' over emphasis of three factors and consequent under emphasis of other factors that are equally important, and even more important, in most fundamental financial analyses. These other areas of finance include running a private business, control investing, most of distress investing, credit analysis and venture capital. The three factors overemphasized in conventional security analysis are as follows:

1. Primacy of the Income Account, i.e., the primacy of flows generated from operations as a valuation determinant – whether those flows are earnings flow or cash flows. Earnings flows are streams of income which create wealth for economic entities while consuming cash. In the corporate world earnings flows probably are more common than cash flows available for securities holders.
2. Primacy of Short-Termism – Prediction of, and reliance, on immediate market prices and changes in those prices. These are

crucial to equity pricing in securities markets dominated by Outside Passive Minority Investors (OPMIs). Determining near-term outlooks for a company tends to be a much more important variable in conventional analysis than is determining underlying value.

3. Primacy of Top Down Analysis – The most important element in predicting market prices in conventional analysis are macro factors such as Gross Domestic Product (GDP), the level of interest rates, technical market considerations, industry sectors and the trends in stock market indices. For conventional analysis, micro factors looked at from the bottom-up, such as loan covenants, appraisals of management, strength of financial positions and access to capital markets are down-weighted compared to top-down considerations.

As to the primacy of the income account, G&D recognized certain of its shortcomings, even though the most important component of their bottom-up analyses was forecasting future earnings. As G&D stated on Page 551 of the 1962 edition of *Securities Analysis, Principles and Technique*:

> *"Most of all security analysts should reflect fully on the rather startling truth that as long as a business remains a private corporation or partnership the net asset value appearing on the balance sheet is likely to constitute the point of departure for determining what the enterprise is 'worth'. But once it makes its appearance as a 'publicly held company – even though the shares distributed to the public may constitute only a small part of the total – the net-worth figure seems to lose virtually all its significance.' 'Value' then becomes dependent almost exclusively on the expected future earnings"*

This overemphasis on forecasting future flows from operations (whether earnings flows or cash flows) would be justifiable in the real world of fundamentalism, i.e., financial activities other than stock market trading, if the businesses being analyzed were strict going concerns; financed as they always have been financed; managed by operators in the same way they have always been managed; not subject to takeovers; mergers, going private or other resource conversion events; and without needs to ever access capital markets. The problem is that there are very few, if any, such companies whose common stocks are publicly traded in existence. Rather than being strict going concerns, virtually all businesses whose equities are publicly traded combine going concern characteristics with investment company characteristics. While income accounts, i.e., flow data, are integrally related to net asset value (NAV), for many companies NAV and changes in NAV are far more important determinants of value than are earnings, or cash flows, from operations. Such NAV-centered companies include Berkshire Hathaway, most mutual funds, most income-producing real estate entities (such as Forest City Enterprises), most control investors (such as Brookfield Asset Management), and most conglomerates (such as Cheung Kong Holdings). In conventional analysis, managements are appraised almost exclusively as operators. In the real world, in which Third Avenue operates, managements are appraised not only as operators but also as investors and financiers. Management roles as investors and financiers are frequently more important than their roles as operators in our analysis.

Even when emphasizing the primacy of the income account, many conventional analysts handicap themselves by failing to consider the importance of NAV in many instances as a tool for predicting future earnings. Graham and Dodd, for example, believe that the past earnings record is the best tool for predicting future earnings, virtually ignoring NAV. However, NAV is an essential tool (though not the sole tool) for predicting future earnings in those instances where data on Return on Equity (ROE) are important to understanding a business. "E", or Equity, by the way, is NAV. Industries where ROE becomes a tool for predicting future earnings include income producing real estate, commercial banks, insurance companies, investment companies, conglomerates and hedge funds. The vast bulk of Third Avenue's common stock investments are in companies where the NAV figure is an important valuation tool. Most of the issues acquired by Third Avenue Funds have been acquired at prices that represent meaningful discounts from estimated NAVs.

Third Avenue's approach to finding values seems to be a lot more broadly based than is the case for conventional stock market analysis. In this regard, Third Avenue seems to be in good company. Others more broadly based in their analyses include those running private businesses, most distress investors, virtually all control investors, most credit analysts and virtually all first and second stage venture capitalists.

Factors considered by Third Avenue and these other economics analysts in appraising a company and its securities encompass the following:

1. Creditworthiness
2. Flows – both cash and earnings
3. Long-term outlook
4. Salable assets which can be disposed of without compromising much, or at all, the going concern dynamics.
5. Resource conversions such as changes in control, mergers and acquisitions, going private, and major changes in assets or major changes in liabilities.
6. Access to capital markets – both credit markets and equity markets.

meltdown, for Third Avenue there has been a primacy of credit-worthiness in analyzing any equity security. At Third Avenue there never has existed a Primacy of Earnings, a Primacy of Short-Termism or a Primacy of Top-Down Analysis.

It seems important to define credit-worthiness, both for private sector analysis and the analysis of sovereigns. Creditworthiness has three elements:

1. Amount of indebtedness
2. Terms of indebtedness
3. How productive are the Use of Proceeds (This third factor is usually the most important.)

It ought to be noted that in the aggregate, indebtedness is almost never repaid by entities which remain credit-worthy. Rather, maturing debt is refinanced and new levels of debt are incurred as credit-worthy entities expand and become more productive. Despite the 2008-2009 economic meltdown, most of the companies held since then in Third Avenue portfolios have grown and prospered, e.g., the Hong Kong Holdings, Brookfield Asset Management and Posco. Today each of these companies has considerably more borrowing capacity than they had when the positions were initially acquired by Third Avenue.

A primacy of earnings approach clearly is in conflict with the desire of most corporations to minimize income tax burdens. Income from operations is taxed at maximum corporate rates. Taxation of capital gains is much preferred, because the taxpayer usually can control the timing as to when the tax becomes payable. And the ultimate corporate tax shelter for businesses which don't need cash return is unrealized appreciation.

In conventional analyses today, there is almost no understanding of risk. The prime example of this is the conventional belief that long-term U.S. Treasury Notes, selling near par, are safe and free from risk. Not so. The U.S. Treasury Notes, paying say 2%-3%, do not carry any credit risk; but, they are replete with several other types of risk, e.g., inflation risk and capital deprecation risk, while at the same time there are no prospects for capital appreciation. The huge amounts of realistic risk inherent in owning U.S. Treasuries today is offset greatly if the portfolio holding these instruments is a dollar-average and will continue to acquire new U.S. Treasuries as interest rates fluctuate. Nonetheless, for most portfolios in 2012, the way to guard against economic risk is to be a total return investor in things such as Third Avenue Funds, rather than to be a cash return investor in U.S. Treasuries.

The common stocks in Third Avenue Funds almost all have the following characteristics:

1. The companies enjoy super strong financial positions, which provide "insurance" to investors and opportunism to management
2. The common stocks were acquired at prices that represent meaningful discounts from estimated NAVs.
3. The companies provide comprehensive, relatively complete, disclosures and operate in markets where regulators provide significant protections for minority investors.
4. The companies seem to have excellent prospects for growing NAV by not less than 10% compounded annually over the next three to seven years.

Short-termism is rampant among market participants. Much of short-termism is appropriate, justifiable and essential for many market participants. It just happens to be irrelevant largely for Third Avenue, which focuses mostly on buy-and-hold, long-term investments.

One had better be very short-term conscious where the portfolio is highly leveraged; where the market participant doesn't know much about the company or the securities it issues; where the market participant uses trading systems, or a technical approach to the market; and where the more important variable in an analysis is what is the near-term outlook, rather than what are the underlying values existing in the company and the company's securities.

Even for the largest institutions, it seems to be impossible to have underlying knowledge about an individual security where the portfolio consists of a huge numbers of securities (say over 500 different common stocks); and those securities are traded frequently. This includes high frequency trading portfolios. If that's where one's interest and attention lies, one should be short term. This is not what TAM does. TAM believes in limited diversification. Diversification is only a surrogate, and usually a damn poor surrogate, for knowledge, control and price consciousness. TAM has to be moderately diversified, because the various Third Avenue Funds are essentially passive, rather than control, investors.

Also, there are certain types of securities – I call them "sudden death" securities – where all the focus has to be short term. These securities are derivatives and risk arbitrage securities, with risk arbitrage being defined as situations where there will be a relatively determinant workout in a relatively determinant period of time, e.g., a publicly announced merger or tender offer.

Even Third Avenue is sometimes short-term oriented, but not most of the time. This occurs where there is a resource conversion event, such as merger or tender offer, where the price to be paid is a substantial premium above the pre-announcement market price. In that situation, Third Avenue fund manager is likely to take his profit and move on to something else. Resource conversions do occur periodically.

For analysts who subscribe to the G&D approach to investing, there is nothing more important in an analysis than to give dominant weight to top-down predictions of the outlook for the economy and the outlook for specific securities markets. Third Avenue, on the other hand, does not ignore top-down considerations but certainly underweights their importance compared with bottom-up considerations. For this, there are two reasons. First, over the long term bottom-up analysis will tend to be a much more important factor in value realization than top-down factors (probably absent social unrest). Second, Third Avenue, like everybody else, doesn't seem to be too accurate as a top-down forecaster, especially when it comes to short-term forecasts.

A good example of how we meld the top-down with the bottom-up lies in the reasoning behind our investments in Hong Kong, China and South Korea. The top-down analysis centers on the belief that over the next three to seven years, that part of the world will grow faster than the rest of the industrialized world, especially Europe and North America. The bottom-up analyses center on the facts that the businesses in which Third Avenue has invested are all eminently creditworthy; that the common stocks were acquired at a significant discount to our estimate of NAV; and that the common stocks are the issues of companies that provide comprehensive, written disclosures; and are regulated by government agencies whose principal interest seems to be investor protection.

Prior to 2008, long-term, buy-and-hold investors did not have to pay too much attention to top-down factors, such as the business cycle. This no longer seems true. Since the meltdown, business cycle factors seem to have become more important than had been the case from the end of World War II until 2008. Despite this, Third Avenue will continue to give more weight in the vast majority of its analyses to bottom-up factors, rather than top-down factors.

CHAPTER 35

Corporate Uses of Cash

APRIL 2012

Throughout the years, I have frequently written about the great emphasis the Third Avenue Management (TAM) investment team places on the quality and quantity of a company's resources when evaluating a potential investment. Put simply, most of the time, we seek to invest in the equity securities of companies with lots of cash and little, or no, debt. This quarter, I thought it might be of interest to my fellow shareholders to expand upon our thoughts on how cash can be most productively used by corporations.

Corporate Uses of Cash

In the broadest context, a corporation has only three uses of cash:

1. Expand assets
2. Reduce liabilities
3. Make distributions to shareholders

       a) Pay dividends
       b) Repurchase outstanding equity securities

For the vast, vast majority of corporations – and from the point of view of the corporation, itself – distributions to equity owners have to be a residual use of cash, distinctly subordinated to having the corporation expand assets and/or reduce liabilities. There are exceptions, however.

Corporations which need relatively regular access to equity markets to raise new funds, will tend to pay out 70% to 80% of earnings as dividends in order to give these companies enhanced ability to sell new issues of common stocks, say every 18 months to two years, at prices reflecting a premium over book value. For most of the post-World War II period, this was the situation that prevailed for integrated electric utilities. Growth in demand ranged from 2% to 7%, per annum, year after year. It took capital expenditures of $5 to $7 to produce $1 of increased revenue. The integrated electrics were financed 60% to 70% with debt, mostly publicly-held first mortgages; 10% preferred stock; and 20% to 30% with common stock.

Obviously given the physical growth, the large amount of capital expenditures and the need to maintain debt-to-stock ratios, companies in the electric utility industry had to raise capital periodically by selling new underwritten issues of common stock every 18 months to two years. What was true for the electric utilities was also valid for water companies, natural gas distributors and many expanding consumer finance companies. These were all, and to a considerable extent still are, high dividend payers.

There are also a large group of companies with flow-through income tax characteristics, i.e., entities which are generally exempt from federal income taxes to the extent that income which would otherwise be taxable at the entity level is paid out to shareholders. These companies include registered investment companies (RICs) and real estate investment trusts (REITs). Master limited partnerships (MLPs) are flow-through entities, whose earnings are taxable, not to the business entity, but to the partners themselves.

However, for most companies it is highly impractical to plan to raise new equity capital by making periodic trips to capital markets. These markets are notoriously capricious. At times, access to equity markets can be had on a super attractive basis – see the 1999 dot com bubble. At other times, there can be no access at all to equity markets at any price – see the 2008-2009 meltdown. In any event, raising new equity by accessing capital markets tends to be quite expensive; gross spreads range between, say, 2 ½% and 7%. Rather, the vast majority of corporations will continue to get most of their new equity capital (and cash) through retained earnings, i.e., profits not distributed to shareholders.

Most of the companies whose common stocks are held in Third Avenue Management portfolios are in an especially good position to make distributions to common shareholders, especially to conduct long-term programs to repurchase outstanding common stock. These companies tend to combine super-strong financial positions with stock market prices that represent a meaningful discount from readily ascertainable, and economically meaningful, net asset value (NAV). Companies in the various TAM portfolios which exhibit such characteristics include the following:

> Bank of New York Mellon
> Brookfield Asset Management
> Capital Southwest Corporation
> Guoco Group
> Hong Kong Property and Holding Companies (Cheung Kong Holdings; Hang Lung Group; Hang Lung Properties; Henderson Land; Hutchison Whampoa; Lai Sun Garment; Sun Hung Kai Properties; Wharf and Wheelock)
> Investor A/B
> Key Corp
> Toyota Industries
> White Mountains Insurance Group

In the above-mentioned list of companies, whose common stocks all are selling at meaningful discounts from NAV and which also enjoy super-strong financial positions, long-term returns to TAM investors would likely be more than satisfactory, if the individual issuers could increase their NAV after adding back dividends by at least 10% per annum compounded.

A stock buy-in program, whereby a corporation repurchases some of its outstanding shares, could make it quite easy for several of the companies cited above to achieve the 10% growth bogey. Most of the managements and Boards of Directors are probably unaware of these benefits from a buy-in program, so it is unlikely to happen in the case of most of the companies on the list (White Mountains Insurance seems a notable exception). A simple example should suffice. Investor A/B reported that at March 31, 2012, its NAV was 167,657,000,000 Swedish Kroner (SEK) on 760,505,872 common shares outstanding, resulting in a NAV of 220 SEK per share. The market for Investor A/B common at the time of this writing is around 130 SEK, or a 40.9% discount from March 31, 2012 NAV. Total debt outstanding was 45,575,000,000 SEK leaving Investor A/B with a stock to debt ratio of 79:21. If Investor A/B, using additional borrowings of 21,000,000,000 SEK, were to tender for 150,000,000 Investor A/B common at 140, (including expenses) and the tender offer succeeded, there would be outstanding 610,505,872 Investor A/B common, with an NAV of 146,657,000,000 SEK or 240 SEK per share, an increase of 9.1% in NAV per share. The basic question ought to be: would such a buy-in be a more productive use of cash than expanding assets? Whether or not such an Investor A/B tender offer attracted 150 million common shares, it seems likely that the immediate aftermarket price for Investor A/B Common would be north of 130.

Mathematically, all of the companies on the list could achieve results consistent with those in the Investor A/B example above but there are other limiting factors. Even for Investor A/B, dividends have an enormous advantage over buy-backs because the dividend payments are tax deductible to Investor A/B under Swedish law at a 28% rate while there are no tax benefits to Investor A/B from most buy backs. Capital Southwest is small and a major repurchase program might cause it to go private; Brookfield Asset Management probably feels its best growth opportunities are in expanding assets; and various Hong Kong control shareholders have been fairly aggressive buyers of common stock for their own personal accounts recently so that for them having their companies buy shares poses something of a conflict of interest.

From a management point of view, share repurchases are a simpler use of funds than expanding the asset base most of the time simply because the research task is so much easier. You are less likely to make analytic mistakes when involved with your own enterprise, rather than an enterprise controlled and managed by someone else.

From a shareholders' point of view, especially the point of view of shareholders affected by daily stock price fluctuations, there are important advantages to these shareholders if cash distributions to shareholders are made in the form of dividends rather than stock buy backs. First, the markets populated by outside passive minority investors (OPMIs) are volatile. However, insofar as a company pays regular dividends which are increased periodically market prices tend to be a lot less capricious than would otherwise be the case because the shares tend to get priced, at least in part, on a return (or yield) basis. Second, many OPMIs rely on regular dividend payments to meet living expenses.

The above shareholder point of view is not the TAM point of view. TAM is basically a long-term buy- and-hold investor. It seeks to invest in the common stocks of companies that have excellent prospects for increasing NAV by not less than 10%, per annum, compounded over the next three to seven years. And TAM would like to have its portfolio companies achieve this goal conservatively and in a very safe manner. To accomplish this, share buy-backs seem an ideal way to go, as long as common shares are available for purchase by strongly-financed companies and priced at meaningful discounts from NAV. The Investor A/B theoretical tender offer cited above demonstrates this.

From a shareholder's point of view, buy-ins do have certain advantages over dividends:

Participating in a buy-in is voluntary for each individual shareholder. Receipt of a dividend, on the other hand, is mandatory to all shareholders.

Generally, a shareholder that participates in a buy-in will, subject to certain conditions, be treated for tax purposes as selling the shares back to the company and the shareholder will be taxed on any gain (proceeds minus cost basis) recognized from such sale. Depending upon the holding period, lower long-term capital gains rates may apply. On the other hand, the full amount of any payment treated as a taxable dividend may be subject to tax. If the qualified dividend rules do not apply, individual taxpayers may be taxed at rates which are higher than long-term capital gain rates. U.S. corporations eligible for the 70% corporate dividends received deductions could be taxed at an ultra-low rate.

Long-term market performance might be better with a buy-in, because weaker shareholders are more likely to sell out in the presence of the corporate buying interest. Buy-ins can cause market liquidity to dry up, a very distinct disadvantage for many OPMIs.

From a company point of view, buy-ins tend to have huge advantages over dividends:

- Regular dividends become, in effect a fixed charge, payable in cash to the corporation. In contrast, management controls completely the timing of buy-ins. It can conserve cash as needed, giving expanding assets and/or reducing liabilities the priorities they deserve at the times they deserve it, versus paying out a regular cash dividend to shareholders.

- Bought-in shares can offset the dilutive effects of issuing employee stock options.

Many, if not most, managements share the TAM view that the long-term object of the company is to grow economically meaningful NAV safely, conservatively and cheaply.

As an aside, it ought to be noted that there are four ways to acquire common stock for cash, whether for buy-in or other purposes:

- In the open market

- In private transactions

- Via tender offers

- By use of the proxy machinery, for cash out mergers or reverse splits

Most purchases are open market purchases made after a Board of Directors authorizes the management of a company to repurchase a certain amount of shares.

Large enough purchases or use of the proxy machinery can result in a company going private or "going dark". This seems unlikely to happen to the various companies in the TAM portfolios, but one never knows. The effect can be disastrous if the going dark price does not reflect a substantial premium over market. I am not too worried on this score. The Hong Kong companies, in particular, seem safe from a take-under because the listing rules in the Hong Kong Stock Exchange make it almost impossible to use proxy machinery to go private. Also, the companies are so big that they are likely to stay public, even though control insiders have been regular and sometimes large, buyers of common stock.

For market participants focused on growth in NAV, there are a lot of differences between the last time the Dow Jones Industrial Average (DJIA) was above 13,000 (December 2007) and the current 13,000 level. Book value for the DJIA is not exactly the same as NAV for the securities listed above; but, it remains a pretty good, albeit rough, surrogate for NAV. The book value for the DJIA at April 30, 2012 was 42.2% greater than the book value at December 31, 2007. More importantly, though, is the probability that the quality of the book value at April 30, 2012, as measured by the financial strength of the thirty companies making up the DJIA, was far superior in April 2012 compared to what it was in December 2007.

Do not rely on OPMI markets for economic logic. In OPMI markets, sponsorship and promotion seem to count much more than does economic logic. Two of the most successful private equity firms acquiring elements of control over the companies in which they invest, based on their long-term track records, are Capital Southwest and Investor A/B. As of this writing, Capital Southwest is trading at about a 43% discount from estimated NAV and Investor A/B is trading at about a 41% discount from estimated NAV. How do these extremely well financed companies compare with private equity limited partnerships and hedge funds, few of which have been as successful as these two in growing long-term NAV?

> 1. The private equity limited partnerships and hedge funds are not priced at any discount from NAV.
> 2. The private equity limited partnerships restrict investors from cashing-in their investments.

Capital Southwest and Investor A/B are marketable as long as securities markets are open (i.e., almost all the time).

> 3. The overall all-in expense ratios for both Capital Southwest and Investor A/B are probably less than 1%. The typical private equity partnership or hedge fund probably charges a management fee of 2%, plus a 20% profit participation after meeting a bogey of, say, 6%, to the limited partners. Most fees earned by a private equity limited partnership or hedge fund (banking fees, home office charges, etc.), probably belong mostly to the general partners, not the limited partners.
> 4. Most private equity partnerships and hedge funds are probably more leveraged, i.e., less well financed, than are Capital Southwest and Investor A/B.
> 5. Investor protections are manifestly greater for market participants holding common stocks than they are for market participants who are limited partners. Especially strong investor protections exist for Capital Southwest, which is registered as an investment company under the Investment Company Act of 1940, as amended.

One final observation. Academics are mostly believers in Modern Capital Theory (MCT). In the efficient market in which they believe, situations like the companies in our list could not exist. For them, efficient pricing would get rid of the large discounts at which each security sells. This MCT view is diametrically opposed to the TAM view. In the TAM view, securities markets populated by OPMIs tend very much to be price inefficient, unless there exist catalysts. Principal catalysts include prospects for changes of control, going private, mergers and acquisitions, spin-offs and major asset or liability restructurings. If there is anything wrong with the TAM list of companies cited, it is a lack of catalysts. Yet, over time, the TAM portfolios have performed satisfactorily even in the relative absence of such catalysts. And, perhaps most important of all, the probabilities seem to be that none of the companies will suffer permanent impairments no matter how unfavorable the various top-down economic outlooks might be.

CHAPTER 36

Financial Accounting

APRIL 2015

Financial accounting is based on one of two protocols – Generally Accepted Accounting Principles (GAAP) used in the United States; and International Financial Reporting System (IFRS) used in the rest of the world.

A principal difference between GAAP and IFRS lies in how each accounts for income-producing real estate. Under GAAP, income-producing real estate is carried on the balance sheet at depreciated historic cost less impairments, if any; income statements reflect periodic charges for depreciation. Under IFRS, in contrast, income-producing real estate is carried on the balance sheet at independently arrived at appraisal values; income statements reflect periodic Fair Value gains (or losses) on investment properties (i.e., periodic changes in appraisal values). In all the reports I've look at where IFRS is used, two earnings figures are disclosed in total and on a per share basis: underlying profit before the fair value change and underlying profit after the fair value change

The vast majority of market participants and security analysts seem to ignore, or down- weigh, the significance of appraised values for income producing real estate by placing dominant weight on underlying profit before the fair value change in their analysis and in making buy, hold, or sell decisions. This is understandable where the emphasis is on short-run predictions of stock market prices, and a belief in the primacy of periodic income or cash flows from recurring operations in determining stock market prices. This seems to be the mind set of most security analysts whether located in New York City, Hong Kong, or elsewhere in developed and developing countries.

As a result of ignoring, or downweighing, IFRS derived Net Asset Values (NAVs), many well-financed, and growing companies have their common stocks selling at 30% to 70% discounts from IFRS reported NAVs. Such issues held in various Third Avenue Management (TAM) portfolios include Henderson Land, Hysan Development, Lai Sun Garment and Wheelock. These discounts compare with the approximately 3x book value where the Dow-Jones Industrial Average and the S&P 500 Average currently are selling.

While IFRS reported NAVs and fair value changes are not helpful in aiding an investor to estimate near-term stock market price changes, for the long-term buy-and-hold investors such as the funds managed by TAM, IFRS reported NAVs are a god-send . First, virtually all independent appraisals rely, directly or indirectly, on an income approach: – the investor gets a cash flow estimate based on the appraiser's estimate of NAV. This is demonstrated in a footnote to the Henderson Land 2014 audit where it is stated "The valuations of completed investment properties in Hong Kong and mainland China were based on income capitalization approach which capitalized the net income of the properties and taking into account the reversionary potential of the properties after the expiring of the current lease." Second, if properties are to be sold or refinanced in bulk, the IFRS-reported NAVs undoubtedly provide a better estimate of what the selling terms will be (or what the new financial arrangements will be) than do stock market prices.

No accounting number, and certainly not IFRS-reported NAVs, determines economic reality for the analyst. Rather, it gives the analyst objective benchmarks which the analyst then uses to determine his or her views as to what economic reality is. I have no question that for income-producing real estate IFRS give analysts far better value benchmarks than does GAAP in helping to determine present values, and what are likely to be future cash flows from existing income producing real estate.

A principal reason such huge discounts from NAVs exist for the income producing entities held by TAM is that for these companies there appear to be little or no possibilities that there will be changes of control or going private (as an aside, such discounts for the common stocks of quality companies seem unlikely to exist in the U.S. for undervalued entities where a very sophisticated investment banking industry continuously promotes resource conversions). Rather, than relying on resource conversions to achieve appreciation in common stock prices, TAM relies basically on long term growth in NAVs. Such growth seems a good prospect, based not only on the long-term track records of the companies in various TAM portfolios but, more importantly, assuming that the independent appraisals represent reasonable estimates of future cash flows for existing properties, then future cash flows should be relatively large compared to the current discount market prices for the relevant common stocks. Incidentally, the various IFRS-reported NAV companies whose common stocks are in TAM portfolios do pay modest dividends, which have been increasing modestly year by year for most of the TAM holdings.

IFRS appraisals are much more meaningful for market participants when such appraisals are used for the valuation of companies that are well and comfortably financed. Investments by TAM in common stocks are pretty much restricted to companies that are quite well-financed.

IFRS would be even more useful if the independent appraisals were publicly available, possibly as a footnote or addendum to periodical financial statements. This is not the case, now.

Another problem many analysts have with relying on appraised values is that appraised values fail to measure directly periodic cash flows for the company whose assets are being appraised. For TAM, this is unimportant. First, investments are pretty much restricted to companies that are well-financed. Second, it is important to recognize what an income statement should reflect. It should reflect a company's cash flows for a period and also its wealth creation during the period. Very often, highly creative and useful wealth creations result initially in cash depletion, not cash generation. IFRS-reported NAV and valuation changes are excellent benchmarks or clues as to what wealth exists for the company, and what wealth creation has occurred during the period for which the accounting statements were issued. Wealth creation, by the way, seems to be the goal of most investors most of the time in managing their own portfolios.

Analysts point out that the discounts from IFRS reported NAVs have always existed. They assume that the discounts always will exist. The analysts are probably right as long as there is an absence of resource conversion activities, e.g., changes of control, going private or massive restructurings such as the impending separation of assets by Cheung Kong and Hutchison-Whampoa into two new companies; one a real estate holding company and the other an industrial-utility holding company. Even if the discounts persist, those discounts seem justifiable only for stock market reasons, and seem in no way justified by underlying business value considerations.

If a company is well-financed, bad times (as currently exist for much of Chinese real estate), provide managements with opportunities to make attractive acquisitions as was the case, for example, in 2012 when Wharf Holdings, a 57% owned subsidiary of Wheelock, made an equity capital infusion into Greentown China, a major mainland Chinese real estate developer.

PART 5

GRAHAM AND DODD FUNDAMENTALS

"Graham & Dodd essentially is analyzing from the point of view of a minority holder of marketable securities seeking high dividends and capital appreciation. Third Avenue is essentially analyzing from the points of view of the company itself, and/or senior creditors and control shareholders, present and potential."

April 1996

CHAPTER 37

A Balanced Approach to Value Investing

OCTOBER 1998

Weight to Performance

The Third Avenue Value Fund (TAVF) had essentially a break-even year in fiscal 1998. What kind of consideration should mutual fund investors give to performance, especially sub-par performance? For buy-and-hold, long-term growth investors such as TAVF, its annual performance ought to be a symptom of one of two things.

Either

1. Poor performance could be a measure of a money manager's incompetence. The investment in LTCB Common would seem to point in that direction. Or,
2. Poor performance could be a measure indicating that terrific values in the portfolio became even more terrific as the common stocks of strong businesses with large long-term potentials became even more attractively priced than when they were acquired initially. I believe that this is the case for the twenty-nine common stock positions which were increased during the just-ended quarter. Pricing for the particular issues seemed more like 1974 or 1982 to me than they did like 1998.

Hopefully, the stockholders of TAVF will give much more weight to the quality of the existing portfolio — and the prices paid to establish these positions — than they will to LTCB. LTCBs do go with the territory. After all, Peter Lynch had Crazy Eddie and Warren Buffett had U.S. Air.

Further, there are other ways to measure performance that may be more meaningful than one-year results overall. For example, our investments in Japanese non-life insurance companies have far outperformed relevant indexes. At October 31, the market value of the Fund's investments in Japanese non-life insurance companies virtually equaled TAVF's cost. Third Avenue had initially invested in these issues in January 1997 when the Nikkei Index stood at 19,446. At October 31, 1998, the Nikkei Index closed at 13,564, for a decline in the January 1997 to October 1998 period of a little over 30%. The experience for the Fund's investments in semiconductor equipment common stocks seems to have been similar — the Fund's investments in semis outperformed easily the semi index.

This is the way it should be. First, the companies in which the Fund has invested enjoy exceptional financial strength. As such, they are unlikely to be victimized by dramatic, adverse, unpredictable business changes. Second, if there is no evidence of permanent impairment of capital, Third Avenue averages down by increasing its positions in the common stocks of solid companies at lower and lower prices. If we do the analysis right, long-term performance for TAVF ought to continue to be satisfactory. I remain optimistic about the issues currently in the Fund's portfolio, both in terms of quality and in terms of appreciation potential.

A Balanced Approach to Value Investing

Third Avenue uses a Balanced Approach in assessing investments. In this regard TAVF is quite different from the vast majority of other mutual funds where, instead of a Balanced Approach, money managers emphasize a Primacy of the Income Account Approach. These other money managers focus on forecasts of future flows – either earnings or cash flows.

It may be helpful to Fund shareholders if they can gain an understanding of how TAVF differs from most others. I try to provide such understanding in the following paragraphs, most of which are excerpted from my new book scheduled to be published by John Wiley & Sons next spring. The title of the book is *Value Investing — A Balanced Approach*.

Wall Street analysts employed in the research departments of broker/dealers and as money managers running mutual funds seem out of step with the rest of the world when it comes to corporate valuations. Wall Street analysts in their valuations emphasize, sometimes to the exclusion of all other considerations, forecasts of future flows — either earning or cash flows. This emphasis does not exist when it comes to the valuation of private businesses, or in the vast majority of Merger and Acquisition (M&A) analyses undertaken by control investors.

Benjamin Graham and David Dodd in the 1962 edition of their classic, *Security Analysis*, describe this difference in analytical approaches. On page 551 it is stated, "Security analysts — should reflect fully on the rather startling truth that as long as a business remains a private corporation or partnership the net asset value appearing on the balance sheet is likely to constitute the point of departure for determining what the enterprise is 'worth.' But once it makes its appearance as a publicly held company — even though the shares distributed to the public constitute only a small part of the total — the net worth figure seems to lose virtually all its significance. 'Value' then becomes dependent almost exclusively on the expected future earnings."

Graham and Dodd were quite insightful in pointing to the strong tendency to look at businesses quite differently when dealing with private entities rather than publicly-traded common stocks. In my view, though, Graham and Dodd overstated the importance of net asset value in appraising private businesses. Rather, those valuing private businesses, or M&A opportunities, tend to have a balanced approach consisting of three general factors:

1. The quality of resources in a business; i.e., the financial strength to be able to either expand, acquire, or refinance, businesses; or to withstand future adversities.
2. The quantity of resources in a business relative to the price paid to acquire equity interests. This is akin to Graham and Dodd's net asset value, or book value, but the accounting figures are almost

always adjusted to reflect a more realistic value for assets — e.g., real estate appraisals for income producing properties, or equities in loss reserves for certain property and casualty insurance companies. The quality of resources and the quantity of resources are then translated into another factor.

3.   The prospects for long-term wealth creation.

Long-term wealth creation for private businesses, or in an M&A context, can come in a number of forms, including improved operating earnings, prospects for Initial Public Offerings, enhanced M&A prospects, abilities to refinance and/or create unrealized appreciation. Except when taking advantage of Wall Street's focus on reported earnings per share from operations, having such reported earnings tends to be the least desirable method by which to create wealth. Operating earnings usually are characterized by huge income tax disadvantages. Such wealth creation usually is fully taxed (in a situation where it is hard for the corporation to control timing of taxable events) as compared with, say, unrealized appreciation which is not taxed at all.

The best investors on Wall Street — Warren Buffett, Carl Icahn, Richard Rainwater, et al — all seem to use the three-pronged balanced approach described above in their investment activities. All are control, or elements of control, investors who do not try to predict stock market prices but rather take advantage of stock market prices whatever they may happen to be at a moment of time. The goal of these control investors seems to be to determine what a business is worth and what the internal dynamics of the business might be. Then they stop.

Wall Street analysts, on the other hand, carry extra analytic burdens. Their object is not so much to determine the underlying worth of a business, though that is part of their job, but, more importantly to predict the price at which a common stock will sell in stock markets in periods just ahead. In doing this, Wall Street analysts become involved in considering a whole gamut of factors that have little, or nothing, to do with determining underlying business values. These non-business value factors include all technical-chartist considerations, predictions about the direction of the general stock market, gauging investor psychology, looking at corporate dividend policy, and studying the supply-demand calculus inherent in figuring out who is buying a particular security and who is selling.

Most buy-and-hold investors, who are interested in analyzing fundamentals, probably can fare very well by emulating the best investors, such as Warren Buffett and Richard Rainwater. It has never been easier for outside, passive, investors to understand most businesses, without the use of inside information. Since Graham and Dodd wrote, there has been a true disclosure revolution. Trained analysts now can make reasonably good decisions about most common stocks an investor wants to hold for the long term simply by reviewing the public record supplemented by interviews of managements and other knowledgeable parties, something that was not possible when Graham and Dodd were writing.

There is a great deal of comfort in investing using a balanced approach. It seems particularly appropriate for investors with true long-term goals — retirement or a child's higher education. Here, rewards ought easily to outweigh risk.

Using a balanced approach, though, is not for everyone.

1. Do not use a balanced approach if you are untrained in fundamental analysis, something true for many research department analysts and money managers.
2. Fundamental investors try to guard against investment risk; i.e., permanent impairment of the capital of the underlying business. In doing this, most fundamental investors end up taking huge market risks, i.e., the price of the common stocks they own may decline. Market risk is particularly pertinent because for most businesses to become attractively priced using a balanced approach, the near-term outlook for the company is poor. If a near-term outlook is poor, near-term stock price performance might be poor also.
3. Don't use a balanced approach where one's job depends on near-term market performance, or where client redemptions are likely to occur based on near-term common stock price performance.
4. Don't use a balanced approach where the portfolio is financed with borrowed money where collateral is marked-t- market daily.

Loans are likely to be called if market prices decline, the
underlying fundamental merits of a business notwithstanding.

CHAPTER 38

Third Avenue vs. Graham and Dodd

APRIL 1996

In past letters, I've contrasted the Third Avenue Value Fund (TAVF) approach with that of academic finance. In this letter, I thought it might be useful for TAVF shareholders if I compared the TAVF approach with that followed by those involved with more traditional fundamental analysis.

Graham and Dodd Revisted

The Graham & Dodd book, *Security Analysis*, is widely recognized as the bible of fundamental analysis. The funny thing about the book, though, is that very few people seem to ever have actually read it.

Graham & Dodd (G&D) in their approach have a number of things in common with the TAVF approach. Both focus on long-term fundamentals and reject all chartist-technical approaches whether promulgated by practitioners or academics involved with efficient markets and efficient portfolios. Both G&D and TAVF have long-term investment strategies but pretty much ignore trading strategies (the newest edition of G&D, however, has a chapter on speculating on short run changes in interest rates and the TAVF approach in this area has been used by TAVF in its sometimes forays into risk arbitrage). Both G&D and TAVF reject heavy emphasis on short-run operating results in analyzing companies and, when it comes to financial accounting, both believe that what the numbers mean tends to be far more important than what the numbers are reported to be most of the time.

Yet, the TAVF fundamental analysis is, by and large, different than the G&D fundamental analysis. G&D essentially is analyzing from the point of view of a minority holder of marketable securities seeking high dividends and capital appreciation. TAVF is essentially analyzing from the points of view of the company itself, and/or senior creditors and control shareholders, present and potential. There seem to be four basic areas of difference between G&D and TAVF:

1. The G&D objective is to estimate prices at which securities will sell in markets populated by Outside Passive Minority Investors (OPMIs); TAVF focuses on what a business could be worth as a private entity or takeover candidate. G&D attempts to guard against market risk. TAVF attempts to guard against investment risk and ignores market risk rather completely.
2. The G&D credit analysis of debt instruments is involved solely with estimating the probabilities of money defaults; the TAVF credit analysis of debt instruments focuses on estimating what values are likely to be realized by a creditor in a reorganization or liquidation assuming that a money default does occur.
3. G&D believe that macro factors are crucial to the analysis of a corporate security (for example, "the economic forecast or a earnings estimate for the Standard & Poor's 500 or other broad index; and Sector and industry earnings forecasts"). TAVF believes such macro factors are irrelevant.
4. In common stock analysis G&D subscribes to a primacy of the income account theory — analysis starts with an examination of the past earnings record, and future returns to stockholders will be measured in part by future operating performance and in part by having acquired a security at a price below "central value," where "central value" is essentially a function of general stock market statistics. For TAVF, there is a primacy of the quality and quantity of resources existing in a business at the time of analysis, and future returns to stockholders will be measured in part by any number of possible scenarios, including future operating performance, mergers and acquisitions, refinancings on ultra-attractive terms, spin-offs, divestitures and going-privates; and in

part by having acquired a security at a price below a private business or takeover value.

Market Risk Vs. Investment Risk

On Page 441 of the 1988 edition of G&D, there is this remarkable statement,

> *"Clearly, the bond contract is inherently unattractive. In exchange for limited rights to share in future earning power, the bondholder obtains a prior claim on cash generated by the borrower and a definite promise of repayment at a stated date. Profitable growth will bring confidence to the investor but no material increase in return. The deterioration of profitability, however, will bring both anxiety and a downward market valuation of the issue."*

Why wouldn't a downward deterioration in profitability bring even greater anxiety and even greater downward market valuation to the holders of that company's common stock issue? As a matter of fact, if the bond is adequately secured or otherwise well-covenanted, no money defaults might occur, and the bondholder would feel no anxiety about his holding regardless of market price. The sophisticated bondholder would probably conclude that he was incapable of predicting bond prices in OPMI markets for lower-rated issues to begin with; TAVF would certainly so conclude.

G&D are probably right that there is a lot of OPMI market risk in holding the bonds of debtors experiencing a downward deterioration in profitability. However, TAVF finds that great investment opportunities are created when market risk is ignored and investment risk is examined and guarded against. Assuming good covenant protections, isn't the bond form inherently attractive when purchases occur subsequent to a downward market valuation caused by anxiety and a downward deterioration in profitability?

Were TAVF unwilling to ignore market risk it never would have acquired, among others, Forest City Enterprises Common in 1991, Inverse Floaters in 1994 and Kmart Debentures in 1995. The investment analyses by TAVF were that Forest City Enterprises has unlimited staying power and an ability to continue to create valuable real estate; Forest City Enterprises Common might be a "home run" by 1997 or 1999 or whenever the real estate depression ends; Inverse Floaters were priced so that a reasonably attractive yield to maturity could be achieved on a reasonable "worst case basis" through owning government agency guaranteed instruments; it seemed likely that an above-average long-term return would be earned on Kmart Debentures whether the instruments were performing loans or participating creditors in a Kmart Chapter 11.

I single out Forest City Enterprises, Inverse Floaters and Kmart because at the time of purchase I thought each issue had huge market risk. It would have been utterly unreasonable to conclude that these issues were being acquired at prices that represented a bottom or even anything close to a bottom because, in each case, the OPMI consensus, which could have proved right, was that the near-term outlooks were horrible.

Credit Analysis

G&D state on page 242 of the 1988 edition, *"Safety is measured by the issuer's ability to meet all its obligations under adverse economic and financial conditions, not by contractual terms of the specific issue."* Also it is stated on page 447, *". . . if a company is creditworthy, the investor should buy the higher yielding issue, which would be the junior or subordinated obligation."* There might be something to buying the junior issue, if the analyst is in a position to determine that a creditworthy company will continue to remain creditworthy until after the bond owned matures. TAVF is just not that good at predicting future corporate outlooks — not even close. Further, many companies, if not most companies, issue junior debt and preferred obligations, i.e., mezzanine securities, because of senior lender requirements that the businesses have expanded borrowing bases. Put otherwise, if these companies were so creditworthy to begin with they never would have issued mezzanine securities in the first place.

In any event, TAVF is covenant driven, the exact opposite of G&D. About $14 million principal amount of Eljer Industries Secured Bank Debt has been held in the TAVF portfolio for several years as a performing loan. A principal subsidiary of Eljer, US Brass, is in Chapter 11 and it remains theoretically possible that a huge amount of product liability claims will be perfected against Eljer. If so, those claims should become unsecured obligations, junior to Eljer Bank Debt. Overall coverage for Eljer obligations could conceivably become quite weak; further, there might even be some market risk in holding Eljer Bank Debt. However, I still have not figured out what the credit risk in holding Eljer Bank Debt might be for TAVF.

Macro Factors

G&D are very involved with macro factors. As is stated on page 9 of the 1988 edition, *". . . the profitability of all business enterprises and the market value of their shares are to some degree affected by (or conditional on) external factors — principally the economy and the stock market."* On page 14 G&D state, *"A competent analyst should be sufficiently familiar with important price patterns of the securities markets to draw intelligent conclusions about probable price movements of different types of securities issues."* And on page 52 there appears the following statement, "Economic forecasts provide essential underpinning for stock and bond market, industry, and company projections."

TAVF believes that, at least for the U.S. Economy, spending a lot of time on macro factors, whether for the overall economy or for securities markets, e.g., the S&P 500, is not only a waste of time but also a refuge for articulate incompetents who are untrained in any aspect of corporate analysis, but can sound intelligent by making predictions about things that are unpredictable. In terms of the general business cycle relationship to the TAVF portfolio, it seems obvious that it will affect directly, and be affected by, the demand for automobiles and heavy duty trucks. As such, Ford Motor and Cummins Engine earnings ought to be influenced by factors such as the Gross Domestic Product (GDP) and the general level of interest rates on a year-to-year basis. However, it is hard for me to figure out what the effect of such "big picture" items ought to be on the rest of the portfolio, positive or negative — credit instruments with strong covenants; the common stocks of very well-financed companies engaged in funds management and insurance; depository institutions; real estate companies; credit enhancers; high-tech manufacturers; medical suppliers; and food purveyors. Some of the issues owned by TAVF might be hurt by "bad times"; some ought to be helped given that they tend to be a lot stronger financially than their direct competitors. Suppose there is rampant inflation. Some issuers owned by TAVF might be hurt because the cost to replace existing assets as they depreciate might skyrocket; others might be helped because the cost of entry into the industry will go up precluding new competition from coming in; further, prices paid to acquire control of certain companies in the TAVF portfolio might increase dramatically.

One reason, but far from the only reason, that TAVF ignores factoring into its investment decisions any views about general economic outlooks, about stock market outlooks, and about interest rate outlooks, is that we are no good at making such predictions and we have never run into anybody who is. Furthermore, we are buy-and-hold investors who are prepared to average down as long as the company in which we have invested continues to appear to be solid. Continuing to appear to be solid is a function of corporate analysis, not market prices. Since we are likely to hold the securities of good companies over their business cycles, and we know that we will rarely, if ever, buy at, or near, a low, why should TAVF be hung up today on attempting to gauge for 1996 and 1997, the levels of inflation, the GDP, the S&P 500 and interest rates?

From the TAVF point of view, securities bargains are created much more by past corporate prosperity than by bear markets. Value is a dynamic concept ever changing, and if TAVF is putting the right issues in its common stock portfolio, ever increasing. For example, SunAmerica, Capital Southwest, Zygo, Raymond James Financial, St. Jude Medical and MBIA Inc. are far more valuable properties today because of their corporate achievements than they were when TAVF first acquired their common stocks. Assume that each of those companies are to have very disappointing operations in 1996 and 1997. Each would still remain far more valuable than when TAVF acquired their common stocks — their ultra-high PE ratios for 1996 and 1997 notwithstanding — provided, of course, that each continues to enjoy exceptionally strong financial positions.

TAVF invests on the basis that there has been a fundamental change in the business cycle since the end of World War II. It is not that industries no longer have depressions that are as bad as anything experienced in the 1930's; but it is that such depressions seem to have little, or no, domino effect. There has been a plethora of severe industry depressions in the last 20 years: energy, automobiles, steel, aluminum, row crops, real estate, retail, savings and loan, and commercial banks. These depressions tend to result in the creation of attractive buy-and-hold opportunities for fundamental investors with a long-term point of view regardless of the levels of the general market as measured by popular indices.

Only infrequently over the years has general market performance been of such overwhelming significance as to overshadow the performance of specific corporations whose common stocks are held in the portfolios of fundamentalist buy-and-hold investors who have staying power. Changes in general market levels became of paramount importance, I suppose, in 1929, 1933, 1937, 1974 and, maybe, 1962 and 1987. These occurrences are just not frequent enough so that fundamentalists ought to worry much about them, even assuming the fundamentalists had useful tools for predicting the timing and severity of draconian bear markets.

I've said in previous letters that TAVF ought to do okay for its shareholders as long as the U.S., or wherever TAVF invests, enjoys political stability and an absence of physical violence in the streets; and TAVF avoids investing substantial funds into outright clinkers. None of these three things seem to me to be "slam-dunks," especially the third one, avoiding clinkers. As to avoiding material clinkers, it's been achieved over the first five years of TAVF's existence. TAVF will continue to stick to its discipline but, believe me, there can't be any guarantees. Corporate futures are just too unpredictable.

In terms of meeting the needs of the TAVF shareholder constituency, analyzing our securities as long-term buy-and-holds seems appropriate for those of us, myself included, who have long-term objectives such as retirements, college educations for children, meeting pension fund obligations, etc. If an investor needs near-term performance, or a fund that will outperform an index or peer group consistently, TAVF is not for him or her.

Micro Factors

The underlying G&D assumption is that a company ought to be viewed as a stand-alone going concern that is going to continue to operate in the future in the same industry as it has in the past. The rewards to the holders of common stock will come from the sale in a public marketplace of the common shares of a business which has increased its earning power and distributable income. Insofar as the common stock was acquired at prices below a "central value," the greater the profit to be realized. Against this stand-alone, going concern background, it is thoroughly understandable that G&D adopt the position that the past earnings record is the starting point for the analysis of an equity security. As G&D state on page 533, "The concept of earning power has a definite and important place in investment theory. It combines a history of actual earnings performance over a period of years with a reasonable expectation that the past level or trend will be approximated unless extraordinary conditions supervene. This performance may be measured in terms of either 1) the earnings per share of common stock or 2) the rate of return earned on the common stock equity." Also the following statement appears on page 595, "In 1962 we stated, 'The basic fact is that except in certain limited parts of the common stock universe, asset values are virtually ignored in the stock market.' Since then there has been a modest shift toward greater use. The rash of mergers and acquisitions has focused attention on asset values, particularly when a portion of the acquired company may be sold off."

Further, the purpose of the G&D fundamental analysis is to make a judgment about what future prices are likely to be in an OPMI trading market. At any time, and for most issues, G&D have correctly observed that for the stand-alone going concern, the market price of its common stock is likely to be influenced much more by current earnings than by current book value. As is stated on page 597, "The asset factor is a primary consideration in valuing most privately owned businesses. This procedure is not followed for publicly traded, marketable common stocks." Thus the G&D emphasis on the primacy of the income account is also understandable.

The TAVF approach turns G&D on its head. TAVF does not think of the companies in which it invests as merely stand-alone going concerns. Given any three-to-five year period, TAVF believes that for most companies whose common stocks are in its portfolio, to use G&D language, "extraordinary conditions are bound to supervene." These extraordinary conditions, or conversion events, encompass mergers and acquisitions, hostile take-overs, massive refinancings, divestitures, spin-offs, refinancings, accessing public or private markets at ultra-attractive prices and going privates. I think the evidence is overwhelming that few, if any, companies remain stand-alone going concerns for protracted periods. This used to be true for electric utilities but such no longer appears to be the case even in that industry. Against this background it is understandable that TAVF would focus first on the quality and quantity of resources in a business, a balance sheet approach, rather than on the earnings record, an income account approach. G&D appraises managements as operators of going concerns; TAVF appraises managements not only as operators of going concerns, but also as investors engaged in employing and redeploying assets and refinancing liabilities.

Also, TAVF does not look to OPMI markets for bailouts from its common stock investments. Rather, TAVF looks for premium prices out of future conversion events such as mergers, spin-offs, divestitures, recapitalizations and share repurchases, including Leveraged Buyouts (LBOs) accomplished via cash tender offers, exchange offers or merger transactions. If such conversion events are to be a long-term norm, it seems logical again that the TAVF approach should emphasize the quality and quantity of resources in a business rather than earnings.

G&D does not ignore asset values. TAVF does not ignore earnings or the earnings record. However, the relative weights assigned to earnings and assets in an analysis tend to be quite different as between G&D and TAVF.

In practical terms, the micro factors G&D concentrate on in most security analyses seem to encompass the following:

- Earnings
- Trend of earnings
- Dividends
- Industry identification
- Return on equity
- Comparative analysis vs. other industry participants.

In practical terms, the micro factors TAVF seems to concentrate on are similar to the variables LBO promoters concentrate on:

- Ability to finance
- Longterm outlook
- Exit Strategies

    a) Future sale to OPMI market
    b) Refinance
    c) Get acquired

TAVF is, of course, in a different position than an LBO buyer who can use corporate assets to help finance his purchase of control. TAVF also gets no control benefits from its passive investment. And TAVF cannot precipitate changes in returns on corporate assets by causing them to be used smarter or more aggressively. TAVF tries to compensate for this by buying much safer and much cheaper than would be the case for an LBO. In virtually every case, the common stocks of companies in which TAVF invests have extremely strong financial positions and TAVF, at the time of purchase, tries to pay no more than 50% of the price we think would be paid for the common stock were the company an LBO or merger candidate.

It ought to be noted too that many control buyers are at times a lot less divorced from the G&D micro standards than is TAVF. Insofar as a control person is looking at exit strategies that entail going public via an Initial Public Offering (IPO), the G&D considerations tend to be a lot more important than the TAVF considerations in both getting better pricing for the IPO, or getting the IPO off at all.

Obviously I think the TAVF methodology has many advantages over the G&D methodology. Two advantages come immediately to mind. First, it's a lot less competitive; there are any number of smart analysts focused on earnings. Not too many seem to care about balance sheets. Second, I'm convinced that those of us who focus on the quality of resources existing in a business are a lot less subject to truly unpleasant surprises than are those whose primary emphases are elsewhere.

CHAPTER 39

Graham and Dodd and the Efficient Market

JANUARY 1998

Sell Discipline

Third Avenue Value Fund (TAVF) is going to continue to be a low turnover buy-and-hold fund, i.e, a reluctant seller. The Fund sells in the open market, rather than waiting for a takeover, when management suspects there might be a permanent impairment of capital. Occasionally, TAVF does make a good sale, such as Apple Computer common stock. More often, though, and especially for large-cap companies, the Fund sold prematurely; i.e., Piper, Digital Equipment Corp. and Kemper Financial. Over the years, Fund performance has been pretty good. However, I suspect, but don't really know, that performance might have been even better if Third Avenue had never sold anything in the open market. I suspect, further, that the Fund's buy criteria are so conservative that the sell side should continue to be used quite sparingly.

Graham & Dodd Breakfast

November 13, 1997

During the last quarter, I was asked to address the Seventh Annual Graham & Dodd breakfast sponsored by the Columbia University Graduate School of Business. Below is a reprint covering my talk at the breakfast.

I am especially honored to be a speaker at Columbia Business School's Seventh Annual Graham & Dodd Breakfast. The writings of Benjamin Graham and David Dodd in *Security Analysis* and *The Intelligent Investor* have had such a dramatic influence on me: the way I invest; the way I think about finance.

Graham & Dodd, in the broad scheme of financial analysis, seems to be a case of arrested development. Since the early 1960's, Modern Capital Theory as embodied in the Efficient Market Hypothesis (EMH) and Efficient Portfolio Theory (EPT) has taken over corporate finance. Graham & Dodd fundamentalism has virtually disappeared so that the financial world seems utterly bereft of the important scholarship that ought to exist to build upon the framework contained in the works of Graham & Dodd (and probably Dewing and others before Graham & Dodd).

It is a shame that Graham & Dodd have been shunted aside for the last 30 years or so. EMH and EPT are not at all useful tools for most value analysis, other than risk arbitrage analysis, a small sized offshoot of value analysis. EMH and EPT seem to be strictly technical-chartist approaches to studies of securities while Graham & Dodd place some emphasis on fundamental analysis. A technical-chartist approach is one where conclusions about securities are drawn from studying the prices of securities and the behavior of securities markets. Fundamentalism exists insofar as there is a focus (even though not always an exclusive focus) on gaining insight into matters internal to the firm which contribute to an assessment of the dynamics of the firms as well as the private, and/or takeover values of the business. Fundamentalism also involves obtaining an understanding of the specific terms existing for securities issued by a company.

EMH is a preferred approach useful where two "special case" conditions exist in concert:

1. The solitary goal of a passive, noncontrol, "investor" is to maximize a risk-adjusted total return consistently. Consistently means all the time. (It seems to me, as it did to Benjamin Graham, that most people or institutions trying to outperform, or even just equal, a market consistently are best described as short-term speculators, not investors).

2. The securities to be analyzed are best analyzed by reference to a very limited number of computer programmable variables. Such securities seem limited to the following:

> a) credit instruments without credit risk, e.g., U.S. Treasuries
> b) derivative securities, including options and convertibles
> c) risk arbitrage securities, i.e., workout securities where the amount of workout value is relatively determinant and where the timing of the workout is also relatively determinant — something that tends to be the case after, say, the public announcement of a merger

The funny thing about Graham & Dodd is that lots of people talk about Graham & Dodd, but very few people seem to have actually read the earlier editions of *Security Analysis* or *The Intelligent Investor*.

In terms of equity investments, Graham & Dodd have given outside passive investors a series of terrific caveats by which to live if the investor really does not know very much about the company with which the investor is involved, or the specific securities issued by that company. The Graham & Dodd caveats provide a margin of safety.

I believe though that today, unlike the Graham & Dodd period, public disclosures have gotten so good that it is now possible for an outsider who is not a very, very short-term trader to know much about many companies just from the public record. Most of the improvements in public disclosures seem to have occurred subsequent to the publication of the pre-1988 editions of *Security Analysis*. There has been a disclosure revolution in this country which I trace to the Securities Acts Amendments of 1964. Now an outsider, who is a buy-and-hold investor trained in fundamental analysis, can know an awful lot about an awful lot of companies just by relying on the public record. For example, look at the overall success in earning excess returns for those involved in hostile takeovers from the 1970's onward. In hostiles, all you have is the public record. Using inside information to acquire securities in a hostile is almost always a "show stopper."

However, after 1964, there seems to have been little or no scholarship to advance fundamentalism beyond Graham & Dodd. All academics seemed to have focused on EMH and EPT. My fellow speaker, Seth Klarman, wrote a book on fundamental analysis, *Margin of Safety*, and I wrote a book on fundamental analysis, *The Aggressive Conservative Investor*. Almost nobody bothered to read either book.

Graham & Dodd were less good in their approach to credit analysis than they were in their approach to equity analysis. Graham & Dodd's credit analysis essentially involved gauging the prospects of whether or not a money default might occur for any debt issue in a corporate capitalization. The analysis was basically quantitative with an emphasis on overall coverage. My fundamental credit analysis, on the other hand, involves the assumption that a money default will occur and then gauging how the security will work out either in an out-of-court restructuring or a Chapter 11. For this type of approach, analysis of debt covenants become crucial, and coverage is measured at various levels of seniority and not on an overall basis (unless you are looking at the most junior issue in a company's debt capitalization).

It seems to me that the most successful people in the financial community — control buyers such as Warren Buffett, Carl Icahn, Ron Perelman and Richard Rainwater — approach securities analysis quite differently from Graham & Dodd or EMH theorists. In investing passively, I try to emulate these control buyers. These successful people analyze what a business is worth and what its dynamics might be; all done from the bottom-up. They then stop. The focus in Graham & Dodd and EMH is different. The Graham & Dodd and EMH goals are to predict where a security will sell in a market populated by outside, passive minority investors. Compared with the best investors, Graham and Dodd seem to carry a lot of excess analytical baggage. This excess baggage is mostly irrelevant to determining an underlying business value. Among these extraneous factors that are irrelevant to valuing a business' fundamentals are the following:

1. Dividend policy
2. Macro market factors
3. General level of interest rates
4. Technical factors, such as supply and demand for marketable securities

Graham & Dodd, along with EMH, undertake virtually all their analysis of companies whose common stocks are publicly traded (other than investment companies whose assets consist of marketable securities) based on a strict going-concern assumption. It is assumed that the company being analyzed will continue to operate in the same industry it always has been in, financed the way the business has always been financed, managed as it has traditionally been managed, controlled as it has been controlled and owned as it has been owned. I am convinced that the strict going-concern assumption is unrealistic. Few, if any, companies are going to go as long as five years without being engaged in mergers and acquisitions, massive refinancings and restructurings, massive asset redeployments, changes in control, and liquidations, in whole or in part. Until the early 1990's, the strict going-concern assumption seems to have been accurate for the electric utility industry but in few other places. The strict going-concern assumption is no longer accurate even for electric utilities.

A logical concomitant of the strict going-concern assumption is that the past earnings record, or in the case of EMH, the past cash flow record, is the best indicator of what future results will be for the company. Thus, there is a belief in the primacy of earnings, or cash flow, as determinants of corporate value. This emphasis on flows, whether cash or earnings, denigrates in importance two other areas where corporate values are created

> a) conversion of assets to other uses and other ownership coupled with refinancings.
> b) having access to capital markets, either debt or equity, on super attractive bases.

In our fundamental analysis of equities, we do not place much emphasis on predicting the future. Rather we try to buy what is "safe and cheap." The companies in whose equities we invest are supposed to have four characteristics:

1. Exceptionally strong financial position, as measured by an absence of liabilities either on balance sheet or off balance sheet; the presence of high quality assets such as surplus cash; and/or the presence of operations that generate unencumbered cash flows available to service the capitalization, e.g., money management firms.
2. Reasonable managements from the outside stockholders' point of view. (This is the toughest area for us in most analyses).
3. An understandable business, which in each case means complete public filings, especially with the SEC, and reliable audits useful to us as objective benchmarks which we treat as tools of analysis. We use financial statements, not because they are Truth, but rather because they are Objective Benchmarks.
4. We try to pay no more than 50 cents for each $1 we think the common stock would be worth, were the company a private business or a takeover candidate.

There are trade-offs involved in following our approach. In almost all cases when we acquire a security, the near-term earnings outlook is terrible. Managements of the companies whose common stocks are in our portfolios tend to be non-promotional and highly conservative, willing in up periods to sacrifice returns on equity and returns on assets for safety. The markets for many securities we own are relatively illiquid.

There are two important respects in which I would like to distinguish Graham & Dodd from EMH:

EMH is information unconscious. EMH theory is that in order to outperform a market, an investor has to have superior information. Graham & Dodd, in contrast, are right on the money in their premise that the route to investment success is to use the available information in a superior manner. As technician-chartists, EMH people seem to have no conception of what corporate information is and how it is used. Some of them even seem to think that algebra is more important than Financial Accounting. In the preface to a leading EMH text, *Principles of Corporate Finance* by Brealy and Myers, there appears this statement, "There are no ironclad prerequisites for reading this book except algebra and the English language. An elementary knowledge of accounting, statistics and microeconomics is helpful, however."

EMH is price unconscious. Market price in EMH represents a universal equilibrium establishing business values for all purposes. Graham & Dodd, on the other hand, point out that market prices can be too high or too low; or to paraphrase Ben Graham, Mr. Market is an extremely emotional fellow, subject to frequent fits of irrationality. The EMH view seems summarized by the statement of William F. Sharpe, a Nobel Laureate, in the Third Edition of his book, *Investments*, "Every security's price equals its investment value at all times." If Bill Sharpe really believes that, I own a bridge to Brooklyn which I would like to sell to him.

CHAPTER 40

Graham and Dodd Revisited

OCTOBER 2011

In the main body of this letter I discuss, after re-reading Graham and Dodd's writings on Value Investing, how the various Third Avenue Fund managers are followers of Graham and Dodd, and how these managers are different. Before doing that, there is one macro point in which I believe strongly, and of which you should be aware. There is no way that I can see that those countries involved with the Euro can be made credit-worthy unless all European Sovereign Debt is assumed, or guaranteed, by each member country including, especially, Germany. Such an amalgamation would make Euro Sovereign Debt more comparable to U.S. Treasuries than is now the case. I do not know how the forthcoming European upheavals will work out. But cash-rich economies with a plethora of investable funds ought to do okay, provided they are opportunistic. It is comforting to know that so much of Third Avenue Management's common stock investments are in companies operating in Hong Kong, mainland China, South Korea, Canada, Brazil, Australia and Sweden.

Graham and Dodd Revised, Updated and Placed in Context

Benjamin Graham and David Dodd (G&D) were prolific writers, publishing volumes in 1934, 1940, 1951, 1962 and by Ben Graham alone in 1971. A principal problem with G&D is that almost everyone in finance talks about G&D but very few seem to have actually read G&D.

This letter is based essentially on the 1962 edition, *Security Analysis Principles and Technique* by Graham, Dodd and Cottle; and the 1971 edition of *The Intelligent Investor* by Graham.

Because so many have such a superficial understanding of G&D, their names have become synonymous with the term "value investing". This, in turn, has led to some confusion about what it is that value investors do, particularly, the way that value investing in equities is practiced at Third Avenue Management (TAM). Though we are influenced by G&D, our methods, developed over the life of the firm, are basically different. Value Investing is one area of Fundamental Finance (FF). It involves investments in marketable securities by non-control outside passive minority investors (OPMIs). The other areas of Fundamental Finance involve the following:

- Distress Investing
- Control Investing
- Credit Analysis
- First and Second Stage Venture Capital Investments

Modern Capital Theory (MCT), like Value Investing, focuses on investments by OPMIs. Unlike Value Investors, MCT focuses strictly on near-term changes in market prices. In a number of special cases the factors important in MCT are also important in Value Investing. MCT is discussed briefly at the end of this paper.

G&D made three great contributions to Value Investing:

1. G&D distinguished between market price and intrinsic value (a concept that still seems alien to MCT).
2. G&D pioneered the concept of investing with a margin of safety.
3. G&D promulgated the belief that investment decisions ought to be based on ascertainable facts. (This was before the modern era – say after 1964, when for OPMIs the amount of factual material exploded and the reliability of factual materials became much enhanced).

The equity analysts at Third Avenue Management tend to follow the basic rule promulgated by G&D: acquire at attractive prices the common stocks issued by primary companies in their industries.

Both G&D and MCT focus on the investment process from the points of view of the OPMI. Little, or no, attention is paid to other points of view; and the particular factors needed to understand the dynamics driving individual companies, particular industries, control persons and putative control persons, as well as creditors. This emphasis on the OPMI is in sharp contrast to other areas of FF – control investing, distress investing and first and second stage Venture Capital. Here, the analysis does not focus on OPMI needs and decisions, but is rather a four-legged stool:

1. Understanding the OPMI's needs and desires.
2. Understanding the company in some depth.
3. Understanding the needs and desires of control persons and entities, present and future.
4. Understanding the needs and desires of creditors.

Open-end funds, i.e., mutual funds (Investment Companies operating under the Investment Company Act of 1940 as amended) are required to operate mostly as OPMIs. Third Avenue, in the management of various portfolios, is basically, but not wholly, an OPMI. But Third Avenue's analytic techniques, unlike G&D's, are the same as control investors, distress investors and creditors. The emphasis is on understanding in-depth, from the bottom-up, the company and the securities it issues; and also the character and motivations of managements, other control entities, and others senior to the common stock, ranging from secured lending by commercial banks to trade creditors to holders of subordinated debentures to holders of preferred stocks. There is a de-emphasis on top-down factors emphasized by G&D and MCT – general stock market levels, near-term stock price movements, a primacy of the income account, a primacy of dividend income, quality or growth as defined by general recognition of such in the general market.

Many of the best value investors graduate into other areas of financial fundamentalism, especially control investing and distress investing. Names of such "graduates" which come to mind are Warren Buffet, Sam Zell, Carl Icahn, Bill Ackman and David Einhorn.

Analysts at TAM think like owners, like private acquirers or like creditors, emphasizing elements of FF that differentiate Third Avenue from G&D. For example, G&D emphasize the importance of dividends for OPMIs. In contrast, FFs look instead at the corporation optimizing its uses of cash. In general, corporate cash can be dispensed in three areas:

1. Expand assets
2. Reduce liabilities
3. Distribute to equity owners

> (a) via dividends
> (b) via stock buybacks

There are comparative advantages and disadvantages for dividends and buybacks, which are never discussed by G&D, because they only mention the stock buyback alternative as it relates to stock options for management. There is no discussion by G&D of stock buybacks as a method of enhancing a common stock's market price over the long run, giving the management the flexibility to retain cash in troubled times, and also increasing the percentage ownership interest of each non-selling stockholder.

From a corporate point of view, distributing cash to shareholders has to be a residual use of cash, compared to expanding assets or reducing liabilities most of the time. Probably the most important exception to this exists where the payments of common stock dividends in cash gives a corporation better long-term access to capital markets than would otherwise exist. This seems to be the case for companies which, by the nature of their operations, consume cash in order to create wealth and are required to raise outside equity capital periodically, e.g., integrated electric utilities and certain financial companies.

G&D in their analysis of common stocks emphasize the following factors:

1. Primacy of the income account – forecast future earnings relying heavily on the past earnings record
2. Dividend distributions
3. The general level of securities markets
4. Outlook for the economy

5. Industry identifications
6. General market opinion as to the quality and/or growth prospects of an issuer

In a G&D primacy of the income account approach (or any other primacy of the income account approach) managements are appraised almost solely as operators. For FF, managements are appraised using a three-pronged approach:

1. Management as operators
2. Management as investors
3. Management as financiers

In appraising managements as financiers, the emphasis is on a primacy of credit-worthiness for either the company or for various securities in the capital structure.

G&D agree that the securities of secondary companies and workout situations can be attractive for Enterprising OPMIs, whom they distinguish from Defensive OPMIs. However, very little is really voiced by G&D as to how secondary situations and workout situations ought to be analyzed, compared with their views on how to analyze the securities of primary companies, other than to state that secondary common stocks should not be acquired except at prices of two-thirds or less of underlying value.

G&D believe it is important to guard against market risk, i.e., fluctuations in security prices. Thus, it becomes important in their analysis to have views about general stock market levels. FF practitioners guard only against investment risk, i.e., the problems of companies and/or the securities they issue. In FF analysis, market risk is mostly ignored except when dealing with "sudden death" securities – derivatives and risk arbitrage securities; when dealing with portfolios financed by heavy borrowing; and when companies have to access capital markets, especially equity markets.

In the analysis of performing credits acquired at or near par, emphasis by G&D is on quantitative data relevant to overall interest coverage, rather than any emphasis on covenants and/or collateral. FF emphasizes covenants and collateral in credit analysis. No matter how favorable the quantitative data, e.g. coverage and debt ratios. FF practitioners examining most corporate credits assume that the quantitative facts are likely to deteriorate over the long-term life (say a five to 15-year life) of a debt instrument. Such an assumption creates a margin of safety for a creditor.

In valuing assets, G&D seem to rely strictly on a classified balance sheet produced according to Generally Accepted Accounting Principles (GAAP). Thus, inventory is viewed as a current asset and real property as a fixed asset. In FF, the analysis tends to get different results. In the case of a retail chain which is a going-concern, inventories usually are a fixed asset of the worst sort – subject to mark-downs, shrinkage, obsolescence, misplacement. On the other hand Class A, fully-leased income-producing office buildings tend to be current assets, probably an area where price agreement can be reached via one phone call.

For FF, GAAP in the U.S. is an essential disclosure tool, the best objective benchmark available to the OPMI analyst in the vast majority of cases. However, GAAP and related accounting measures, unadjusted by the analyst, are almost always misleading, in one context or another.

G&D stress the importance of adjusting GAAP to determine "true earnings" for a period. In FF, the analyst always adjusts GAAP, not only to determine earnings from operations, but also to determine credit worthiness and asset values.

GAAP recognizes three classifications on the right hand side of the balance sheet: liabilities; redeemable preferred stock; and net worth. In economic fact, there are many liabilities that have an equity component. It is up to the analyst to decide what percentages of certain liabilities are close to equivalent to payables and what percentage are close to equivalent to net worth. Take the liability account, deferred income taxes payable, in a going concern. If the cash saved from deferring income taxes are invested in depreciable assets, the tax may never become payable. However, the deferred tax payable account can never be worth as much as tax paid retained earnings (part of net worth) because the tax may someday become payable, especially if the company engages in resource conversion activity, such as being acquired in a change of control transaction. So, maybe there is as much as a 90% equity value in the deferred income tax accounts payable. On the other hand, deferred income taxes payable can never be as much of a liability as current accounts payable or interest bearing debt. Maybe, at the maximum, there is a 5% to 10% equity in the deferred tax payable account. GAAP is based on a rigid set of rules; it is no longer principles based. The appraisal of an account, such as deferred income taxes payable, is in the province of the users of financial statements, not the preparers of financial statements.

For G&D, values for stockholders are created by earnings which are then valued in the market by a price earnings ratio (or capitalization rate) and/or dividends, which are valued by the market on a current yield basis.

In FF, stockholder values flow out of creating corporate values. There are four different ways corporate values are created:

1. Cash flows available to security holders. This is probably created by corporations fewer times than most people think.
2. Earnings, with earnings defined as creating wealth while consuming cash. This is what most well-run corporations do and also most governments do. Earnings cannot have a lasting value unless the entity remains creditworthy. Also, in most cases, in order to maintain and grow earnings the corporation or government is going to have to have access to capital markets to meet cash shortfalls.
3. Resource Conversion. These areas include massive asset redeployments, massive liability redeployments and changes in control. Resource conversion occurs as part of mergers and acquisitions, contests for control, the bulk sale or purchase of assets or businesses, Chapter 11 reorganizations, out of court reorganizations, spin-offs, and going privates including leveraged buy outs ("LBOs") and management buy outs ("MBOs").
4. Super attractive access to capital markets. On the equity side, this includes initial public offerings ("IPOs") during periods such as the dotcom bubble. On the credit side, this includes the availability of long-term, fixed rate, and non-recourse financing for income producing commercial real estate.

G&D do not distinguish between cash return investing and total return investing. In cash return investing, returns are measured by current yield (or dividend return), yield-to-maturity, yield-to-worst or yield-to-an-event. In total return investing, returns are measured in price paid relative to cash returns plus (or minus) capital appreciation (or depreciation) in given periods of time. Many portfolios have to be invested only for cash return into high-grade credits, e.g., bank securities portfolios; insurance company portfolios, at least as to the amount of liabilities; certain pension plans. (In the current low interest environment, it seems almost impossible to be a rational cash return investor). For G&D, the higher the dividend, the higher price at which a common stock would sell. G&D imply that the higher dividend issue should be acquired. G&D ignore that the lower priced security may be more attractive to the total return investor because of the lower price and the larger amount of retained earnings.

Two facts stand out in comparing dividend income in the U.S. with interest income:

- Dividends are generally tax-advantaged in the U.S., with individuals currently subject to a maximum federal tax rate of 15% on qualified dividends; and corporate taxpayers are generally entitled to a 70% exemption from income tax on dividends from domestic companies.

- In the U.S., as a practical matter, no one can take away a creditor's right to a contracted interest payment (or other cash payment) unless that individual so consents or a court of competent jurisdiction, usually a bankruptcy court, suspends that payment.

Most OPMIs involved with common stock believe in substantively consolidating the company with its common stock owners. They believe they are buying General Electric (GE), not GE common stock. In FF, the company is a standalone, separate and distinct from its shareholders, its management, its control group and its creditors. Essential for understanding the dynamics of many companies are not only consolidated financial statements but, also, how financial statements are consolidated. In many cases, it is important to know which liabilities of particular parents or subsidiaries are assumed or guaranteed by other companies which are part of a consolidation.

There are crucial differences between the analysis of companies as going concerns and the analysis of companies as investment vehicles. Most companies have both going concern characteristics and investment company characteristics. For both going concerns and investment vehicles, credit-worthiness is paramount for the company and its securities holders (except perhaps for adequately secured creditors). In going concern analysis, great weight is given to flows: whether cash or earnings. In investment vehicle analysis, great weight is given to asset values, especially realizable asset values. G&D emphasize going concerns except for a short description of Net-Nets, which focuses only on classified balance sheets and never mentions credit-worthiness or prospects for resource conversion, especially changes of control or going private.

The importance of market price depends primarily on two factors:

1. The form of investments in the portfolio
2. How the portfolio is financed

Generally, market prices are much less important if a portfolio consists of performing loans. Indeed, in some portfolios, e.g., high-grade municipal bonds held by individuals, almost no attention is paid to market prices. Market prices are almost always important in evaluating common stocks, except in instances where the common stocks are being accumulated with the idea of obtaining control or elements of control. Market prices are almost always of critical importance where the portfolio is financed by margin borrowings where the collateral for the borrowing are the securities that make up the portfolio.

Analysts really ought not to use the word "risk" without putting an adjective in front of it. G&D really do not distinguish often enough between market risk and investment risk, even though they recognize in measuring market risk that "Mr. Market" tends to be utterly irrational some of the time. Market risk refers to short-term fluctuations in securities prices. Investment risk refers to something going wrong with the company issuing securities or with the securities (e.g., dilution).

Sometimes analysis takes funny turns. In a poorly financed company, would one prefer to have had the company issue subordinated debentures or a preferred stock which is, of course, subordinated to the debentures? If there is a failure to pay interest or principal on a subordinated debenture, the one remedy available to the subordinated creditor is to declare an event of default. Then, either the indenture trustee, or usually 25% of the subordinated creditors, can accelerate the debt, declaring it due and payable. For a subordinate class, the right to accelerate most often is the right to commit suicide, because this action would likely result in a reorganization or liquidation where almost all, or all, the value will go to senior creditors. In contrast to an event of default, the preferred shareholder accumulates dividend arrearages. The company has less need to reorganize or liquidate. If an investor is making a capital infusion into a troubled company, the investor frequently is much better off from a safety point of view by having the issuer issue a preferred stock, rather than a subordinate.

G&D seem utterly silent about the compensation of promoters, which has to be understood if one is to understand Wall Street and/or corporate managements. Economists have it wrong when they say, "There is no free lunch". What they should say is, "Somebody has to pay for lunch". Those who most commonly pay are OPMIs.

In writing of growth stocks, G&D seem to define growth as that which is generally recognized in the marketplace as growth. Many growth stocks do not have general recognition and so they sell at very modest prices. Current examples include Applied Materials, Brookfield Asset Management, Cheung Kong Holdings, Hang Lung Group and Wheelock & Co.

While ignored by G&D, I am of the strong opinion that common stock prices never have to be rational in the absence of catalysts that are the bedrock of resource conversion. The most important catalyst seems to be changes of control and/or potential changes of control. In a conservative, non-control, FF investment, the common stocks contained in many TAM portfolios are those of blue-chip companies selling at substantial discounts from readily ascertainable net asset values (NAV). The exit strategies are based on the belief that NAVs will grow over the next three to seven years and that the discounts from NAV will not widen materially. Without catalysts, though, it appears as if the discounts from NAV are just a random walk at any particular time.

Where there are no prospects for changes of control or no Wall Street sponsorship (induced by generous compensation arrangements for managers and securities sales persons), prices in OPMI markets can be utterly irrational persistently. The very best companies whose common stocks are publicly traded and where no catalyst exists usually sell at discounts to NAV. Sometimes these discounts from NAV reach 50% or greater.

Many of these companies are extremely well financed and have most impressive long-term records of increasing NAVs and earnings per share persistently. Such companies include Brookfield Asset Management, Capital Southwest, Investor AB, and Cheung Kong Holdings. In contrast, there is a huge market for private equity that OPMIs spend billions of dollars to get into and which are priced at substantial premiums above NAV. These are the hedge funds. Typically, their premiums above NAV are reflected in the present value of promotes paid to hedge fund managers. Those promotes normally run to 2% of assets under management plus 20% of annual profits after the OPMIs receive a preferred return of, say, 6%. Further, lengthy lock-up periods tend to exist for OPMIs owning hedge funds, while the publicly-traded common stocks cited above are all marketable. From a value point of view, there does not seem to be any rational reason why the publicly-traded issues mentioned above should sell at steep discounts, while the hedge funds are priced at premiums.

In FF, potential resource conversions, catalysts, and access to capital markets are included in the valuation process. FF puts a great premium on the value of control, something ignored by G&D. Asset values are very important insofar as they are readily ascertainable and exist in well-financed companies. Asset values are of limited importance in companies which are not well financed and where the principal assets are single purpose assets useful only to a going concern. These asset values can have a positive or negative effect on underlying value. They can help predict that future earnings will be high based on an ROE analysis (book value equals E) or they can indicate, and often do, very high overhead and very high fixed costs.

I largely disagree with G&D as to when low pricing creates a margin of safety. For G&D the margin of safety is created mostly by depressed prices in the general market. For FF, the margin of safety is derived largely from micro factors affecting a company and its securities, not general stock market levels. G&D seem to have a valid point in terms of guarding against market risk. FF is involved with investment risk, not market risk.

Diversification, quite properly, is key in a G&D analysis. It is an OPMI analysis which relies heavily on predicting future earnings and future dividends, something extremely hard to do well. In FF there is much less need for diversification which is viewed in FF as only a surrogate, and usually a damn poor surrogate, for knowledge, control and price consciousness. Non-control investors need a modicum of diversification, but nowhere near to the degree emphasized by G&D, MCT and academics in general.

G&D is mostly a tool for top-down analysis; while FF, in contrast, is almost completely bottom up.

G&D describe how to forecast for a coming five to ten-year period:

- Formulate a view as to the general economic climate
- Anticipate future earnings from the Dow Jones Index and the S&P 500
- Forecast earnings for individual companies

In FF, the essential analysis is of the individual company and the current price of the security versus its estimated intrinsic value. Instead of just forecasting earnings, in FF, prognostications are made about:

- Operations
- Potential resource conversions
- Access to capital markets

There are always trade-offs in FF investing. For example, a strong financial position in 2011 means one is dealing with a management willing to sacrifice returns on equity, for the safety and opportunism inherent in a strong financial position. Also, and this is a possibility that G&D do not consider, there are incentives for certain control people to prefer low prices for publicly-traded common stocks:

1. Those doing estate planning

2. Those contemplating taking the company private, including LBOs; Going private entails cashing out public shareholders. To go private two conditions have to be fulfilled:

> a) Low, to reasonable, price
> b) Strong finances – usually by the company itself, or it could be by the buyer or both

3. Control person is insulated from changes in control.

MCT, like G&D, is focused on looking at economic and financial phenomena from the point of view of OPMIs. Unlike G&D, the entire focus of MCT is on near-term changes in market prices. MCT operates on the false assumption that markets are efficient for all participants. Unlike one of G&D's great conceptual teachings, MCT does not distinguish between market price and intrinsic value.

When it comes to corporate finance, MCT offers a valuable approach to project finance, but contributes little to corporate finance as visualized by FF participants. The concept of net present value (NPV) is essential for understanding project finance. For a project to make sense, estimates of the NPV of cash outflows has to exceed the NPV of cash inputs. In terms of corporate finance, there can be other reasons for undertaking (or not undertaking) a project than positive (or negative) net cash generation. In terms of capitalization, most MCT believers sign off on the Modigliani-Miller Theorem that if a management is working in the best interest of shareholders, the capitalization is a matter of indifference. The Modigliani-Miller Theorem is an absolute non-starter in FF. One can't measure credit-worthiness without also appraising capitalizations.

In FF, quarterly earnings reports tend to lack significance. However, there are instances where quarterly earnings reports can be important. This tends to be the case for most poorly financed companies, which need virtually continual access to capital markets. FF and MCT tend to coalesce when dealing in "sudden death" securities or absolutely credit worthy debt obligations. Such securities seem a special case and encompass the following:

1. Credit instruments without credit risk
2. Derivatives
3. Risk arbitrage, with risk arbitrage defined as situations where there is likely to be a relatively determinant workout in a relatively determinant period of time

In much of what MCT and G&D do, the goal is to estimate the probable effect of certain items on near-term market prices in OPMI markets. Thus, G&D emphasize the importance of determining "true" earnings for a period. In contrast, for FF, the possible or probable effect on OPMI market prices is pretty much ignored in most, but not all, cases. Rather, the goal in FF is to understand the underlying values of a business as well as the business' dynamics. Such understanding requires a study not only of flows – whether cash or earnings – but also, resource conversion possibilities, access to capital markets and the quality and motivations of management and control persons.

As practiced at Third Avenue, Value Investing is a component of Fundamental Finance that stresses intellectual rigor and a long time horizon. The contributions of Graham and Dodd to this approach have been valuable, but they are only part of the story.

PART 6

ACADEMIC FINANCE

"In the financial world it tends to be misleading to state, 'There Is No Free Lunch.' Rather the more meaningful comment is, 'Somebody Has to Pay For Lunch'."

April 2005

CHAPTER 41

Modern Capital Theory and Fundamental Investing

APRIL 1993

More on The Third Avenue Value Fund's Investment Philosophy

The Third Avenue Value Fund (TAVF), in its investment processes, is strictly fundamentalist. The analyses used by TAVF for the purpose of making passive securities investments are virtually the same analyses as those used by businessmen to buy and sell businesses, and by Wall Street activists engaged in mergers and acquisitions, leveraged buyouts (LBOs), the restructuring of troubled companies, going private, and venture capital. In particular, technical market factors, and the teachings of technicians, are completely ignored. Technicians are those who reach investment, or more likely trading, conclusions by studying the behavior of securities prices and securities markets. Technicians are of two types: practitioners and academics.

Also, TAVF fundamental analysis is always bottom-up. There is a concentration on factors peculiar to the business, and minimal weight is given to top-down factors such as predicting business cycles or interest rate movements, or the shape of the new tax bill overall, or the level of the general stock market. On the other hand, fundamental securities analysis, as embodied in the classic Graham & Dodd text, *Security Analysis*, is essentially top-down. Further, Graham & Dodd is not about understanding businesses. Rather, it is about excellent caveats to follow if you can't, or don't, understand particular firms.

I thought it might be helpful to the Fund's shareholders if I briefly contrasted the TAVF approach with the approach that is central to academic finance, to wit, Modern Capital Theory (MCT). This spring, I conducted a seminar at Yale University's School of Organization and Management entitled "Restructuring Troubled Companies." The participants in the seminar seemed concerned that most of their work in my seminar was in sharp contrast to what went on in other finance courses. Consequently, I reviewed somewhat systematically the key literature of MCT, and then wrote a paper for my seminar, entitled "Reconciling Modern Capital Theory and Active Investing."

It seems useful in this letter to share a few thoughts with you about MCT because I believe it has a huge influence on most money managers with whom TAVF ostensibly competes. Further, MCT obviously is becoming highly influential in many financial areas where there are important public policy issues, ranging from reform of the U.S. Bankruptcy Code to accounting for employee stock options under Generally Accepted Accounting Principles (GAAP). MCT, in fact, ought to be applicable, if at all, to a few narrow special cases. It has nothing to do with what TAVF does or, I daresay, with at least 98% of the investment activities in the financial community, excluding mutual fund managers and other strictly passive investors. To the extent one is trained to obtain fundamental knowledge about companies and their securities and to the extent one is an activist investor, promoter, or business buyer, MCT and its practitioners are best described as being straight out of "Looney Tunes."

In the MCT scheme of things, the entire investment process (including the management of companies) revolves around the needs and desires of Outside, Passive, Minority Investors (OPMIs) who can never have special knowledge of anything, or control of anything, and whose needs and desires are fulfilled by continuously outperforming, in the stock or bond market, similarly situated OPMIs, risk adjusted. MCT might be useful for such OPMI traders. That agenda has nothing to do with TAVF. It may have a little to do with trading. It also has nothing to do with long-term investing. MCT does not involve fundamental analysis. Rather, its practitioners are technicians with PhDs. For MCT to be useful in security analysis, the application of its teachings must be limited to those securities which are readily tradeable and which can be analyzed by reference to a few simple, computer programmable, variables. In my view, those securities are limited to the following: a) credit instruments without credit risk; b) derivative securities, including synthetics, warrants and convertibles; and c) pure risk arbitrage situations, i.e., situations where there are relatively determinant price realization events in relatively determinant periods of time.

As to other precepts of MCT, e.g., diversification theory and measurement of the riskiness of assets, these are merely surrogates, and usually very poor ones, for knowledge and control. From a "money grubbing" point of view, I'd strongly suggest to those who invest on the basis of MCT theories that they, and their clients, would be well served by placing a portion of their portfolios in TAVF as an alternative investment. I'll bet such an investment would be a lot more productive than would be, say, an investment in an index fund. More importantly from a public policy point of view, now that I've read the MCT literature, I can't fathom why any respectable authority would give any weight to MCT in coming to terms with optimizing the U.S. Bankruptcy Code, U.S. securities law and regulation, Generally Accepted Accounting Principles, and the valuation of businesses. In these areas (indeed most areas) MCT ought to be viewed as irrelevant.

CHAPTER 42

The Third Avenue Approach vs. The Conventional Academic Approach

JULY 1995

The Third Avenue View Vs. The Conventional View

Generally speaking, most shareholders seem to prefer high, and increasing, dividends to modest, or no, common stock dividends. As is pointed out on page 549 of a leading academic text on finance, *Corporate Finance* (3d ed.) by Ross, Westerfield and Jaffe ("Ross, Westerfield"), "The stock market reacts positively to increases in dividends (or an initial dividend payment) and negatively to decreases in dividends. This suggests that there is information content in dividend payments." Although situations have to be examined on a case by case basis, TAVF generally favors a no cash dividend policy, especially for companies, like Ryan Beck, having a demonstrated ability to earn huge returns on reinvested capital.

I continue to be struck by the fact that the Third Avenue Value Fund (TAVF) view of the financial world, in almost all respects, is almost 180 degrees different from conventional views, especially views expressed by scholars such as Ross, Westerfield. Furthermore, these academic views, which are discussed at some length below, seem to have been adopted virtually in their entirety by most money managers, including the managers of most mutual funds, especially those who are non-fundamental, top-down asset allocators. In addition, each and every manager of an index fund accepts the academic theories. These theories are, after all, the *raison d'être* of index funds.

Corporate dividend policy is just one area of difference separating TAVF from the conventional "plain vanilla" world of passive, non-control investments in marketable securities. It seems to me that if I can do a reasonable job of explaining to you, the Fund shareholder, where the TAVF approach fits in, and where the conventional academic approach fits in, you ought to come away with a pretty good idea of what TAVF is and is not. The downside to my having spent so much time and effort on academic finance is that this quarterly letter to Fund shareholders will be dull, boring and unimportant — hardly an earth-shaking event. Hopefully, though, the analysis of the basic differences in approach between TAVF on the one hand, and conventional academic finance as embodied in Modern Capital Theory (MCT), and its component parts, the Efficient Market Hypothesis (EMH) and Efficient Portfolio Theory (EPT) on the other, will be useful for you as a Fund shareholder.

Insofar as the Fund invests for cash return, it invests in debt instruments, not common stocks. TAVF follows this policy because where cash return is an investment objective, the buy-and-hold portfolio manager, and the portfolio, tend to be far better served if that cash return is received from the ownership of securities on which cash payments are a contractual requirement, i.e., credit instruments, rather than from non-guaranteed common stock dividend payments. TAVF restricts its investments in credit instruments to issues containing strong protective covenants; where the prospects of a money default are remote, where the Fund would fare at least okay in the subsequent reorganization in the event of a money default; and where the cash return appears to be at least 500 basis points better than can otherwise be obtained from a credit of comparable quality.

TAVF remains reluctant to hold the common stocks of highly leveraged holding companies whose principal assets, on a parent company basis, are the common stocks of highly leveraged, highly regulated subsidiaries. If academics analyze financial statements at all, they seem to focus on estimating cash flows on a consolidated basis. TAVF not only does not focus on one number, e.g., cash flow from operations, but the Fund also emphasizes different accounting entities depending on context, sometimes focusing on consolidated financials and sometimes focusing on parent company financials.

The Third Avenue Approach Vs. The Conventional Academic Approach

The characteristics I impute to the conventional academic approach comes from reading substantial amounts of academic literature. In writing this quarterly report, I cite largely from three books: Ross Westerfield (mentioned previously), *Principals of Corporate Finance* (4th ed.) by Brealey and Myers ("Brealey and Myers"), and *Corporate Valuation-Tools for Effective Appraisal and Decision Making* by Cornell ("Cornell"). Not every academic who basically subscribes to MCT will agree with everything contained in the three texts: MCT believers are not monolithic. Each of the three texts seems to lack internal consistency and some of my citations could be modified by other citations. Nonetheless, I believe I have stated fairly below the academic positions regarding market efficiency, price equilibrium, substantive consolidation, structural subordination, information flows, agency costs, risk, valuation, and the uses and limitations of financial accounting.

Before contrasting the TAVF approach with the academic approach, it is helpful to examine the conditions under which MCT theories appear to be wholly valid. This happens when two special conditions exist in concert:

1. The securities, or assets, being examined are simple to analyze, with prices being determined by reference to a very limited number of computer programmable variables. In the securities arena such instruments appear limited to the following:

   a) credit instruments without credit risk, e.g., treasury bills.
   b) derivative securities, including options, warrants and convertibles.
   c) risk arbitrage securities, i.e., situations where there are reasonably determinable workouts within reasonably determinable periods of time.

2. The sole objective of the beneficial owner of the asset is to maximize a risk-adjusted total return, convertible into cash at any time, consistently. Consistently means short term, probably daily, or even weekly or monthly.

Given these two conditions, there exists an efficient market for Outside Passive Minority Investors (OPMIs) who are traders seeking to maximize total return consistently. TAVF may be an OPMI, but it is not a trader; it is a buy-and-hold fundamentalist. OPMI traders are neither insiders, nor people trained in fundamental analysis, such as would be the case where the analysis is activist. The MCT approach also makes sense for money managers with little, or no, training or interest in fundamental bottom-up analysis; and who are required by clients, or circumstances, to value the portfolios they manage exclusively, or almost exclusively, by marking to market (i.e., pricing) on a daily basis.

The Cornell book points to three elements of the Efficient Market Hypothesis:

1. *"Neither technical investors who rely on mechanical trading rules, nor professional money managers, as a group, are able consistently to earn rates of return greater than those earned by a simple buy and hold strategy."* (pages 40 and 41)
2. *"Because the current stock price reflects all currently available information, the EMH predicts that changes in stock prices are caused by the arrival of new information."* (page 41)
3. *"Stock prices must respond immediately and without bias to the response of new information."* (page 42)

Incidentally, while TAVF, as an OPMI, relies exclusively on public disclosures in its fundamental analyses, so too do many non-OPMI control investors. For example, public (i.e., non-inside) information has to be relied on exclusively when one is attempting a hostile takeover.

The underlying problem with MCT is that it takes these narrow special cases, which are especially useful for passive day traders who ought to restrict their dealings to securities susceptible to simple, mathematical analysis, and tries, based on unproven anecdotal assumptions, to promulgate general laws of universal applicability. These general laws, based solely on studies of securities prices arrived at in markets populated by OPMIs, are used to reach conclusions and recommend courses of action, not only for buy-and-hold fundamental investors such as TAVF, but also for those involved with non-OPMI markets such as the markets for leveraged buyouts (LBOs), mergers and acquisitions and venture capital promotions; for financial managers who run companies; for the promulgation of Generally Accepted Accounting Principles (GAAP); for determining liabilities and damages in securities litigation (as for example, "fraud on the market" theories); for promulgating regulations of financial institutions; and for setting national fiscal policies (the balanced budget being one example).

Being a believer in MCT is not very helpful for portfolio managers who are buy-and-hold fundamentalists, but that consideration seems relatively unimportant in the overall scheme of things. The Fund really is not affected much, one way or the other, by MCT except that MCT disciples probably would never invest in TAVF Common Stock, except as "hot money" which TAVF management does not want anyway. From a public policy point of view, though, MCT appears to be downright dangerous insofar as MCT influences the decision making of corporate managements not seeking access to equity markets on a regular basis; GAAP (e.g., see the stock options controversy or the rules on the carrying values for portfolios consisting only of performing credits); securities law and litigation; financial institution regulation; and national fiscal and monetary policies.

Specifically, MCT appears to be largely irrelevant for that minority of portfolio managers, including the TAVF manager, trained to deal in fundamentals. MCT, EMH and EPT are chartist-technical approaches to security analysis, similar to all other systems based on studies of securities prices and securities markets. MCT does virtually nothing for analyzing corporate fundamentals, the behavior of activists and promoters, and the characteristics of corporations. MCT appears to be based on 10 propositions:

MCT Proposition 1: MCT examines all financial phenomena strictly from the point of view of the OPMI short-term trader, even when it comes to corporate, non-stockholder, matters. One example of this is contained on page 398 of Brealey and Myers where the authors state, "The choice of (corporate) capital structure is a marketing problem, find the combination of securities that has the greatest overall appeal to investors." TAVF, on the other hand, puts its first emphasis on the point of view of the corporation in which it is investing, not the point of view of short-term OPMIs. For TAVF, the choice of capital structure is an internal, corporate problem revolving around giving the typical corporation comfort to be able to operate with some margin of safety in uncertain future periods; reasonable assurances of access to capital markets; and reasonable prospects of enjoying a "good enough" ROE. TAVF has a company point of view, first and foremost, not a stockholder point of view. Thus, TAVF thinks Ryan Beck would be better off retaining earnings, rather than paying large dividends in cash on its common stock, regardless of the immediate effect on the Ryan Beck common stock price of implementing that policy.

Examining financial practices strictly from the point of view of the OPMI trader is akin to examining the marine food chain by restricting the study to observing the reactions of kelp and plankton which float passively on the surface of the sea and serve as the tail-end of a very complex food chain. One is really not going to understand the marine food chain unless one also studies systematically the actions, and reactions, of the myriad marine life existing beneath the surface. The players beneath the surface who, unlike the OPMIs, are basically actors rather than reactors, in the financial "food chain" include managements, control shareholders, creditors, deal promoters, investment bankers, securities salespersons and attorneys, among others.

OPMI traders and corporations have both communities of interest and conflicts of interest in their relationships with each other. The one time that a community of interest tends to predominate is when the corporation needs, or desires, access to equity markets. Here, treating the OPMI trader well may give the corporation better access to new equity capital than otherwise would be the case. Incidentally, the price at which a corporation can sell new issues of non-dividend paying common stock, as distinct from whether the corporation can issue new equity securities at all, is consideration of great importance to stockholders who might suffer from dilution, but it is not *per se* a corporate issue of much consequence. I've never seen this point made in any academic literature, probably because MCT does not view the corporation as a constituency separate and apart from the stockholder constituency.

One reason MCT concentrates so much on the OPMI and OPMI markets seems to be that the OPMI market is the only financial market where prices are always readily available on an instantaneous basis. Such precise prices are what MCT people need to undertake their algebra-based studies of past prices. Yet, there are numerous other markets populated mostly by activists who, unlike OPMIs, act rather than react. These other markets include LBO markets, merger and acquisition markets, first and second stage venture capital markets, markets for consensual plans when restructuring troubled companies, getting to be lead plaintiffs' counsel in stockholder litigation markets, securities salespersons compensation markets, and markets for money management fees.

Each of these markets tends toward a price efficiency, but in many instances that tendency is so weak as to be negligible. Furthermore, a price efficiency in one market is, per se, a price inefficiency in another market. Put otherwise, a huge number of participants in financial processes earn, on average, excess returns including, so far, TAVF and a number of other funds concentrating on passive investments.

MCT Proposition 2: MCT assumes the existence of a substantive consolidation between the firm and its stockholders for almost all purposes. The corporation and its stockholders are treated as if they were one in examining investment opportunities, appropriate capitalizations, discount rates, and return on investments. This is demonstrated by Ross, Westerfield on page 69: "Suppose that firms are just ways in which many investors can pool their resources to make large-scale business decisions. Suppose, for example, that you own one percent of some firm. Now suppose that this firm is considering whether or not to undertake some investment. If that investment passes the NPV (i.e., net present value) rule, that is, if it has a positive NPV, then one percent of that NPV belongs to you. If the firm takes on this investment, the value of the whole firm will rise by the one percent and your investment in the firm will rise by one percent of the NPV of the investment." If, as I think they are, Ross, Westerfield are saying that substantive consolidation is so pervasive, and OPMI markets are so efficient, that changes in underlying corporate values get reflected efficiently in OPMI market prices, then they have an utterly different view of the real world than does TAVF.

Further, in having corporations deal with their security holders it is apparently hard, under MCT, for there to be "win-win" situations. As Brealey and Myers state on page 289, "If selling a security generates a positive NPV for you (the corporation), it must generate a negative NPV for the buyer." TAVF, of course, thinks this is an entirely unrealistic view of the real world where, in effect, deals get done by showing each constituency that it is obtaining a positive NPV for its purposes. Such constituencies include bank lenders, outside professionals, employees, OPMI investors, and investment bankers, among others.

The one possible exception to substantive consolidation under MCT is in the methodologies used for valuations. Here, corporations are to be valued strictly as going-concerns based on forecasted cash flows from existing operations. Stock-holders, on the other hand, are to be valued as investment vehicles rather than going-concerns; the methodology here is to value by marking net assets to OPMI market prices consistently, rather than examining operating cash flows, i.e., dividends and interest from investments.

Under MCT, too, the changes in the going-concern performance of a business, as measured by periodic cash flows from operations and/ or reported accounting net income, is deemed to be substantively consolidated, i.e., strongly correlated, with changes in the OPMI market price of a common stock, something that happens instantaneously. TAVF, on the other hand, does not tend to believe that such a substantive consolidation, if it does exist, is particularly important. As a buy-and-hold investor, TAVF analyzes most companies as a combination of strict going-concerns engaged in day-to-day operations, and investment companies deploying and redeploying assets in new areas from time to time, as well as undertaking financing and refinancing activities from time to time which are well outside the ordinary course of business. These investment company activities, as well as going-concern activities, cause changes in the underlying values of businesses. TAVF does not operate under the assumption, or belief, that such value changes get reflected in market prices, whether instantaneously or even over any definable time period.

For TAVF, substantive consolidation does not exist on Planet Earth. Even if there were price equilibrium for non-OPMIs (which I doubt), control issues on behalf of corporate managers, differentials in knowledge as between insider-activists and outsider-passivists, differences in tax structures, and differentials in the ability to finance, would preclude corporate decision makers from examining investment and reinvestment opportunities in the normal course of events on the basis of whether or not the corporation could earn better returns, risk adjusted, on moneys not distributed to shareholders than could the shareholders, especially where estimated shareholder returns on "risky assets" are measured by things like Beta, a study of the relative past price volatility of an OPMI traded common stock. The corporations whose securities are held by TAVF seem to make their NPV decisions based on the corporate universe, not the OPMI universe. Without considering OPMI NPV, corporations frequently do make massive cash and other property distributions to shareholders, but only a few of those distributions seem to bottom on a theory that stockholders have better risk-adjusted investment opportunities than the corporation. Rather, those distributions are undertaken in the context of delivering far above average returns to some other non-OPMI constituency such as promoters of leveraged buy-outs and management buy-outs.

MCT Proposition 3: MCT assumes the existence of structural subordination, where all other interests are junior to those of OPMIs, i.e., corporations and managements work in the best interests of OPMI traders. With the exception of agency costs, discussed below, the corporation and its management are supposed to work to maximize the near-term prices of the corporation's common stock trading in OPMI markets. Indeed, in MCT, the normal tendency is to view the corporation and its stockholders as one entity.

If any reader believes such structural subordination actually exists for the vast majority of publicly traded equities, except in special cases where control of the corporation goes "into play" or, sometimes, when insiders are looking to cash-out of control positions, then I would like to sell that reader a certain bridge to Brooklyn.

MCT Proposition 4: MCT assumes the existence of agency costs between the stockholders on the one hand, and management on the other. Stockholders are the principals, and managements are the agents of the OPMI principals. There are conflicts between the principals and the agents. As Ross, Westerfield points out on page 18, "The costs of resolving the conflicts of interest between managers and shareholders are special types of costs called agency costs. These costs are defined as the sum of (1) the monitoring costs of the shareholders and (2) the incentive fee paid to the managers." As an aside, the above statement again demonstrates the unrealistic MCT focus on substantive consolidation. Agency costs are not borne by stockholders; they are borne by corporations.

From the TAVF point of view, academics don't have clue about agency costs. To begin with, there are myriad constituencies within the financial world, each of which has communities of interest and conflicts of interest with the others. Conflicts (and communities) are not limited to managements and OPMI traders. Other important constituencies include the corporation itself, long-term buy-and-hold OPMIs, non-management control shareholders, trade creditors, other creditors, customers, employees, governments, etc. In TAVF's analysis, it is crucial to recognize the existence of the multiplicity of constituencies and the communities and conflicts of interest between and among each of them. Financial phenomena cannot be understood by restricting an examination to the relationship between managements and OPMIs, especially when the crucial examination ought to be between managements and corporations; the real world is far more complicated than MCT assumes. There are even distinguishable constituencies within the OPMI community. Certainly the Fund, as a buy-and-hold OPMI, finds itself with both communities of interest and conflicts of interest *vis-a-vis* OPMI traders.

Second, academics seem to believe that stockholders control companies because they can elect a Board of Directors, and thereby put a limit on agency costs. As Ross, Westerfield states on page 20, "Shareholders determine the membership of the board of directors by voting. Thus, shareholders control the directors, who in turn select the management team." The fact, though, is that boards of directors are de facto elected, not by stockholders, but rather by those who control the proxy machinery and those who get the corporation to finance proxy solicitations. Such people are virtually never non-management, non-control stockholders. In general, if there has been any corporate (not stockholder) expense that has been uncontrolled in recent years, it appears to have been top management compensation (albeit, by and large, agency costs for most of the companies in the TAVF portfolio appear to be reasonable).

The Fund is always looking at distinct constituencies. To TAVF, the company is the company; it is not its stockholders; and it is not management. Among stockholders, the OPMI is the OPMI; the OPMI is not the company; and it is not the control group. The company, as the company, has conflicts of interest with each of the other constituencies, all of whom tend to want things, such as high Ryan Beck type dividends or management entrenchment provisions, which detract from corporate feasibility. However, the company, as the company, tends to have a unique community of interest with each and every other constituency, since each of these other constituencies likely would suffer if the company did not maintain a minimum standard of feasibility.

MCT Proposition 5: A price equilibrium exists. The price of a common stock in the OPMI trading market is, by far, the best measure of value for all purposes, whether such purposes are for OPMI trading, mergers and acquisitions, hostile takeovers, leveraged buyouts or restructuring troubled companies. As William F. Sharpe, a Nobel Laureate, and typical exponent of MCT, states on page 67 of the Third Edition of his book, *Investments*, "Every security's price equals its investment value at all times." Ross, Westerfield on page 363 states, "Because information is reflected in prices immediately, investors should only expect to obtain a normal rate of return. Awareness of information when it is released does an investor no good. The price adjusts before the investor has time to trade on it." And also on page 363, "Firms should expect to receive the fair value for securities that they sell. *Fair* means that the price they receive for the securities they issue is the present value. Thus, valuable financing opportunities that arise from fooling investors are unavailable in efficient capital markets."

TAVF utterly rejects any views that OPMI market prices are indicators of value for all purposes. The Fund also rejects any views that information is properly reflected in OPMI market prices at all, much less instantaneously. There is no question that the efficiencies inherent in price equilibrium and the disclosure of information do, in fact, exist for OPMI traders seeking to earn superior returns consistently. However, such efficiencies just do not exist for participants with other agendas, such as TAVF and for all others in other markets, despite the fact that there will be tendencies toward efficiency, however weak and unimportant, in any market. For example, at the time an LBO of a public company is to be undertaken, the price of the common stock in the OPMI market, say $20 per share, is an inefficient price compared with the premium price, i.e., the price in the LBO market necessary to get the LBO done, say $25 or $30 per share. By definition, the LBO promoter has to view the $20 OPMI price as an inefficient price for his purposes and his calculation of his NPV (and the NPVs of those who are financing the LBO promoter). If the "fair" value in the LBO market were not different, and higher, than the "fair" value in the OPMI market, then no LBO transactioh likely could be consummated.

Few corporate managers believe that OPMI markets determine universal true values, which are valid in all contexts. Sometimes these managers view OPMI market prices as ridiculously high. They then cause companies to go public in events such as IPOs, and/or sell their personal holdings, and/or have the corporation use the overpriced common stock as a currency, a "Chinese Dollar," to be issued in a merger transaction. Sometimes these managers view OPMI markets as notoriously underpriced; and they, perhaps in association with LBO promoters, acquire common stock in going-private transactions, or they place "shark repellents" in corporate governance documents driven, at least in part, by a desire to protect shareholders from being forced to part with their shareholdings at an unfairly low price.

Furthermore, the LBO buyer (and as an aside, TAVF) looks at different information, or weights the same information differently, than does the OPMI trader analyzing a going concern. For OPMI traders, the dominant considerations are likely to be reported earnings, especially forecasted earnings over the next quarter or two, industry identification, comparative analysis of this issue with others in the same industry, sponsorship, stock promotion activity, market liquidity for the particular security, technical market considerations, and predictions about macro factors such as the level of the Dow Jones Industrial Average, forecasts of interest rates and GDP. In the LBO (and TAVF) context, though, the concentration in the use of information will tend to be on ability to finance the proposed transaction, the long-term outlook for the specific company, exit strategies and, if the LBO is not a purely financial transaction, strategic fit. (LBO promoters, incidentally, ought to be characterized as information creators, rather than information reactors, *vis-a-vis* their relationships with the OPMI trading community.)

The fact that an efficient price in the LBO, or takeover, market is different than an efficient price in an OPMI market is an alien concept under MCT. MCT adherents believe there is a "true value." As Brealey and Myers state on page 294, "Competition among investment analysts will lead to a stock market in which prices at all times reflect true value" — true value "means an equilibrium price which reflects all the information available to investors at that time."

Interpreting information is a difficult task for which OPMI traders and MCT academics seem untrained and ill equipped. Take one information example out of thousands. Suppose new public disclosures are needed about replacement costs. Suppose, further, that an inflationary situation exists where the replacement value of the Property, Plant and Equipment (PPE) used in a capital intensive company is far above the depreciated cost basis at which the PPE is being carried on the company's books. This means that accounting depreciation charges are inadequate and the corporation is overstating earnings, at least by the amount of underdepreciation. This also may mean, however, that the corporation is insulated against new competition coming into the industry because the cost of entry into the industry has become prohibitive. Is the new information about replacement cost bullish or bearish? It depends; but, I doubt that the OPMI market prices can reflect an accurate analysis from the point of view of buy-and-hold OPMIs or anyone actively involved with the particular corporation and its industry.

In terms of the information content of financial statements, MCT people seem very worried about the fact that GAAP frequently does not reflect economic reality. As a matter of fact, financial statements rarely reflect economic reality. For TAVF, accounting statements are something entirely different. They are, by far, the best objective benchmarks available for use by buy-and-hold fundamentalists as tools essential, most of the time, for reaching reasonable conclusions about what economic reality might be. TAVF cares about what the numbers mean, rather than what the numbers are.

One of the key questions that passive, non-control investors such as the Fund almost always must resolve in any analysis relying strictly on the public record is, "What am I missing?" If GAAP audited financial statements did not exist, this probably would become a nearly impossible question to answer, certainly in terms of what contingencies might be important, and what documents (e.g., loan agreements or acquisition agreements) ought to be reviewed in detail. Interestingly, MCT never asks the question; MCT assumes the OPMI market already has answered the question.

In justifying the alleged existence of a universal price equilibrium, Ross, Westerfield states on page 370, "All the efficient market hypothesis really says is that, on average, the manager will not be able to achieve an abnormal or excess return." This statement seems to be the result of sloppy analysis and is offered without proof. The proven valid statement is, instead, that, "All the efficient market hypothesis really says is that few, if any, OPMI traders will be able to achieve an abnormal or excess return consistently." TAVF, on its almost five-year record, has outperformed the market on average. So have a large number of other passive money managers, especially others who are also buy-and-hold fundamentalists.

TAVF cannot, and has not, outperformed the market consistently; I don't think the Fund ever will. To outperform the market consistently one has to load up the portfolio with those securities which the analyst believes are the most popular or are about to become the most popular. This is the very antithesis of value investing. Going forward, TAVF would like to be able to enjoy, on average, an ROE of at least 20% per annum regardless of what happens in the general market. To continue to meet this 20% bogey the Fund managers are going to have to be both good and lucky regardless of what happens in the general market.

MCT Proposition 6: Generalized risk is measured, at least in part, by examining "the riskiness of assets." The riskiness of assets is measured essentially by looking at past price volatility in OPMI markets, with such measures encompassing the concepts of Beta and the Capital Asset Pricing Model. If one were to look into companies, rather than market prices, riskiness of assets would be measured by the quality of the issuer and the terms of the issue. It has to be this way for MCT because price of the issue would not be a consideration since price is always in equilibrium.

TAVF rejects any concept of general risk, or any concept that the information content of past price performance in OPMI markets tends to be material. Risks are specific, and one always must put an adjective before the word "risk" to differentiate between and among the different types of risk: market risk, investment risk, inflation risk, excess leverage on the right hand side of the balance sheet risk, and new competitors coming into a market risk, among many others. TAVF takes huge market risks in that it pretty much ignores OPMI markets. The Fund focuses on avoiding investment risk by being extremely price conscious and by trying to buy well-covenanted credits and the equities of financially strong companies.

MCT guards against generalized risk by causing portfolios to be diversified according to the precepts of EPT. TAVF believes that diversification is only a surrogate, and usually a poor surrogate, for knowledge, control, price consciousness and, in the case of a passive investor such as the Fund, restricting equity investments to well-financed companies which would have unquestioned staying power when, and if, things do go wrong. Diversification is clearly the correct course for OPMIs untrained in fundamentals who assume that, at any particular time, security prices are in equilibrium. At the other extreme, diversification would make no sense at all for a young person starting out and using all his resources to start up a new business. TAVF, as a matter of common sense, would always diversify, at least to a modest extent, because it is a passive, non-control, investor. The Fund, however, is much less diversified than other mutual funds of similar size run by managers who concentrate on macro top-down considerations and are not price conscious.

When one is price conscious, as the Fund is, the analysis of risk becomes the exact opposite of the MCT view. In the MCT view there is a risk/reward ratio; if one desires greater returns, one has to take greater risk. The TAVF view is the cheaper the security, the less the risk; the cheaper the security, the greater the profit potential; therefore, the lower the risk, the greater the reward potential.

MCT Proposition 7: Value is determined essentially by a corporation's forecasted free cash flows discounted to present value at an appropriate rate. As Ross, Westerfield states on page 37, "In determining the economic and financial condition of a firm, cash flow is more revealing [than net income]."

Here MCT becomes utterly confusing by failing to distinguish between values for individual assets and groups of assets on the one hand, and values for going-concerns on the other. For individual assets or groups of assets to have a reliable positive value, those assets, as used in operations, ought to generate a positive cash flow. However, most going-concern corporations (and incidentally all growing national economies) are cash consumers, not cash generators. What are the real elements that go into a corporate valuation from the TAVF point of view? There are four such elements:

1. free cash flow from operations; or
2. earnings, with earnings defined as creating wealth while consuming cash. This is what most growing economic entities do. Earnings, as defined, can have no value unless they are also combined with access to capital markets, whether those markets are credit markets, equity markets, or both; and
3. the existence of separable and salable assets which can be disposed of without reducing cash flow or earnings, or as a substitute for cash flow or earnings; and
4. access to capital markets — both credit markets and equity markets — on a highly attractive basis
5. *MCT Proposition 8:* Comparative analysis, especially as embodied in the concept of NPV, is the key to all valuations.

NPV is a very important and valid concept but its usefulness in the real world seems more limited than is assumed under MCT. Since substantive consolidation is a myth, corporations are unlikely to undertake an NPV analysis using as a standard ideas of what shareholders could earn, risk adjusted, on funds distributed to them rather than retained by the firm. The usefulness of NPV is further limited by questions of control and knowledge, and above all by the feasibility of particular deals. In looking at the common stocks of potential takeover candidates, TAVF is much more influenced by whether or not a deal at a substantial premium over market might close, as compared with which of several attractive securities is priced more attractively as a going-concern based on an NPV analysis.

The TAVF objective is to enjoy at least a 20% ROE regardless of the performance of other mutual funds with which the Fund might be compared. This absolute standard for TAVF, rather than any comparative analysis calculation, probably leaves a lot to be desired. However, I don't think that TAVF is all that comparable to most other funds and to the general market. More importantly though, if the Fund can earn 20% on average, then I think most TAVF shareholders will conclude that such results are good enough.

MCT Proposition 9: All portfolios ought to be marked to market since total return is the one thing that counts most.

Most investors probably invest for assured cash return, not total return. For TAVF both total return and cash return count, with different weights at different times. For example, the Fund's rather successful investment in Inverse Floaters was based on a duality of objectives. First, a minimum yield to maturity could be locked-in regardless of price performance of the Inverse Floaters in the market. Second, TAVF could get lucky and earn a super total return if interest rates went down. Unlike MCT, we were willing to have two objectives; either an above average yield to maturity, or an above average total return. To get to this "win-win" situation, TAVF had to ignore the market risk it was taking; the Inverse Floaters (it bought at 50) could have sold in the OPMI market at 30 shortly thereafter, even though the Fund had locked in a pretty good minimum yield to maturity. One of the reasons the Fund had to take such huge market risks with the Inverse Floaters is that I am not equipped, by background or training, to forecast the general level of interest rates, and the near-term market performance of Inverse Floaters was strictly a function of short-term interest rates.

MCT seems to fail to understand that there are huge numbers of portfolios in which maximizing a risk-adjusted total return becomes unimportant. This includes, besides TAVF as an Inverse Floater investor, most life insurance companies, most pension plans, and most high net worth individuals who acquire tax-exempt securities. Insofar as such entities continually have new funds to invest and reinvest in performing credit instruments, the worse the current market performance for the portfolio, the greater the future investment income on the portfolio will be. This occurs because the new investments will enjoy higher interest returns as a result of declines in market prices. Of course, this negative weight for market prices does not exist for all portfolios. It certainly does not exist for OPMI portfolios financed with borrowed money. Put otherwise, there are few, if any, meaningful general laws in portfolio management. Each one ought to be approached on a case by case basis.

MCT Proposition 10: The worth of any common stock is the present value of all future dividends to be received plus the present value of the exit price.

For TAVF, the theoretical value of any stock has two components: either the present value of any future cash bail out and/or the present value of control arising out of common stock ownership. TAVF, as a non-control investor, always has to visualize a cash-out exit strategy. For common stocks this almost always means sale to a market, though not necessarily an OPMI market. For performing credit instruments the market is far less important than in the case of equities. The Fund will have a cash bailout of credits it holds, as long as each credit instrument performs in accordance with the money terms of the instrument as they exist at the time they were acquired, or as they might be modified. Furthermore, in the case of performing credits acquired at a discount from the principal amount, time alone can correct market mistakes, something that does not have to happen with common stocks. Just hold the credit instrument to maturity and the discount at which the security was purchased will disappear.

I've now reviewed a fair amount of the MCT literature. I remain amazed at how flawed almost all the MCT analysis is, especially where MCT authors write about topics in which I have special expertise. Two areas that are particularly striking to me are MCT explanations of why most closed-end investment company common stocks sell at discounts from net asset values, and MCT theories about restructuring troubled companies. The literature about closed-ends is, I think, mind-boggling in terms of the intellectual contortions scholars go through to defend the indefensible; why, if the OPMI market prices efficiently, should closed-ends sell at a discount, or even come into existence in the first place? Many academics and money managers seem to be staking their careers and livelihoods on continuing to stress the basic tenets of the EMH: there exists a unitary true value, and there exists a universal price equilibrium. Maybe so, but not for TAVF.

CHAPTER 43

Third Avenue and the Efficient Market

JANUARY 2001

There is the tale about a finance professor and a student who came upon a $100 bill lying on the ground. The student stooped to pick up the bill. "Don't bother," says the professor, "If it really were a $100 bill, it wouldn't be there." This story misses the main point relevant to financial analysis. Neither by training, nor by background, would the finance professor be able to identify what the piece of paper lying on the ground was — a $100 bill or a scrap of worthless paper. Trying to distinguish between the two is what fundamental value analysts, and most control investors, do. Academics, on the other hand, are technician-chartists with PhD's. They study markets and securities prices, not fundamentals. You need to be literate about fundamentals if you are to have any hope of distinguishing between $100 bills and garbage in the field of security analysis.

Starting in the 1960's, the theories embodied in Academic Finance which revolve around the study of security prices, have taken over security analysis rather completely. The quants rule the roost; Graham and Dodd is mostly dead except for the small minority of outside investors who have a Third Avenue type of approach.

If one signs off on the assumptions underlying Academic Finance, the investment techniques that are an outgrowth of Academic Finance make sense. Indeed, most common stock investment today follows academic precepts. It dominates investment styles. Most investment techniques used by passive investors bottom on the academic theories of the Efficient Market Hypothesis (EMH) and Efficient Portfolio Theory (EPT) as for example:

- Indexing
- Asset Allocation
- Top Down Market Strategies
- Diversification
- Value is determined strictly by forecasts of discounted cash flows (DCF)

The bedrock of Academic Finance is the assumption embodied in EMH that the market is efficient, or to put it in Third Avenue Value Fund (TAVF) language, the market attains instantaneous efficiency.

TAVF has a markedly different view of efficiency than the academics. It ought to be helpful to Third Avenue shareholders to explain the differences:

The Academic View

1. The market is efficient, or achieves instantaneous efficiency. The market is defined as trading marts populated by "investors," i.e. Outside, Passive, Minority Investors (OPMIs). The principal trading marts for securities are sites such as the New York Stock Exchange and NASDAQ.
2. Without access to superior information, no OPMI can hope to outperform the market, or relevant benchmarks, consistently. Consistently means all the time, or almost all the time.
3. Market prices value any business at any time more correctly than any other measure that might be used. Thus, if a debt free company has 50,000,000 common shares outstanding, and the shares are quoted at $10, the best measure of the value of the company for all purposes is $500,000,000 (50,000,000 shares times $10 per share price).

The TAVF View

1. There exist myriad markets, not one. There are OPMI markets, hostile takeover markets, Leveraged Buyout (LBO) markets, Strategic Buyer Markets, Merger and Acquisition markets where new common stock issuances rather than cash are the "coin of the realm," etc. Each market has its own pricing parameters. A market is defined as any arena in which participants strive to reach agreement on price, and other terms, which each participant believes is the best reasonably achievable under the circumstances.
2. All markets tend toward efficiency. Very few markets, though, ever achieve instantaneous efficiency. Those that do achieve instantaneous efficiency seem to be "special cases." In many markets the tendency toward efficiency can be quite weak, especially where efficiency is defined as appraising a business or a security at a price that approximates an underlying value.
3. Most market actions are driven by activists — promoters, investment bankers, attorneys, salesmen, management — who, by most definitions, earn excess return relatively consistently. For most OPMI's, the nongenius ones, the path to earning excess returns is not to obtain superior information, but rather to use the available information in a superior manner. For example, most analysts, most of the time, ignore the corporate balance sheet in their analyses. There is no way that TAVF would have invested so heavily in the common stocks of AVX, KEMET and Vishay, unless each company enjoyed, as they do, superb financial strength as reflected on their balance sheets. This balance sheet emphasis ought to mean that the Fund is using the available information in a superior manner.
4. An efficient price in one market is, most often, an inefficient price in another market. For example, any activist operating in an LBO market, knows that in the vast majority of cases, a buyout will not be a doable transaction unless the price offered in the takeover represents a meaningful premium over OPMI market prices.

Reconciling the Two Views

There are markets that are characterized by instantaneous efficiency. These markets, however, seem to be narrow special cases. The underlying problems of Academic Finance here seem to be two-fold. First, academia takes these special cases and tries to make a general law out of them covering all, or almost all, securities investments. Second, academics look at investments only from the viewpoint of the OPMI, rather than the varied viewpoints of the many participants in the investment process.

TAVF does not, with rare exceptions, participate in those markets characterized by the existence of instantaneous efficiencies; markets achieving instantaneous efficiency seem to have two characteristics:

1. The "Investor" is a trader seeking to maximize a marketrisk adjusted total return realizable in cash, consistently (TAVF is a buyandhold investor with little or no demonstrated skill in short-run trading)
2. The securities (or commodities) being analyzed, can be analyzed by reference to only a limited number of computer programmable variables. These special case securities seem to be limited to three types of issues:

    a) Credit Instruments without credit risk (e.g., U.S. Treasuries)
    b) Derivatives (e.g., options, convertibles, warrants, swaps)
    c) Risk arbitrage (e.g., situations where there will be relatively determinant workout events in relatively determinant periods of time). An example of a risk arbitrage is an announced corporate merger where the common stock of the target company is priced below the indicated market value, or cash value, that will be received if the transaction closes. Most TAVF investments do not have risk arbitrage characteristics though some do, such as the Fund's investments in certain distressed credits (see the recent purchase of USG 9 ½% Notes maturing September 15, 2001).

If one believes that all markets attain instantaneous efficiency, one also has to believe that in all markets, there exists instantaneous, or almost instantaneous, convergence. Convergence refers to the belief that like securities trading in the same, or different, markets will end up selling at the same price. For example, Tecumseh Class A common selling at $49.44 per share at January 31 is exactly the same security as Tecumseh Class B common selling at $45.38, except that only the Class B common has voting rights. Under convergence theory, market forces will buy Tecumseh Class B increasing its price; and market forces will sell Tecumseh Class A decreasing its price. In short order, both Tecumseh A and Tecumseh B ought to be selling at, say, $47. The truth is that the discount at which Tecumseh B sells, has persisted for a long time and probably will continue to exist until, say, an activist Tecumseh Board makes the "B" stock convertible into "A" stock on a share for share basis.

Convergence pricing seems to approach instantaneous efficiency most of the time in the "special case" markets I've identified above. For most of what Third Avenue does, however, there is no instantaneous efficiency. Almost all of the convergence that actually takes place, takes place because active players act rather than because amorphous market forces identify disparities in value between related securities; and then cause the spreads to narrow, or disappear, as if an invisible hand uses "magic."

Unlike academics, Third Avenue management and similar fundamentalists are probably pretty good at identifying $100 bills, for which we, at TAVF, try to pay not more than $50. Our problem, and the problem of other fundamentalists similarly situated, is not so much in identifying the $100 bills, but rather in how to get enough efficiency into one, or more, markets, so that the realization on the $100 bill can be $100, or even $65 or $70. Most investors comparable to TAVF try to do this by either identifying catalysts or becoming catalysts themselves (See Mutual Shares in pressing Chase Manhattan Bank to sell out, or Gabelli in encouraging a bidding process in connection with the sale of control of Paramount Pictures). At Third Avenue, management spends little time identifying, or seeking, catalysts. Rather the TAVF approach revolves around relying on a long-term tendency toward efficiency. The fund owns a large number of common stocks of well-financed companies that have been acquired at what seem to be steep discount prices. The view is that while Fund management cannot time when individual situations will work out, enough situations in the Fund's portfolio are likely to work out on a lumpy, rather than consistent, basis, so that overall the TAVF portfolio ought to perform okay.

The TAVF portfolio seems to be loaded with $100 bills acquired for $50 or less. It is much easier for Fund management, and I suspect everyone else, to identify $100 bills using a balance sheet, rather than an income account, or cash flow statement, approach, albeit any good security analyst considers all elements that go into the accounting cycle. Common stocks in the TAVF portfolio that appear to be $100 bills bought at large discounts include the following:

> Toyoda Automatic Loom Works, Ltd. ("TAL")
> Alico, Inc.
> Arch Capital Group, Ltd.
> Capital Southwest Corp.
> C.I.T. Group, Inc. Class A
> Harrowston, Inc.
> Forest City Enterprises, Inc.
> Liberty Financial Companies
> Liberty Homes, Inc.
> Japanese NonLife Insurers
> Stewart Information Services Corp.
> Tejon Ranch Co.
> Weis Markets, Inc.
> Woronoco Bancorp, Inc.

TAL serves as a good example of how instantaneous convergence does not work in complicated situations. At January 31, 2001, TAL Common closed at $19.26 per share. Its assets consisted of holdings of Toyota Motor Common with a market value of approximately $21 per TAL share; other marketable securities with a market value of about $8–$9 per TAL share; and magnificent, world-wide, operating businesses with a probable present value of $6–$9 per TAL share after deducting all debt. If Toyota Motor, which owns 22% of TAL Common, and/or TAL, as activists, do not undertake one or more of the several corporate actions available to them, the disparity between the market price of TAL Common and the underlying net asset values inherent in TAL, more likely than not, will persist.

There are all sorts of real world frictions that argue against the elimination of convergence, at least in the context of instantaneous efficiency. One example revolves around the near-universal existence of management entrenchment provisions embodied in corporate charters and by laws; state corporate laws; and certain Securities and Exchange Commission regulations. The costs to an outside activist trying to cash in that $100 bill the business would really be worth if there were a change of control can be prohibitive even where the activist might be able to acquire non-control common stock in the OPMI market for, say, $30 or $40. Other frictions discouraging convergence include management stock options; huge administrative costs for attorneys and investment bankers; and traditional corporate policies such as those that seem to govern the actions, and non-actions, of TAL and Toyota Motor.

The belief in instantaneous efficiency, and that the prices in the OPMI market reflect economic reality better than anywhere else pervades many areas of American life, including law and sociology as well as finance. There are now many proposals being floated to privatize partially social security on the theory that Wall Street is better able to identify attractive common stock investments in an efficient market then could government investing in credit instruments without credit risk. TAVF would never trust any of its investments to mainstream Wall Street. After all these are the same people, trained in academic finance, who brought us the dot.com madness of 1997 to early 2000, probably the greatest speculative bubble in the history of mankind.

CHAPTER 44

Generally Accepted Accounting Principles and the Enron Mess

JANUARY 2002

There is plenty of blame to go around for the apparent accounting frauds that led to Enron Corporation filing for relief under Chapter 11 of the U.S. Bankruptcy Code. In assessing blame, though, it would be a shame if conventional security analysts, conventional money managers and conventional finance academics were left out of the mix. Whatever their other talents — and these people tend to have many other talents — analysts, money managers and finance professors seem notoriously unqualified to be intelligent, responsible users of GAAP who actually understand the uses and limitations of financial statements.

The 1960's were a period of great ferment in finance. Two divergent trends took hold. One affected bottom-up fundamentalists, and one affected conventional top-down security analysts and money managers.

The Securities Acts Amendments of 1964 sparked a disclosure revolution that is still ongoing. Today, for trained, bottom-up fundamentalists, GAAP has never been better, more informative or more reliable, the Enrons of this world notwithstanding.

Starting in the 1960's and continuing to date, Modern Capital Theory (MCT) has increasingly dominated conventional security analysis and conventional money management. MCT is based on views that there exists an efficient market where the market knows more than any individual, or group, of investors; where day-to-day stock market price fluctuations are highly material; where there is a primacy of the income account with a consequent denigration of the importance of examining balance sheets and financial positions; where generally recognized growth is worth premium prices in the stock market; and where the GAAP earnings or cash flow number, as reported, is deemed to be far more important than what can be learned from studying and interpreting all of the other GAAP numbers available for a corporate analysis.

In MCT, an investor guards against market risk through diversification and asset allocation. In bottom-up fundamentalism, certainly as practiced by Third Avenue Funds, investment risk is guarded against by obtaining detailed knowledge about companies and the securities they issue and by being acutely price conscious when acquiring securities.

Enron-type promotions fare much better in the MCT environment than in a bottom-up fundamentalist environment.

In the old days when I was growing up as a security analyst, there was a pervasive principle of GAAP which stated, in effect, that financial statements were to be prepared under the assumption that the users of GAAP were intelligent, informed persons who expected financial statements, taken as a whole, to be objective benchmarks which the user could then employ in an analysis. After the 1960's, this approach was increasingly discarded, as MCT took hold as the approach of choice for outside, passive, minority investors. Today, it is expected in security analysis that GAAP tell the truth (rather than provide objective benchmarks) to the average investor about those particular numbers deemed most important to the average investor, i.e., those numbers most likely to have an immediate impact on stock market prices. The particular numbers deemed important under the present paradigm are quarterly earnings per share from normalized operations, or quarterly cash flow per share from normalized operations. If these quarterly flow numbers have been growing rapidly, the common stock is seen as a "growth stock," likely to sell at a premium price in stock markets populated by outside, passive, minority investors. The average investor focuses on what the operating earnings numbers are rather than what all the numbers mean simply because the earnings numbers, as reported, are likely to have a major, immediate, influence on stock market prices for a common stock.

Enron took advantage of this average investor approach. It apparently tried to maximize reported earnings per share from operations by booking as income the present value of long-lived transactions even though there never existed "reasonable assurances" that such income would be realized. Enron also benefited from the conventional view that there actually exists a primacy of the income account, and that premium prices would be paid for the common stocks of companies exhibiting a growth trend. This emphasis on earnings from operations as reported and on perceptions of growth by analysts and money managers permitted these people to ignore rather completely other factors that tend to be extremely important in any balanced analysis for which GAAP is useful: e.g., strength of financial positions; understanding the underlying business; and appraising management not only as operators and stock promoters, but also as investors of corporate assets and financiers of businesses.

At each of the Third Avenue Funds, common stocks are analyzed the old fashioned, pre-MCT, way. Despite shortcomings in the Funds' approaches, it remains extremely unlikely that any of the Funds would ever acquire an Enron type common stock simply because Fund management does not focus on quarterly earnings as reported and growth trends. Rather, the Third Avenue criteria for acquiring common stocks encompass the following:

> The first thing examined is the quality of resources in a business. If a common stock is to be owned, the company ought to enjoy an exceptionally strong financial position. Financial position, in turn, is measured by one, or a combination, of three factors: a relative absence of liabilities whether disclosed on the balance sheet, in the footnotes or in the world in general; the existence of high quality assets, usually cash or assets such as fully rented office buildings which appear to be convertible into cash; or, free cash flow from operations available for stockholders, something that is a relative rarity.

It is comforting to invest when the quantity of resources in the business is near to, or in excess of, the price paid for the common stock. A good deal of the time, Fund management is hard put to estimate what realistic net asset values (NAVs) are using GAAP book value as an objective benchmark and starting point. The ease with which NAV can be estimated varies with the company being analyzed. It tends to be difficult to estimate NAV for manufacturing companies, and much easier to estimate NAV for financial institutions and real estate companies holding income producing properties. In evaluations, Fund management gives much more weight to NAV than to earnings insofar as the underlying businesses' *modus operandi* is to try to create wealth by means other than having operating, and therefore taxable, earnings. These other methods of creating wealth include mergers and acquisitions, refinancings, asset redeployments, and having access to capital markets on a super attractive basis. Insofar as the business being analyzed is pretty much restricted to creating wealth by having operating earnings, Fund management gives much more weight to earnings than to NAV. In no corporate analysis, however, are either NAV, or operating earnings, ignored completely; each is weighted.

In order for any of the Funds to invest in a common stock, the underlying business has to be *understandable* to at least one of the current 11 analysts who make up the Funds' in--house research team. Understandable can mean lots of things, but at Third Avenue, no issuer can be understandable unless the following conditions exist: The issuer has to have made full documentary disclosures which appear to be reliable; and there has to exist audited financial statements, which are objective benchmarks usable as a tool of analysis. Lack of understanding has kept the Funds from investing in Enron Common, dotcoms, telecoms, almost all emerging markets, new inventions and new discoveries. This is likely to continue to be the case.

Lastly, our investment criteria described above afford the Funds opportunities to buy "what-is" cheaply. Fund management also speculates about the future. The difference between Fund management and conventional money managers is that at

Third Avenue we try to not pay up for our predictions of the future. At present, our purchasing criteria for common stocks are as follows:

- For issuers which are primarily earnings companies, the Funds do not pay more than 10 times past peak earnings provided that Fund management believes that the next peak earnings, whenever that might occur, will be better than the last peak.

- For issuers which are primarily wealth-creation companies, Fund management strives to buy in at, at least a 20% discount from readily ascertainable NAV. Such common stocks are acquired only when Fund management believes that corporate management has reasonably good prospects for growing NAV on a long-term basis.

Unlike an analysis undertaken by conventional analysts and conventional money managers, a Third Avenue analysis is strictly bottom-up. Fund management looks at the company and its securities — period. Fund management does not have a view about when the current recession might end or a focus on technical analysis in decision-making. We had better understand the company, and understand it well. That is why corporate financial accounting is so crucial at Third Avenue. In contrast, the convention is to be primarily top-down, to forecast the outlook for Gross Domestic Product, interest rates, and the Dow Jones average or technical stock market factors. Many conventional analysts are successful though they have no detailed knowledge about securities they own, or trade; and are "babes in the woods" when it comes to understanding the uses and limitations of financial accounting. Indeed, when managing a high turnover portfolio, no investing institution, even if otherwise qualified, can be in a position to study individual companies and their securities in depth. This failure to study by the users of financial statements seems ordained to create many Enrons and Enron type situations. But probably many portfolio managers, and their portfolios, don't suffer too much from their inability to use corporate accounting. As a substitute for knowledge about specific securities, many money managers have well-developed top-down programs for investing centering on portfolio diversification and asset allocation. For this, the precepts of MCT are valid and highly useful. Third Avenue is much less diversified than conventional portfolios. We think diversification is only a surrogate, and usually a poor surrogate, for knowledge, control and price consciousness. Third Avenue does diversify some; it is not a control investor, but we do try hard to bring to any common stock investment knowledge and price consciousness.

The Third Avenue goal in acquiring a common stock is to attempt to acquire the security at a price that represents a substantial discount from the price which would exist were the company a private business or a takeover candidate. In contrast, the goal for most conventional money managers seems to be to achieve near-term price appreciation for the common stock and/or to outperform a benchmark as consistently as possible. If one's goal is the short-run outperformance of a benchmark, there is much to be said in favor of investing in companies with rapidly growing earnings per share as reported, without critically examining how these earnings are derived or what they mean. Such an approach just isn't Third Avenue, and never will be.

In brief, conventional security analysts and conventional money managers frequently seem to employ the following approach:

- There exists an equilibrium price. In an efficient market, a common stock's price at any moment in time is the right price reflecting the only real value extant. That price will change as new events unfold. Here, the principal analytic ability sought is the ability to predict the future. After all, maximum stock price appreciation will occur insofar as earnings from operations, and/or cash flow from operations, grow

- Quarterly earnings statements are always highly important

- What the numbers are, as reported, especially the earnings number, is much, much more important than what the numbers mean

- Ignore the balance sheet; indeed, in many contexts, a high book value is a negative factor

- Portfolios will tend to have a high turnover. Third Avenue portfolios average a turnover of under 20%. Most conventional funds seem to exceed 100%

- In buying into growth, buy generally recognized growth. There has been no way in stock markets of buying into generally recognized growth without paying up. In contrast, at Third Avenue, we try to buy into future growth that is overlooked or misunderstood. We don't pay up.

- Rely much more heavily, sometimes exclusively, on management interviews and other interviews than on in-depth reviews of documents
- Emphasize the importance of top-down variables.

Financial accounting is crucially important to the U.S. economy. If financial statements are seen as unreliable, or untrustworthy, the whole economy could fall apart because corporate credit grantors — e.g., commercial banks, finance companies, and life insurance companies — would no longer be in a position to make safe loans to businesses. The United States has been steadily losing its manufacturing base, and as a consequence, suffers massive merchandise trade deficits. But in a double-entry world, the U.S. economy does not have to focus on the fact that it is characterized by a growing excess of merchandise imports over merchandise exports. Rather, the U.S. economy is benefiting from the export of participations in its capital markets — the best, most efficient, most honest, most informed in the history of mankind.

Fortunately for Third Avenue and similar institutions trained in the use and limitations of GAAP, financial disclosures have never been more complete, more informative, or better benchmarks than is now the case. This seems true despite the tremendous waste of the past 25 or 30 years in trying to have GAAP fulfill the needs of the types of people who speculate in securities such as Enron Common. Without reliable audits, all these "bests" and "mosts" might well disappear. I think no one can ever design financial statements to be more than objective benchmarks. Accounting, in general, just can't tell the truth about quarterly income accounts. The standard for disclosure ought not to be, "Financial Statements for Dummies."

GAAP has to be based on a relatively rigid set of limiting assumptions, which frequently are going to be unrealistic. For example, depreciation charges are based on historic cost, not replacement cost. GAAP, realistic in one context, has to be unrealistic in another context. For example, cash accounting omits descriptions of a company's wealth creation, i.e., accrual experience. Accrual accounting, on the other hand, fails to describe a company's cash experience. Both cash accounting and accrual accounting give valuable objective benchmarks to analysts trained to use all the numbers in an accounting. Determining what the numbers mean has to be the province of the users of financial statements, not the province of preparers of financial statements. The duty of the auditor ought to be to approve financial statements prepared in accordance with a conservative bias, and which statements are comparable and reconcilable while being sure that all material liabilities are disclosed in either the balance sheet or footnotes whether the liabilities are firm or contingent.

A company, for example, has an obligation to pay out $100 million cash in the future. Depending on the form of the transaction, the obligation will be recorded under different forms under GAAP, even though the true economics will be similar. The obligation will appear as a balance sheet liability if it's a borrowing but not if it's an operating lease, a put option written by the company, or even a credit insurance policy written by the company. Under GAAP, inventories, say of a department store chain, are classified as "current assets." The inventories are current assets only in a liquidation analysis or if the analyst is looking at individual items of inventory rather than at inventory in the aggregate. If the department store chain is to stay operating as a going concern, its inventories in the aggregate tend to be fixed assets for any economic purpose.

GAAP can never provide a statement of true earnings. Earnings are subject to interpretation if one is to arrive at an analyst's version of the truth. I think that in the case of most of the companies in which TAVF holds common stocks, GAAP data result in material understatements of true earnings.

Toyota Industries ("Industries") has a huge portfolio of marketable securities, principally a 5%-plus interest in Toyota Motor Common. Industries' income account reflects only dividends received from portfolio companies. As such, Industries' reported earnings under GAAP for the 12-month period ended September 30, 2001 were $0.65 per share, assuming a yen value of 133 to the dollar. Had Industries' income account also reflected Industries' equity in the undistributed earnings of its portfolio companies, almost all of which are business affiliates, earnings on the same yen to dollar basis would have been approximately $1.45 per share.

Electronic component and semiconductor equipment suppliers in the 21st century are much like auto suppliers were in the 1960's and 1970's in that long-term growth trends for these cyclical enterprises seem favorable so that current expenditures are likely to result in materially enhanced future earnings power. Auto suppliers anticipated participating in future growth mostly by making capital expenditures for property, plant and equipment. In the case of electronic component and semiconductor equipment suppliers, the comparable expenditures are for Research and Development ("R&D"), not capital facilities. In the case of the auto suppliers, capital expenditures are capitalized and then charged against income by annual depreciation charges over the life of the capitalized assets. In sharp contrast, the electronic component and semiconductor equipment manufacturers expense all R&D expenditures by contemporaneous charges, as incurred, against the income account. Compared with auto suppliers, and indeed almost all of the old economy manufacturing companies, issuers such as Applied Materials, AVX, KEMET, and Electro Scientific Industries seem to be materially understating their true earnings, especially during periods when R&D expenditures are on an uptrend, i.e., most periods.

As The St. Joe Company develops its vast landholdings in Florida, there is a strong tendency for adjacent, undeveloped properties, also owned by St. Joe, to appreciate in value, sometimes markedly. This increase in unrealized appreciation is rarely, if ever, reflected in annual income accounts, whether for St. Joe, Tejon Ranch or other companies whose common stocks are in the Fund's portfolio and which own developable properties.

GAAP income accounts also fail to fully reflect the annual increase in Adjusted Book Value for MBIA, or the value of annual increases in Assets Under Management for Legg Mason.

Determining whether GAAP earnings overstate, or understate, true annual (or even quarterly) earnings is a job for trained analysts, not CPAs or average investors. Fortunately, in the case of Third Avenue

Funds, I think there is a strong tendency for GAAP financial statements to result in an understatement of true earnings and true net asset values as well as realistic disclosures about all liabilities, something that hardly seems to have been the case for Enron.

In the desire to fulfill the needs of the average investor, GAAP has become about as complex as the Internal Revenue Code. Complexity seems necessary for the Internal Revenue Code because its purpose is to determine an actual number — the taxpayer's tax bill. GAAP is complex because of attempts to determine one number — true earnings per share. In fact, the goal of GAAP should be much simpler — provide the user with objective benchmarks, not truth.

Arthur Levitt, the former Chairman of the Securities and Exchange Commission (SEC), is a principal proponent of GAAP for the average investor. I think this is an unproductive goal. Incidentally, in citing who effectively regulates GAAP, Mr. Levitt seems to leave out the most important group that has been policing the accounting profession, for better or for worse, the Plaintiffs' Bar. The awards attorneys have received in stockholder lawsuits and payments made to class member plaintiffs for accountants' liability have profoundly influenced the audit profession. My experience in dealing with public presentations of accounting data is that the first question asked is, "How should this be presented so that we avoid stockholder suits, or, in any event, successful stockholder suits?" Arthur Andersen seems to have ignored this in the Enron matter. The vast majority of auditors don't.

My suggestion for accounting reform is to go back to the old, pre-MCT, days. Financial statements ought to be aimed at people equipped to use them, not stock market speculators focused on earnings per share from operations. Financial statements should be, as a practical matter, designed to meet directly the needs of creditors; and all creditors need a conservative bias when examining financial statements. Companies should be viewed as stand-alone entities, separate and distinct from the shareholder constituency. In seeking to have GAAP serve the needs of creditors, similarities are found in other accounting systems. For example, Statutory Accounting for insurance companies is designed to protect policyholders, not owners; and broker-dealer accounting under SEC rules is designed to protect customers.

I am not a CPA. I am a user of financial statements. I admire the audit profession, the independence of most accountants, their knowledge, and their ability to provide all of us analysts at Third Avenue with the tools we need to do our job.

CHAPTER 45

Reconciling Modern Capital Theory and Value Investing

APRIL 2003

Huge amounts of the moneys invested in mutual funds have been placed in Index Funds. The *raison d'etre* for Index Funds arise out of the underlying assumptions of Modern Capital Theory (MCT). For MCT, it is fruitless to hope to outperform benchmarks, e.g., the general market, because trading on the New York Stock Exchange and NASDAQ results in efficient, or correct, prices (the Efficient Market Hypothesis or EMH). Rather, investors should eschew any fundamental analysis but rather allocate assets to an appropriately diversified portfolio (Efficient Portfolio Theory or EPT). MCT is summarized by William F. Sharpe, a Nobel laureate and typical efficient-market believer, when he stated in the third edition of his book, *Investments*, that if you assume an efficient market, "every security's price equals its investment value at all times" (page 67).

Value Investing, on the other hand, bottoms on the assumption that through sound fundamental analysis based on knowledge of companies and the securities they issue, as well as price consciousness, a passive investor can usually outperform an index over most periods of one year or more. I remain convinced that over the long term, an investment in TAVF will combine both greater upside potential, and much less downside risk, than would an investment in an Index Fund such as the Vanguard 500 Index Fund. I believe that my conviction is supported by the long-term performance of TAVF. The remainder of this letter explains why I believe this is so by examining some of the underlying assumptions of MCT.

For MCT, the proof of the existence of an efficient market centers on the observation that no individual investor, or institution, has ever outperformed a market, or a benchmark, consistently. Consistently is, of course, a dirty word: It means "All The Time." Academics seem to be absolutely right in their observation that no one outperforms any market consistently. However, it seems asinine to offer this as evidence that fundamental analysis is useless or nearly useless. Lots of investors, especially value investors, outperform markets or benchmarks on average, or usually, even if no one from Warren Buffet on down can outperform a market or a benchmark consistently. Further, many, if not most, MCT acolytes seem sloppy in their observations in that a good deal of the time they conveniently ignore the "consistently" condition in describing the uselessness of fundamental research.

EMH seems to be absolutely valid in a special case. The basic problem with MCT believers is that they assume wrongly that this special case is a general law. EMH describes the investment scene accurately only when two conditions exist in tandem:

1. The solitary goal of a passive, non-control investor is to maximize a risk-adjusted total return consistently.
2. The security, or commodity, being analyzed can be best analyzed by reference to a limited number of computer programmable variables. In the securities field, these instruments seem limited to three types of securities:

    > a) Credit instruments without credit risk, e.g., U.S. Treasuries
    > b) Derivatives, e.g., options, futures, convertibles, swaps, warrants
    > c) Risk arbitrage situations. Risk arbitrage situations exist where there are to be relatively determinate workouts in relatively determinate periods of time. An example of a risk arbitrage situation is one where there is an announced proposal to acquire 100% of a common stock issue at $30 per share when that common stock is selling at, say, $27.50

per share. Risk arbitrage situations don't exist most of the time for most common stocks. Common stocks represent ownership interests in corporations with perpetual lives

EMH seems to be the most appropriate approach for participants in the securities markets who combine one or more of the following characteristics, none of which are applicable to Third Avenue Funds, and, hopefully, to the vast majority of Third Avenue Stockholders:

1. The security holder is playing with borrowed money and might be subject to margin calls if market prices decline. Such a person, or institution, has to be vitally interested in day-to-day market prices.
2. A securities trader with a technical, or chartist, approach. The underlying belief of such people is that the market knows more than I do and that to perform well one needs only study securities prices, not corporate fundamentals. TAVF would not invest in any security except in the belief that Fund management understands the situation better and more completely than the market; and that the Fund understands the business in which it invests as well as the securities issued by that business. In a very meaningful sense, academics who subscribe to the MCT approach are nothing more than technician-chartists with PhDs. In a leading text, *Principles of Corporate Finance* by Brealey and Myers, Seventh Edition ("Brealey and Myers"), it is stated on page 365 under the heading "The Six Lessons of Market Efficiency" that one ought to "Read the Entrails. If the market is efficient, prices impound all available information. Therefore, if we can only learn to read the entrails, security prices can tell us a lot about the future."
3. The person's livelihood depends on being mostly right about near-term stock price movements. This group includes many analysts in broker-dealer research departments, many securities salespeople, and many financial advisers.
4. People with no training whatsoever in fundamental corporate analysis.

There are many underlying assumptions of MCT and Index Funds that are just plain wrong from a TAVF point of view. Among the most important are the following:

For MCT, there is a risk-reward ratio, i.e., the more (market) risk one takes, the more the possible rewards. This view traces to a belief in price equilibrium. At any moment of time, a security's price is the correct price for all valuation purposes. For TAVF, the risk-reward ratio trade-off is non-existent; the lower the price in a given situation, the less the risk and the greater potential for reward. For Third Avenue, there does exist a risk-reward ratio insofar as the quality of the company, and the terms of the securities issued by the company, are concerned (e.g., typically a first mortgage obligation of an issuer has a lesser risk element than that company's common stock issue, other things being equal). However, for TAVF, the existence of a risk-reward ratio implicit in the quality of the issuer, and the terms of issue, are more than counterbalanced by the fact that most of the time securities prices represent a material disequilibrium. There is a huge safety factor inherent in buying in at a bargain price.

MCT misdefines risk. For MCT, the word risk means only market risk, i.e., fluctuations in prices of securities. In fact, one can't really use the word "risk" without putting an adjective in front of it. There is market risk, investment risk (i.e., something going wrong with the company), credit risk, commodity risk, failure to match maturities risk, terrorism risk, etc. At TAVF, we try to avoid investment risk. We pay less attention to market risk.

Insofar as MCT theory is concerned, the only source of corporate value is Discounted Cash Flows from operations (DCF) and the only source of value for stockholders is the present worth of future dividend flows. These MCT views are utterly naive. In focusing on DCF, the academics confuse project finance (where any project has to have a positive net present value as measured by cash flows in order to make sense) with corporate finance. This can be seen in Brealey & Myers' statement on page 119, "Only Cash Flow Is Relevant." In fact, the vast majority of prosperous corporations consume cash; they do not generate positive DCF. Rather, the prosperous corporations have earnings, not DCF. Earnings are defined as creating wealth while consuming cash.

For TAVF purposes, corporations can create value in four different ways:

1. Positive DCF, something that very few corporations enjoy.
2. Earnings, which are how most prosperous going concerns create wealth. For most companies consuming cash, earnings can have a value over the long term only insofar as earnings are combined with corporate access to capital markets, either for borrowing or for the sale of equity.
3. Resource conversion: asset redeployments, liability redeployments, and changes in control. These activities are the results of mergers and acquisitions, leveraged buyouts, Chapter 11 reorganizations, spin-offs, contests for control and liquidations.
4. Access to capital markets — whether credit markets or equity markets — on a super attractive basis. I suspect more corporate fortunes have been created by fortuitous access to capital markets than from any other source. See the number of fortunes created out of the dot com bubble, or in real estate where there has been access to low interest rate, long-term, non-recourse mortgage financing.

The MCT view of common stock value is summarized on page 118 of the text *Corporate Finance* by Ross, Westerfield and Jaffe, Fourth Edition ("Ross, Westerfield"): Investors "only get two things out of a stock: dividends and the ultimate sales price, which is determined by what future investors expect to receive in dividends."

For TAVF, in contrast, the value of a common stock is the estimated present worth of any future cash bailout whatever the source. The cash bailout can come from one of three sources:

1. Cash payments by the company for dividends or to repurchase outstanding common stock.
2. Sale to a market, with the market price determined by any number of factors: e.g., estimated future dividends; increases in corporate wealth for businesses which will never pay dividends; or speculative enthusiasm for a particular group of common stocks.
3. Control, or elements of control, of a company.

For MCT, diversification is a must; EPT governs. For TAVF, diversification is only a surrogate, and usually a damn poor surrogate, for knowledge, control and price consciousness. Because the Fund is a non-control investor, a certain amount of diversification is essential, but Third Avenue is far more concentrated in its investments than are Index Funds.

Much of MCT is based on utterly unrealistic views of the real world. For example, Ross, Westerfield state on page 17, "Shareholders determine the membership of the board of directors by voting." The fact in the real world is that, in 99%-plus of the cases, membership of the board of directors is determined by those people who control the corporate proxy machinery — management and/or people friendly to management. Shareholder votes almost all the time are equivalent to what elections used to be like in the U.S.S.R., where incumbent Communists received from 99% to 100% of the vote.

Ross, Westerfield also state on page 17, "Fear of a takeover gives managers an incentive to take actions that will maximize stock prices." The universal fact is that fears of takeovers have caused almost all managements to put in place "shark repellents" such as poison pills, staggered boards, blank check preferreds, fair price provisions, and friendly state laws, in order to insulate themselves in office. These entrenchment provisions tend to depress, not enhance, common stock prices.

While not wholly free from doubt, MCT seems to say that except for agency costs, managements do work in the best interests of stockholders. For TAVF, a much more productive approach is to understand that all participants, in all financial processes, including the relationships between managements and stockholders, combine communities of interest and conflicts of interest. For the vast majority of companies in the TAVF portfolio, the managements seem quite cognizant of the interests of Third Avenue and other outside stockholders. Nonetheless, the only situation of which I am aware where one might expect management to work exclusively in the interests of stockholders to the exclusion of other constituencies, is the one where the CEO and his family own all the outstanding common stock.

MCT and Index Funds are based on two premises. First, there is only one securities market, the places where Outside Passive Minority Investors (OPMIs) trade, e.g., the New York Stock Exchange and NASDAQ; and second, the market is efficient, or to put it otherwise, securities prices almost always reflect an instantaneous efficiency. TAVF, on the other hand, believes there exist myriad markets, and that all markets tend toward efficiency, but that few actually achieve instantaneous efficiency except in the special cases previously cited. A market is an arena in which participants arrive at agreements as to price, and other terms, which each participant believes is good enough under the circumstances. Disparate markets include OPMI Markets, leveraged buyout Markets, Merger and Acquisition Markets, Managerial Compensation Markets, and Markets for Reaching Agreements about Consensual Plans of Reorganization in Chapter 11. Sometimes price efficiency is attained slowly. I've noticed that it took the better part of 10 years for the pricing of first mortgage bonds of troubled regulated electric utilities to become priced efficiently. An efficient price in one market, say the OPMI Market, is, *per se*, an inefficient price in another market, say, the Leveraged Buy-Out Market.

MCT — and Index Funds — operate under the assumption that OPMIs cannot outperform a market, or index, because all relevant information gets impacted into common stock prices instantaneously. At Third Avenue, we do not rely on receiving superior information but rather we strive to use the available information in a superior manner. For example, most practitioners, from MCT theorists to Graham and Dodd, believe that there is a primacy of the income account; the balance sheet is virtually ignored by these analysts, who instead concentrate on the past earnings record or forecasts of future flows, whether earnings flows or cash flows. In contrast, a majority of the common stocks held in the TAVF portfolio are issues of companies with ultra-strong balance sheets where the issue was acquired at prices that represent a substantial discount from readily ascertainable net asset values; e.g., Toyota Industries, Tejon Ranch, MBIA, Millea Holdings, Forest City Enterprises, Radian Group, St. Joe, and Brascan. These common stocks will have substantial appreciation potential if managements can keep growing net asset values, even if such growth comes from sources other than having operating income or cash flow, such as appreciating land values.

The goal of MCT seems to be to find general laws which will explain market price fluctuations and securities price fluctuations. At TAVF, in contrast, we focus on individual differences. The tools and variables involved in analyzing securities vary case by case. Our standards for investing in the common stocks of high-tech companies are quite different than our standards for investing in the common stocks of real estate companies or banks; and the criteria we use in investing in distress credits are quite different than our common stock criteria because in the case of common stocks, we restrict investments to companies with strong financial positions while in the case of distress credits, corporate balance sheets are almost always very weak.

CHAPTER 46

Characteristics in Modern Capital Theory

OCTOBER 2013

Academics involved with finance restrict their studies to analyzing markets and securities prices. As far as they are concerned, the study of companies and the securities they issue are someone else's business. To me, it is disappointing to have a Nobel Prize awarded to an academic, Eugene Fama, who studies only markets and prices; and who, it appears to me after reading his work, may never have read a Form 10-K or the footnotes to a corporation's audited financial statements. In fact there is no way of determining whether any market is efficient or not in measuring underlying values unless the analyst understands, and analyzes, the specific securities that are the components of that specific market.

Market participants make two types of decisions: – market decisions and investment decisions. Market decisions involve predicting security prices and are virtually always very short-run oriented. Investment decisions involve, *inter alia*, determining underlying value, resource conversion probabilities; terms of securities; credit analysis, and probable access to capital markets particularly for providing bailouts to public markets at high prices (vs. cost) for promoters, insiders and private investors.

Modern Capital Theory (MCT) concentrates on market decisions and provides valuable lessons for specific markets consisting of Outside Passive Minority Investors (OPMIs) who deal in "sudden death" securities, i.e., options, warrants, risk arbitrage, heavily margined portfolios, trading strategies and performing loans with short-fuse maturities. MCT is of little or no help to those involved primarily with making investment decisions: value investors, control investors, most distress investors, credit analysts, and first and second stage venture capital investors.

The most basic problem for MCT, and all believers in efficient markets is that they take a very narrow special case – OPMIs dealing in "sudden death" securities – and claim, as the Nobel Prize winner does, that their theories apply to all markets universally. What utter nonsense! Most of the activity – and money – on Wall Street is in the hands of people making investment decisions, not market decisions. For the activist, and value investor, the market is a place for a bailout at high prices (vs. cost) not a place where underlying values are determined. MCT, in looking at Wall Street, concentrates on mutual funds which trade marketable securities. MCT seems oblivious to activists, not studying what activists do, and why they do it.

MCT, not only misdefines markets, but also seems to be sloppy science. Their theory embodies the correct observation that almost no one outperforms relevant market indexes consistently. Consistently is a dirty word; it means all the time. In justifying and promoting Index Funds, MCT points to this failure to outperform consistently. MCT acolytes, however, forget that many managed funds – such as the five Third Avenue Funds – do tend to outperform relative benchmarks, over the long term, on average, and most of the times, notwithstanding their higher expense ratios. It's just plain stupid to state that the quality of money management is tested by looking at consistency. Insofar as MCT identifies what it describes as performance outliers, e.g., Berkshire-Hathaway, no attempt is made to study what it is that outlier's do that make them outliers, since this would entail the detailed analysis of portfolio companies and the securities they issue. How unscholarly!

MCT cannot possibly be helpful almost all the time to those focusing primarily on investment decisions, i.e., understanding a company and the securities it issues. This is because in MCT four factors are overemphasized to such an extent that economic reality is blurred.

1. A belief in the primacy of the income account with some emphasis on cash flow from operations rather than earnings. (Earnings are defined as creating wealth while consuming cash). If there is a primacy of anything. in understanding a business, at least subsequent to the 2008 financial meltdown, it is credit-worthiness, not periodic cash flows or periodic earnings.

2. An emphasis on short-termism. I think it is impossible to be market conscious about publicly traded securities without emphasizing the immediate outlook at the expense of a longer term view.

3. Overemphasis on top-down macro-factors such as forecasts for the economy, interest rates, the Dow-Jones Industrial averages with a consequent de-emphasis of bottom up factors such as the financial strength of an enterprise, the relationship of a securities price to readily ascertainable Net Asset Value (NAV), or the covenants in loan agreements. It is easy to appear wise and profound, for example, by forecasting outlooks for the general economy. Forecasting about the general economy almost all the time tends to be a lot less important for long-term buy-and-hold investors than are nitty-gritty details about an issuer. Indeed, it seems as if macro forecasts dominated in importance in the last 85 years only in 1929, 1974 and 2008-2009. Even in those years of dramatic down-drafts in the U.S., macro factors tended to be non-important (outside of immediate market prices) for adequately secured creditors seeking interest income or for well financed companies with opportunistic managements seeking acquisitions.

4. A belief in equilibrium pricing. An OPMI market price is believed to value correctly and OPMI market prices change as the market receives new information. Such a view, though widely held, is ludicrous. The fact that the common stocks of many well-financed, growing companies sell at 25% to 75% discounts from readily ascertainable NAV is mostly lost on finance academics who believe in efficient markets. They do not believe that such pricing can exist, though it does.

The Third Avenue portfolios are replete with the common stocks issues of companies which have great financial strength and are selling in the OPMI market at 25% to 75% discounts from readily ascertainable NAV. Such discounts would not exist if the companies could be involved in changes in control, whether hostile or friendly. If there were to be changes in control, the prices in many, if not most, cases would reflect a premium over readily ascertainable NAV. Which is the efficient price? Is it the prevailing price in the open OPMI market or the price likely to be obtained if there were a control market? As a long-term buy-and-hold investor, I would suggest that the price to be realized in a control market is the more efficient price insofar as efficiency reflects economic value.

Insofar as an OPMI's ability to make sound investment decisions about underlying values exists, it is important to note that it is easier and more productive to make such decisions today than it was in the Graham and Dodd (G&D) era that ended in the 1970's. Starting with the Securities Act of 1964 as amended, there has been a continuing disclosure explosion. It is now possible for trained OPMI's, like the various Third Avenue analysts and portfolio managers, to learn from public records tremendous amounts of pertinent information about a tremendous number of issuers. This disclosure explosion exists today not only for U.S. issuers, but also for companies listed or traded in Canada, Hong Kong, the UK and also for companies issuing American Depositary Receipts (ADR's). This disclosure explosion seems of little or no benefit to financial academics, ETF managers, or high frequency traders. Mostly, these people seem unaware of the existence of these disclosures. In any event, the vast majority of them seem to have no training in how to use the disclosure system that is in place assuming they ever would want to take advantage of available disclosures.

Behavioral science has many shortcomings in that it postulates that people in markets do a lot of things that are emotional and irrational. However, much of what those making market decisions do are rational in a market context but irrational for investment decisions. If market players tried to do what Third Avenue does, most of them probably would be wiped out. Much of what Third Avenue managers do seems irrational from a market point of view. For example, Third Avenue managers tend to invest when the near-term corporate outlook is bad; the managers are value conscious rather than outlook conscious. The manager's talents lie in identifying long term values not in gauging immediate market outlooks. It is hard to be a well-capitalized value investor if one doesn't buy aggressively as market prices are declining. This factor, alone, prevents most value investors from outperforming markets consistently.

Very few Wall Street fortunes are made by OPMIs who buy general market securities in the open market. Rather, the fortunes are made by those able to obtain cheap stock prices for a company going public; certain opportunistic creditors; promoters who earn large managerial fees; investment banking fees; trading commissions, and carried interests. In a recent book, of which I am co-author, *Modern Security Analysis*, there are three chapters describing how OPMIs, through private placements, were able to enjoy huge returns – say 10 baggers to 20 baggers – by being early investors:

1. The limited partners in the three groups which acquired control from Ford Motor Company of Hertz Global Holdings in 2005. While Hertz has not prospered, the returns to limited partners have been huge because the sponsors – Clayton, Dubilier & Rice; Carlyle Corp.; and Merrill Lynch have been so skillful in accessing capital markets.
2. The sponsors and promoters of Schaefer Brewing who received common stocks for $1 before Schaefer went public at $26 in transactions which allowed the Schaefer family to extract large sums from the company while still maintaining control of the company.
3. The Leasco transaction where Institutional OPMI's obtained a huge return by financing committing to finance transactions whereby Leasco was able to obtain control of Reliance Insurance without putting up any meaningful amounts of money unless Leasco, did, in fact;, obtain control of Reliance Insurance.

As an aside Twitter went public November 2013 at $26 per share. On the first day of trading Twitter Common closed at $45.90. The prospectus discloses, *inter alia* that 42,708,824 options on common shares, exercisable at an average price of $1.84 per share, were outstanding on June 30, 2013.

Occasionally the above types of returns are available to OPMI's in the general market, e.g., Google Common, selling at $1,000 went public at $85. For us at Third Avenue, we ape the Berkshire Hathaway mode in an attempt to obtain such returns. What Berkshire Hathaway concentrates on is increasing NAV over the long term, albeit Berkshire is basically a control investor rather than an OPMI.

A meaningful number of common stocks in Third Avenue portfolios enjoy Berkshire-Hathaway characteristics, i.e., finances are strong, the companies have superior managements and the prospects for NAV growth appear very good. Unlike Berkshire-Hathaway, the various common stocks in the portfolio are priced at meaningful discounts from readily ascertainable NAVs. Such issues include Brookfield Asset Management, Capital Southwest, Cheung Kong Holdings, Exor, InvestorA/B, Leucadia, Pargesa Toyota Industries and Wheelock and Company.

A large number of the Third Avenue Portfolio investments – especially in the Real Estate Fund, the Value Fund and the International Fund – have the following four characteristics:

1. The Companies enjoy super strong financial positions.
2. The common stocks are priced at discounts of from 25% to 75% of readily ascertainable NAV. (In contrast the Dow-Jones Industrial Average is selling at about 3 times book value).
3. Full disclosures, including reliable audits, are given to the OPMI and the securities are traded in markets that are highly regulated with substantial investor protections (e.g., U.S., Canada, Hong Kong, England).
4. The businesses have good prospects for growing NAV after adding back dividends, by not less than 10% compounded annually over the next three-to-seven years.

One shortcoming of this approach is that there is probably little chance of resource conversion (especially changes of control) that would result, almost immediately, in the elimination, or sharp reduction, in the discounts from NAV. However, this shortcoming will be ameliorated if the businesses grow. There is one macro-factor that seems to put the odds in favor of the OPMI achieving satisfactory, long term, investment returns, even if NAV growth is less that than 10%

compounded. The macro is that perhaps 80% of the time for at least 90% of the companies which are well financed, readily ascertainable NAV will be larger in the next reporting period than it was in the last reporting period. While not determinative of security prices in itself, these steady increases in NAV ought to put the odds in favor of the buy and hold OPMI who bought in to equities at substantial discounts from NAVs.

Good companies, with good growth prospects, selling at discounts of greater than 45%, are not uncommon. I think mainland China has relatively bright long term growth prospects. Five issues with direct or indirect presences in Mainland China and selling at such discounts are as follows:

Issuer and Discount from NAV as of the Latest Reporting Date:

Henderson Land	48%
Lai Fung Holdings	72%
Lai Sun Development	76%
Lai Sun Garment	78%
Wheelock & Company	52%

CHAPTER 47

Going Concerns and Investment Type Companies

OCTOBER 2015

At Third Avenue Management (TAM), companies, the securities they issue, and their managements and/or control groups are appraised from three different angles:

1. As going concerns with perpetual lives engaged in day to day operations, managed as they always have been managed and capitalized pretty much the way they have always been capitalized
2. As investors buying and selling assets in bulk as well as buying and selling controlled companies and affiliates
3. As financiers funding going concern operations as well as resource conversions such as hostile takeovers, mergers and acquisitions, going privates, starting up new activities; and also restructuring capitalizations for either healthy or distressed companies

Virtually all companies are involved in the three activities and combine elements of being both Going Concerns (GCs) and Investment Type Companies (ITCs). Most companies probably are focused on recurring operations, i.e., being GCs, and in analysis, principal weight is given to the primacy of the income account to determine periodic earnings and cash flows from recurring operations. Such companies include Walmart and Pfizer.

Here most analysis seems to be conventional Graham & Dodd. For other companies the emphasis is on increasing readily ascertainable Net Asset Values (NAVs) over time. Here the emphasis is on analyzing the company as an ITC. Such companies include Berkshire Hathaway, Loews Corp. Wheelock & Company, Brookfield Asset Management, all mutual funds, most other Registered Investment Companies (RICs), and virtually all hedge funds.

While TAM invests in the common stocks of companies which are predominantly GCs, it is probable that TAM concentrates more heavily on equity investments in companies that are predominantly ITCs. For this there are a number of reasons:

ITCs tend to be easier to analyze, especially if the common stocks are available at prices that reflect deep discounts from readily ascertainable NAV, and the company is strongly financed, i.e., eminently credit worthy. ITC-type analysis seems especially useful in appraising financial institutions (such as Keycorp and Comerica) and income producing real estate (especially non-US real estate where income producing assets are carried in financial statements at independently appraised net asset values such as is the case in Hong Kong, China, Canada, England and Germany).

An investor in ITCs usually has less need for diversification than is the case for GCs, in part because the portfolios of ITCs tend to already be quite diversified as is the case for Brookfield Asset Management, Loews Corp., and a majority of the portfolio securities held by Third Avenue Real Estate Value Fund. Earnings are not ignored in an ITC analysis. The Return on Equity (ROE) for TAM's ITC investments seems to be comparable to the ROE's for general market investments as represented by the Dow-Jones Industrial Average (DJIA). The DJIA is selling at around 3x book and about 17x latest twelve month earnings. In contrast, the common stocks of most Hong Kong and Chinese income producing real estate companies are priced at least at 30% discounts from NAV and usually around 2x to 6x latest 12 month reported earnings. ITC analysis seems more suitable for long term investors than does most GC analysis. Much of GC analysis, including Graham & Dodd analysis, is not too helpful in appraising long term prospects for four reasons:

1. There is an emphasis on the primacy of the periodic income account rather than on creditworthiness.
2. There is a concentration on short-termism. It seems impossible to focus on stock price movements without being a short termer or even a trader.
3. There is a concentration on macro factors, such as the DJIA, Gross Domestic Product, interest rates, employment numbers, with a consequent denigration of important micro factors, such as appraisals of managements, appraisals of a company's ability to finance its activities and analysis of a company's competition, and appraisals of a company's ability to innovate.
4. There is a belief in equilibrium prices, i.e., there exists an efficient market whose pricing represents a true valuation price which will change only as the market obtains and digests new information.

Graham and Dodd in common stock analysis are not overly helpful for long term investing because of their emphasis on three factors in common stock analysis: the macro outlook, earnings from operations and dividends.

ITC analysis however is not very helpful to investors when the entity being analyzed is not credit worthy. Creditworthiness seems to be a function of three factors:

1. Cash flows from operations
2. Strength of current balance sheet and other credit factors whether disclosed in footnotes or elsewhere or not disclosed at all
3. Access to capital markets ranging from availability of senior credits to an ability to raise equity capital

Access to capital markets seems to be quite capricious. Loss of such capital market access by companies which needed continuous access was the precipitant for a large number of the biggest insolvencies in U.S. history: Drexel Burnham, Enron, Bear Stearns, Washington Mutual and Lehman Brothers.

In ITC investing, there is an emphasis on guarding against investment risk, i.e., something going wrong with the company or the securities it issues. Market risk – securities price fluctuations – is pretty much ignored in ITC investing. Thus using borrowed money, i.e., margin, to be an ITC investor is dangerous: too much market risk is entailed if an investor is on margin.

In a sense, GC analysis is distinguishable from ITC analysis by what the analyst is seeking to learn. GC analysis concentrates heavily on forecasts of results for the immediate future and the intermediate future. These forecasts are quite subject to error, sometimes gross error. In ITC analysis, the concentration is on acquiring "what is" safe and cheap, an activity much less prone to error than forecasting future profitability or future resource conversions.

GC analysis has to have major weight in most analysis (albeit TAM as an investor has available a myriad of ITC securities in which its funds might invest). NAV tends to be a not very useful tool for investors when individual assets of the GC are not separable and saleable; or where assets are hard (or impossible) to value. Industries where NAV tends to lack importance include retail, most manufacturing companies, most service companies, transportation companies and many natural resources extraction companies.

Diversification is a surrogate, and usually a damn poor surrogate, for knowledge, control and price consciousness. At TAM, its concentration, whether GC or ITC, is exclusively on outside minority passive investing with deep knowledge of companies and the securities they issue, and also price consciousness in trying to buy at big discounts from intrinsic value for companies with good outlooks. Thus TAM has less need to diversify than finance academics and traders, most of whom study only markets and security prices, and have little or no knowledge about companies and the securities they issue. Also, TAM, as an outside passive minority investor, has more need for diversification than do control investors and most active investors.

For financial academics and Efficient Market Theorists, their intellectual appeal is to traders, an almost non-existent activity at TAM. Most activity on Wall Street, however, involves not trading, but knowing much about companies and the securities they issue.

Those activities encompass the following:

- Value Investing
- Distress Investing
- Active Investing
- Control Investing
- Credit Analysis
- 1st and 2nd Stage Venture Capital Investing

It is hard to think of efficient market theorists as knowledgeable about important matters. Indeed, when it comes to understanding companies and the securities they issue, these people seem to place a premium on being ignorant.

Most markets are efficient in one sense or another, and the same markets are inefficient in one sense or another. For analytical purposes, there are three types of efficiencies for securities markets:

- Value Efficiencies
- Transaction Efficiencies
- Process Efficiencies

Value efficiencies reflect the price and other terms, that would be arrived at in transactions between willing control buyers and willing control sellers, each with knowledge of the relevant facts and neither under any compulsion to act.

Transaction efficiency exists in markets for "sudden death" securities and the analysis involves a relatively few computer programmable variables. Sudden death exists where there is to be a final disposition of the situation within a relatively short period of time. Sudden death includes trading strategies, options, warrants, exchange offers, tender offers, merger arbitrage and certain liquidations.

Process efficiency (or lack of process efficiency) exists in markets where there are prospects (or no prospects) for changes of control, going private, mergers, massive recapitalizations and some liquidations.

Process efficiency can also exist in the markets where there is a lack of trading volume and/or a lack of compensation for securities salesmen and securities promoters. Here the process efficiency price may only be a fraction of the value efficiency price. TAM invests in GCs and ITCs where there is a belief that a wide discrepancy exists between the value efficiency price and the lower process efficiency price.

While most ITCs sell at large premiums over readily ascertainable NAVs, many are not only priced at meaningful discounts from readily ascertainable NAVs but also are the common stocks of quality companies with good outlooks. TAM is invested in many of the best ITCs which are both blue chips and steadily growing. Such investments include the following:

> Hong Kong –mainland China real estate Companies
> Investor A/B
> Toyota Industries
> Loews
> Brookfield Asset Management
> Pargesa

Creditworthy companies almost never repay debt in the aggregate. While individual debt instruments mature, credit-worthy companies are able to refinance, and expand, their indebtedness as they become more and more creditworthy. This seems true for most TAM equity investments. Never repaying debts in the aggregate ought to be part of the underlying assumption in financial accounting which bottoms on the fact that most corporations are going concerns with perpetual lives.

CHAPTER 48

Value Investing

April 2005

This year, I led seminars on value investing at the Schools of Management at both Syracuse University and Yale University. At the first session of the seminar programs, I contrasted the underlying assumptions pervading value investing with the underlying assumptions that seem to govern both academic finance and conventional research department analyses. Hopefully, it will be useful for Third Avenue Value Fund (TAVF) shareholders if I share with them what I said at these first sessions, as well as how I believe the Fund's investment approach comports with a number of the underlying assumptions.

Academic and research department concepts that are part and parcel of value investing revolve around Net Present Value (NPV) and Present Value (PV). NPV is pervasive in value analysis and is used much more broadly than merely measuring Discounted Cash Flows (DCF). In Value Investing one tends to PV everything: asset values, liabilities, earnings, EBITDA, expenses; often converting fixed expenses into liabilities; and assured earnings and cash flows into asset values. For example, see the table below "Closed End Fund X." An above normal expense ratio (4% rather than 1.5%) is capitalized as a liability and the present value of the excess is deducted from Closed End Fund X's NAV. For value purposes Closed End Fund X's common stock is deemed to be selling at a 6.7% premium over NAV, even though based strictly on Generally Accepted Accounting Principles (GAAP), it appears to be selling at a 20% discount from NAV.

Closed End Fund X

NAV	$100,000,000
# shares outstanding	10,000,000 Shares
NAV Per Share	$10
Annual Operating Expenses	$4,000,000
Expense Ratio	4%(a)
Market Price of Common	$8
Market Price as Discount from NAV — as reported under GAAP	(20%) Adjust NAV to exclude Expense Ratio in excess of 1.5%
from NAV $2,500,000 capitalized at 10%	$25,000,000
Adjusted NAV	$75,000,000
Adjusted NAV — Premium over market price	6.70%

(a) TAVF expense ratio was 1.12% for fiscal 2004

37 Underlying Assumptions of Value Investing

Organized Under Five Titles:

- Efficient Market Hypothesis (EMH)
- Efficient Portfolio Theory (EPT)
- Disclosure and GAAP
- Economics and Markets
- Security Analysis

Efficient Market Hypothesis

1. The General Theory of Market Efficiency Some markets will tend toward instantaneous efficiency. Some markets will tend toward long term efficiency but rarely achieve it. Some markets are inherently inefficient. Which market exists is a function of four variables:

> Who the market participant is
> ii. How complex is the security, or the situation, being analyzed
> iii. What are the time horizons of the participants
> iv. How strong are the external forces imposing disciplines on a market:

a) Government external forces;
b) Private sector external forces.

In markets where instantaneous efficiencies exist, participants do not earn excess returns. In other markets, earning excess returns is to be expected. TAVF, a buy-and-hold cash investor, tends to invest in complex securities where the work-out horizon is five years, or more. As such, the Fund operates in markets that rarely approach instantaneous efficiency.

2. Financial markets almost never approach instantaneous efficiency unless they are strictly regulated.

3. A market is defined as any financial, or commercial, arena where participants reach agreements as to price, and other terms, which each participant believes is the best reasonably achievable under the circumstances.

Efficient Portfolio Theory

4. Diversification is a surrogate, and usually a damn poor surrogate, for knowledge, control and price consciousness. At April 30, 2005, the Fund had 104 common stock positions and the top ten issues accounted for approximately 40% of TAVF's portfolio. Most mutual funds of similar size seem to hold 300 to 400 positions.

5. The objective of some securities holders is total return; others emphasize cash return; and some holders seek elements of both. TAVF is strictly total return conscious in its common stock investing. However, much of Third Avenue's investments in credit instruments is cash return driven.

6. Portfolio analysis differs from individual securities analysis. For portfolios, there is no such thing as a value trap.

Disclosure and GAAP

7. GAAP provide objective benchmarks, not truth, except in several special cases. For example, see Toyota Industries ("Industries"). Over half of Industries' assets at market prices are in a portfolio of marketable securities, principally Toyota Motor Common. For GAAP purposes, Industries reports only dividends and interest received from

portfolio companies. On this basis, Industries Common is selling at around 22 times earnings. If Industries' income account is adjusted to include Industries' equity in the undistributed earnings of portfolio companies, Industries Common is selling at less than eight times earnings. GAAP for Industries is a good first approximation of periodic cash flow. Picking up the equity in undistributed earnings of portfolio companies is a good first approximation of Industries' periodic wealth creation.

8. Every GAAP number is derived from, modified by, and a function of, other GAAP numbers.

9. Documentary disclosures to creditors and investors have never been better, or more complete, than they are now, at least in the U.S. Some of the credit for this goes to the Plaintiffs' Bar.

10. In value investing and control investing, what the numbers mean tend to be much more important than what the numbers are.

11. GAAP are more useful insofar as this accounting system is designed to meet the needs of long-term creditors rather than stock market speculators. Fund management basically analyzes all securities, including common stocks, as if the securities were long-term debt instruments.

Economics and Markets

12. The concept of risk is not useful unless a modifying adjective precedes the word "risk." Market risk — fluctuations in securities prices — is a different animal from investment risk — changes affecting a business' operations or investments. Other risks include commodity risk, terrorism risk, credit risk, failure to match maturities risk, weather risk, reorganization risk. See the contrast discussed above under cash management between credit risk on the one hand and capital risk on the other.

13. Once instantaneous efficiency is not present, measuring investment risk and market risk involve three factors:

i. Quality of the issuer
ii. Terms of the issue
iii. Price of the issue

Assuming price equilibrium, there is no need to factor in price of issue. If one factors in price, the lower the price the less the risk of loss and the more the potential for gain. When factoring in price, no risk/reward trade-off exists. Fund management is first safety conscious, and then, price conscious.

14. The basic interest of most market participants is wealth creation, an asset value concept, not DCF. DCF is just one method of creating wealth, and frequently a method that carries tax disadvantages. Over 80% of TAVF's common stock portfolio consists of securities, which were acquired at prices well below estimates of readily ascertainable NAVs. Current and immediately prospective Price Earnings Ratios are either downplayed in a TAVF analysis or completely ignored.

15. Debts — whether incurred in the private sector or by governments — are usually never repaid. Rather they are refinanced by those wealth-creating entities which are able to remain creditworthy. The Fund sells common stocks immediately when the businesses no longer appear to be creditworthy. To Fund management, this spells a permanent impairment.

16. There is a long-term arbitrage between business value and common stock prices:

Common stock prices high relative to business value — Go Public
Common stock prices low relative to business value — Go Private, or semiprivate

17. Assets can have an in-use value separate and apart from any market value.

18. Fairness in financial dealings is that price, and other terms, that would be arrived at in a transaction between a willing buyer and a willing seller, both with knowledge of the relevant facts, and neither under any compulsion to act. In a going private situation, one is faced with a willing buyer (who frequently is also a fiduciary)–coerced seller

situation. Fairness opinions are then used, and should be based on simulating the prices and other terms that would have existed were there actually a willing buyer-willing seller situation. TAVF, and its sister funds, complain loudly and/or take other actions when we become a forced seller at prices we think constitute a "takeunder" rather than a "takeover."

19. You can't understand corporate finance if all you do is look at corporations and securities wholly, or mostly, from the point of view of common stockholders who are Outside Passive Minority Investors (OPMIs). To understand corporate finance, you have to be cognizant of the interests and beliefs of other important constituencies — Managements, Creditors, Promoters, Underwriters, Governments.

20. Assuming relative political stability and an absence of violence in the streets, macro factors tend to be unimportant for value investing. The Fund's satisfactory investment experience after 1997 in Japanese non-life insurance common stocks is a good example of this. At the time these investments were made, Fund management had no idea that the Japanese business depression would turn out to be as deep and protracted as it was, and that interest rates would stay so low for so long.

21. Any and all resource conversion activities (e.g., mergers and acquisitions, initial public offerings, restructuring troubled companies, refinancings) involve huge costs payable to investment bankers, brokers, lawyers, accountants, lenders, and promoters. This is something Fund management has to consider for most of its investments. This expense problem seems exacerbated for small-cap companies.

22. There exist strong Wall Street pressures to have periodic IPO booms:

> i. Huge gross spreads
> ii. Exclusive Product
> iii. Easy Sell

23. Passive investment products tend to be sold by salesmen, rather than bought by investors.

24. The markets for top management compensation and top management entrenchment tend to be inefficient. Therefore, top managements, as a group and individually, earn excess returns. This, too, is a factor in Fund management's decision making.

25. All financial relationships combine communities of interest and conflicts of interest. Agency costs are a non-starter.

26. In the financial world it tends to be misleading to state, "There Is No Free Lunch." Rather the more meaningful comment is, "Somebody Has To Pay For Lunch."

Security Analysis

27. Substantive Consolidation of the interests of the Company itself and its OPMI stockholders is a relatively rare special case. The Company is the Company. The Company is not the management. The Company is not its stockholders. All TAVF analyses treat the company as a stand-alone. For example, Fund management recognizes that stock options are a stockholder problem, and only rarely, a company problem.

28. The worth of any security is the present value of the future cash bailouts to be received by security holders. Cash bailouts come from three sources:

> i. Cash Distributions by issuers in the forms of interest, principal, premium; dividends, and securities repurchases
> ii. Sales to a market
> iii. Control

29. Passive securities, for most economic purposes, are a different commodity from control securities, albeit they are identical in legal form. From a TAVF point of view, if a passive security is to become a control security, the holder (hopefully Third Avenue) is entitled to a premium price.

30. Outside of a Court Proceeding, usually Chapter 11, no one in the U.S. can take away a creditor's right to a money payment for interest, principal, or premium unless that individual creditor so consents. A creditor has only contract rights, not residual rights.

31. Equities represent ownership and only very rarely require cash service. Equity owners have residual rights *vis-à-vis* the company and its management; e.g., management has a duty to deal fairly with stockholders.

32. In all transactions, consider the use of proceeds. Corporations can only use cash proceeds in four ways:

> i. Pay expenses
> ii. Expand the asset base
> iii. Service and/or repay liabilities
> iv. Distribute to equity via dividends and/or buybacks

Distributions to equity are almost always a residual use of corporate cash. The principal exception is where the payment of dividends gives capital hungry companies better access to capital markets than they otherwise would have. (TAVF tends not to invest in the common stocks of such companies.) Excluding this consideration, buying in common stock is almost always a preferable method of distributing cash to shareholders from both a company point of view and a TAVF point of view compared with paying cash dividends. This tends not to be the case from the point of view of short run oriented OPMIs.

33. In passive investing, decisions should be based more on a "reasonable worst" case basis than on a "base case" basis.

34. Management appraisals involve looking at managements not only as operators but also as investors and financiers.

35. Weighted Average Cost of Capital (WACC) is a non-starter for two reasons:

> i. From a creditor's point of view (and without getting into the issue of effective differences in cost between, say, short-term senior secured issues and long-term subordinates), the cost of creating corporate creditworthiness is very different in the case where the company issues debt securities which have a required cash cost on the one hand, and where the company issues equity securities which don't require cash payments on the other hand.
> ii.The vast majority of equity financing takes place via having

the company retain earnings, rather than having the company market new issues of common stock. The PE ratio, or cap rate, at which a common stock sells in an OPMI market, has no particular meaning for a company increasing its equity base through retaining earnings. Here Return on Equity (ROE) gives a better estimate of the "cost" of equity capital to the company than does a cap rate measured in part by OPMI market prices, albeit many cash conscious managements and companies will view retaining earnings as a cost free method of increasing equity capital.

36. The liability side of the balance sheet is a lot more than obligations and net worth. Rather, it is a layer cake consisting of at least the following:

  i. Secured obligations
  ii. Unsecured obligations
  iii. Subordinated obligations
  iv. Liability reserves which analytically have an equity component:

    a. Preferred Stocks
    b. Common Stocks
    c. Common Stock Derivatives

Whether an issue is debt or equity depends on where you sit. To senior lenders, subordinated debt is a form of equity. To common stockholders, subordinated debt is debt.

37. Many disciplines can be helpful in contributing toward making one a successful value investor. There are three areas, though, where it is essential that the participant needs to be well informed, i.e., needs to be knowledgeable enough so that at the minimum, the analyst can be an informed client. These three disciplines are as follows:

    1. GAAP
    2. Securities Laws and Regulation
    3. Income Tax

A Differentiated Approach to Value Investing

About Third Avenue

For over 30 years, Third Avenue has consistently pursued a fundamental, bottom-up approach to deep value investing: we focus on the company's balance sheet, the value of its underlying assets, and the discounted price of its securities.

This fundamental conviction defines our singular investment culture, which was pioneered by our founder and revolutionary value investor Martin J. Whitman. Marty's early career established him as an expert witness in shareholder litigations, and turnaround specialist for bankrupt companies. In 1974, Marty formed M.J. Whitman & Co. and his first notable investment was in the mortgage bonds of then-bankrupt Penn Central Railroad. Marty recognized the value of the company could be realized through the fulcrum security–the security in the capital structure that gives the investor control over the reorganization process. The success of this investment created the foundation of Third Avenue. Today, Third Avenue manages assets across four core equity strategies — Value, Small-Cap, Real Estate, and International –which are all rooted in the differentiated, high conviction investment approach established by our Founder. To learn more about Third Avenue, please visit our website at www.thirdave.com